PN97 L765

GROMCHIK

and Other Tales
from a Psychiatrist's Casebook

By the same author

MANAGEMENT OF EMOTIONAL DISORDERS, 1962

MANAGEMENT OF EMOTIONAL PROBLEMS
OF CHILDREN AND ADOLESCENTS, 1965,
Second Edition, 1974

TEXTBOOK OF CLINICAL PSYCHIATRY,
An Interpersonal Approach, 1967,
Second Edition, 1975

PUT-OFFS AND COME-ONS, 1968

SEXUAL MANEUVERS AND STRATAGEMS, 1969

THE PHYSICIAN'S GUIDE TO MANAGING
EMOTIONAL PROBLEMS, 1969

THE GAMES CHILDREN PLAY, 1972

THE INTERPERSONAL BASIS
OF PSYCHIATRIC NURSING
(with Elza M. Almeida), 1972

MARITAL BRINKMANSHIP, 1974

IT'S ALL ARRANGED: 15 Hours
In A Psychiatrist's Life, 1975

GROMCHIK

AND OTHER TALES

from a Psychiatrist's Casebook

by A. H. Chapman, MD

Author of *It's All Arranged*

G. P. Putnam's Sons
New York

To the memory of Karl Young
Late Sterling Professor of English, Yale University
and for
Todd Chapman

Contents

Preface

DURING the twentieth century, in the context of medical practice, a profession with unprecedented opportunities for studying human experience has evolved, and for almost thirty years I have been engaged in it. In these years of work as a psychiatrist I have seen, in treatment or consultation, hundreds of patients, and I have recorded the stories of five of them in this book.

They are not run-of-the-mill cases. They are persons whose difficulties, or their abilities to put their thoughts and feelings into words, make them of special interest. I shall tell their stories as simple narratives, in most cases as they were unfolded to me. Names and some other data have been changed, since all these patients are still alive.

There are in psychiatry no simple cases, no cut-and-dried problems. There are patients whose inner turmoil blocks them in their efforts to talk, and patients whose agony we do not grasp because of our own shortsightedness. But if a patient can scrutinize his life well enough, and if the therapist can comprehend him sufficiently, each person is absorbing and different from all others. In many cases, moreover, there is, at one or many points, an uncanny awesomeness, an abrupt encounter with the unexpected, an eerie twist.

A. H. CHAPMAN

Gromchik

WHEN David Ross came to see me for his first visit, I doubted that he would come for more than a couple of sessions. As
his family physician had explained when he telephoned to
set up the appointment, David stated that he had "bombed
out" with two psychiatrists in California and two more in
Kansas City. By that David meant that he had gone to see
each of them for one or two interviews, had spent most of his
time in silence, and had quit.

When I went to the waiting room to meet him for his first
interview, I found a tall, black-haired boy in blue jeans and a
bulky gray sweater. He toted a green cloth book bag with half
a dozen books in it into my office and slumped into the sofa
chair. He was twenty; he had flunked out of the University of
California at Berkeley five months earlier and had spent
most of his time since then reading in his bedroom at home.
His family physician had told me this, and I knew nothing
more about him.

I offered him the bottle of a cola drink that I offer all
adolescents at the beginning of each session. He took a swig
out of it and placed it on the table beside him. I drank some
of my cola drink out of the bottle and set it on a plastic coast-
er on my desk.

"I suppose that's to take care of my unmet oral needs," he
said.

"It's supposed to break the ice," I replied.

"Carbonated breast milk," he commented.

"I see you know some of the lingo."

"Lingo," he said. "An archaic word. It went out about nine-

11

teen hundred forty. You ought to be able to do better than that, Soaper."

"What word would you prefer?" I asked.

"Oh, come on, Soaper, you don't expect me to do your homework for you, do you?"

"No, I guess not. Incidentally, I take it that this title of Soaper is a condensation of soft-soap, or soft-soaper, which is more or less how you see me."

"Oh, Soaper, you've crashed again. It's Soaper because that's your function. You are to cleanse me of my filthy complexes and make my ego lily white. For that you need soap, or the finest type of detergent. So you're the Soaper. Are you with me, Soaper?"

"Yes."

"Really, Soaper," he went on, "you disappoint me. You've been around all these years and you don't even know what your own name is. Doesn't that strike you as being rather sick?"

"Well, I suppose it could be interpreted that way," I replied.

"Soaper," he said, "you disappoint me more every minute. You don't really 'suppose' anything of the kind. You just said that because you couldn't think of anything else to say, and it's not considered good technique to argue with adolescents. Meet them on their own ground, talk to them in their own jargon, don't repeat with them the sick patterns of interaction they had with their parents. Isn't that the way it goes?"

"Yes."

"Ahhhhhh," he said. "Very cautious of you, Soaper. Very clever. There's not much I can do with a simple, plain, old yes."

"No," I said.

"Bull's-eye again, Soaper. I didn't think you could do it twice in a row. After a brilliant yes, you come up with a magnificent no. May I suggest the next one?"

"Of course."

"That's very good, too," he said. "Three in a row. 'Of

course.' I can't do anything with that. But that's not what I
had in mind."

"What did you have in mind?"

"Maybe," he replied. "Maybe. There's a word that ought to
be added to your vocabulary of meaningless noises. What do
you think of it, Soaper?"

"I'll note it down."

"Talking of notes, Soaper, are you bugged?"

"Bugged?" I repeated.

"Bugged," he said. "Everybody knows what 'bugged' is.
However, I shouldn't press you on the point. 'Answer a question with a question.' Isn't that the first rule in 'The Psychiatrist's Handbook'?"

"I admit that we sometimes use that little technique," I replied.

"You mean, 'that little trick,' Soaper."

"Very well, we use that trick," I responded.

"But you haven't told me yet."

"Told you what?"

"Soaper, how old are you?"

"I'm well over forty," I said.

"And you're already getting senile? Tsk, tsk, tsk. It's a pity.
All those years of education and medical experience going
down the drain. I ask you a simple question, and you can't
even remember it one minute later."

"What was the simple question?" I asked.

"Whether or not you're bugged. In other words, is this interview being recorded by some electronic device in the closet, controlled by a button under the edge of your desk? In
brief, Soaper, are we on tape?"

"No. This interview is not being tape-recorded."

"Honest injun?"

"Honest injun," I answered. "We don't do that in our
work."

"Dr. Millman did."

"Did what?"

"Taped my interviews with him," he answered.

"I take it Dr. Millman was one of your former psychiatrists."

"You take it correctly, Soaper. But come clean, Soaper, don't you have nice photocopied reports on me from at least three of the shrinks I've seen?"

"No, I don't."

"Soaper, would you like to know a secret?"

"Fascinated," I replied.

"The secret is: I don't believe you."

"You mean you don't believe that I have no reports on you from some of your former psychiatrists?"

"That is correct, Soaper."

"I don't have any reports on you. All I know is that you've seen two psychiatrists in California and two in Kansas City, and that it didn't work out with any of them. You saw none of them more than a few times. You flunked out of Berkeley about five months ago, and haven't done much since then. Your father is Arthur Ross, a lawyer, and I have your home address and telephone number in my records. That's all I know about you."

He squinted at me. "And nobody's ever offered you any records on me?"

"Well now, that's another matter," I said.

"What kind of other matter, Soaper?"

"Well, to be quite frank, when Dr. Wilner referred you to me, he said that your father had a rather impressive pile of reports on you from these four psychiatrists and offered to send them to me; or, more accurately, he said that your father would send them to me from his office. But I turned him down."

He laughed. "Soaper, you have one thing going for you. You're the most original shrink I've met yet. Most of the rest of them, or at least the four with whom I've had personal dealings, are lousy liars. They tell all the conventional fibs. But you, Soaper, tell really fantastic ones. It shows either incipient psychosis or true genius."

"In other words, you doubt my veracity when I tell you that I turned down a peek at all those records?"

"Exactly, Soaper. You have stated the matter admirably."

"Well, it so happens that I told you the truth."

"Motive, Soaper, motive. *Cherchez le motif*, as the sleuths say. What possible motive would you have for turning them down? No letters to write, no permits to sign, nothing to do but say yes. Then the referring physician says, 'Ah, Soaper is a good psychiatrist. I'll send him more patients,' and my father says, 'Soaper is thorough, a good man to have around.' Talk at cocktail parties soon confirms to the community that Soaper is not only a good psychiatrist but also a good man to have around. Soaper thrives. Soaper's family thrives. Fade-out, with rising crescendo."

"Well, I shall quite frankly tell you my motive," I said.

"That's the second time you've used the phrase 'quite frankly,' Soaper. Do you work your way through med school as a used car salesman?"

"No," I replied. "I figured it this way: If the patient has not stuck with four previous psychiatrists, he probably won't stick with me. In fact, he may not even show up for the first appointment. So why read all those records? I told Dr. Wilner exactly that and said that if you came to see me for four or five sessions, I'd call him and have your father send over the records."

He looked at me in silence for a few moments.

"You know, Soaper, I believe you."

"Thank you," I said.

"Don't mention it."

After a pause I said, "Would *you* like to know a secret?"

"Love to, Soaper."

"I know why you believed me."

"Ah, an interpretation. A healing device. Do tell me why I believed you."

"Because my motive for not accepting the reports was cynical. It showed little respect for you as a person; I didn't think highly enough of you to bother to get the reports, let alone read them. Such cynicism and low regard for other people is something you can understand, because that's the way you view the world. So you believed me. If I had given you an altruistic, dedicated motive, you would not have believed me, no matter how hard I tried to convince you."

He studied my face for half a minute. "Soaper, you have possibilities. Another twenty years at this and you may become a halfway decent psychiatrist."

"Thank you," I said.

"Don't mention it. I like to spread good cheer and help my fellow man."

We sat in silence for a few moments.

"Soaper," he said.

"Yes."

"You still haven't answered my question."

"You mean about whether this room is bugged?"

"Soaper, you're improving."

"The answer is no. This interview is not being recorded."

"The machine is broken?" he suggested.

"No."

"Hmmm. You haven't paid your electric bill and they've turned off the juice on you?"

"Wrong again."

"You felt that nothing of importance would come up in this session and saw no point in taping it?"

"Wrong again," I said. "You're not doing very well."

"Soaper, I give up. Tell me. Why isn't this interview being taped?"

"Very simple," I replied. "No machine."

"The credit company repossessed it because you got behind in your payments?"

"No," I said.

"Your teen-age son or daughter took it to a pop festival and some kid accidentally stomped on it?"

"No.'

"Then where is your machine, Soaper, and what is your problem?"

"I don't own one."

"Ah," he said, "you rent one, and the rental company is cleaning it today."

"Wrong again. I've never used one."

"Never, Soaper?"

"Never."

"Then how do you remember all this crap?"

"I have a very good memory."

"Oh, Soaper, you are a caution, as I think they said in the time of the late Queen Victoria. Do you mean to say that you sit here six or more hours a day and listen to all this drivel and, by a feat of sheer photocopy memory, remember it all, year in, year out, time without end, amen?"

"It's not quite that way," I said. "I make notes in front of most patients, especially during the first few interviews, but not with children and adolescents. I hope I don't offend you by putting you in this category, but you do demand the utmost candor from me. Until you are twenty one or so we classify you as an adolescent."

"Apology accepted," he said. "Please go on."

"When I am particularly interested in a patient, and he absorbs my attention fully, I can more or less reconstruct his interviews as they occurred. It's a matter of attention; complete concentration is the trick. I remember some interviews with a high degree of accuracy for several hours, or even a day or two. At the end of such an hour or at the finish of my day's work I can dictate an extremely detailed account of such a session. I may dictate rapidly for up to twenty minutes, giving a good deal of dialogue verbatim. I am aided in this by a reasonable degree of intelligence; I have college transcripts and other documents to prove it."

"You think rather well of yourself, Soaper."

"No. I know my weaknesses, or at least I think I do. Some of them handicap me badly in certain situations. But I also have my strong points."

"Soaper, you are either a genius or the most egregious fraud I've ever met."

"I am neither," I said.

"It's pronounced nee-ther, Soaper, not nigh-ther."

"I'm sorry," I said. "Nee-ther.'

"Is one of your faults a slight tendency to affectation at times? Are you, in your weaker moments, a bit of a poseur?"

I took a deep breath. "That could be one of my little weak-nesses."

"Little? It seems rather big to me. It smells of hypocrisy. Sham. Humbug. Deceit. Arrogance."

"You make me a little uncomfortable at times," I replied.

"'I wants to make your flesh creep.'"

"Fat boy, Dickens," I said.

"Careful, Soaper, you're showing off. A bit of the old po-seur coming out."

I did not reply.

"Soaper, when you see affectation and arrogance in peo-ple, doesn't it make you want to go out and puke?"

"It is disgusting," I said, "but I don't puke."

"Soaper, where's the toilet here? I feel like puking."

"You are hitting me below the belt," I said. "And you are also wasting your father's money."

"And whatever else we do, we must not do that," he re-joined. "Lord knows I've heard enough of that since I flunked out of the Berk."

A minute passed in silence.

"Well, Soaper," he said, "do you think you'll remember this interview with what you call your 'high degree of accura-cy'?"

"I rather think so."

"I *rah-ther* think so," he said. "Where did you pick up that English accent, Soaper? Took a six-week postgrad course one summer at Oxford, perhaps?"

"My mother was Canadian, the daughter of English immi-grants," I said. "When I am under tension my speech has a tendency to regress to the diction of my childhood."

"And you're under tension now?"

"I'm alert.'

"Do I make you tense, Soaper?"

"You keep me on my toes," I replied.

"A nice return," he said.

More silence.

"Well," he said, "let us proceed to talk about me. Like you

said, we don't want to waste my father's money talking about your personality defects, do we?"

"No."

"Now, Soaper, you said you remember interviews with interesting patients with what you call 'a high degree of accuracy,' and you further stated that you *rah-ther* think you'll remember this particular interview with this 'high degree of accuracy.' It therefore follows that you consider me an interesting patient. Is that so?"

"Yes."

"'Oh, doctor,' said he with a boyish giggle, 'I bet you tell that to all your patients.'" And he made a grimace.

"'No, no,' retorted the physician earnestly, 'it is not so,'" I retorted. And I made a grimace at him.

He looked at me with a slight smile.

"Well, Soaper, as I said, you are a caution."

"I'll take your word for it," I replied.

There was another minute of silence.

"Soaper," he said softly.

"Yes, David," I answered in a similar tone.

"David!" he shouted.

"That, I believe, is your name," I said, "or do you prefer Dave or Davey. We aim to please."

"Then never call me David again."

"All right," I said.

"My name is Gromchik."

"What?"

"Gromchik," he repeated, and he spelled it out, "G-r-o-m-c-h-i-k.'

"Let me write that down," I said. "My memory for unusual names is visual rather than auditory."

He spelled it out again as I wrote it on a pad.

"All right, Gromchik," I said. "May I ask how you got this name and what it means."

"You may ask, Soaper, but that can only be revealed if we get to know each other very well and become quite chummy. Only my most intimate friends know that."

"How many intimate friends do you have, Gromchik?"

"Well, Soaper, now that you mention it, I have none at all."

"Then I am the only one who knows that your true name is Gromchik?"

"Yes," he responded.

"Well, I feel flattered."

"You feel nothing of the kind, Soaper."

"You are wrong, Gromchik. I do feel flattered."

"Well, perhaps you do. Maybe you're the type that is easily flattered.'

"I take it," I said, "that you don't like the name David."

"I do not."

"Why?"

"Well, that's complicated," he replied.

"That's my stock in trade, Gromchik. I am a dealer in complicated things."

"Well, Soaper, first of all I don't like the name David because that's what my parents call me."

"And you perhaps have occasional differences with them?"

"Continual, Soaper, continual."

"All the time?"

"All the time," he replied.

"Are they aware of this?"

"No. They think we get along fine. As they see it, everything is fine, except that I flunked out of the Berk." He paused for a moment. "There are, of course, other reasons why I don't like David."

"Tell me about them."

"You're all ears, Soaper?"

"One hundred percent."

"Well, you see, Soaper, I'm one of the chosen people."

"Jewish?"

"Right, Soaper."

"And you don't like that?"

"No, Soaper."

"And why don't you like that?"

"Many reasons. First of all, my parents are Jewish. That sours it for me right there. Secondly, all my relatives are Jewish, and that makes it even worse. On top of it all, most of my friends are Jewish, which completely turns me off on the whole tribe."

"Isn't that a little discriminatory, Gromchik?"

"Not at all. I'm not against all Jews. I'm just against all the Jews I personally know. I don't have anything against the rest of them."

"Well," I said, "I'm glad to hear that. We must all work hard to stamp out prejudice wherever we find it."

"Exactly what I expected of you, Soaper. You're noble. You're true-blue. You're also slightly a fraud. That's another of your little weaknesses, isn't it?"

"We are all slightly a fraud, Gromchik. In that I am no worse than anyone else."

"Including me?"

"Perhaps."

Silence.

"Being the observant chap you are, Soaper, you might want to know how our name became Ross. Well, when my father graduated from law school in the late nineteen hundred thirties, Hitler was running around Europe, and so Daddy shortened it from Rosenberg to Ross; he didn't want people to think we were German. Fine old Scottish name, Ross. I've always meant to go down to the main public library and see what our tartan is, but I never got around to it."

"I take it you're not a strong proponent of the Jewish religion," I said.

"It is the most egregious hoax ever perpetrated on any people in the history of the human race," he replied. "You notice that's the second time I've used the word egregious. It's one of my favorites."

"And you feel that this egregious hoax has been perpetrated against you?"

"Precisely. We are the only people whom a god ever chose. Now, mind you, I would have nothing against this if I could see any tangible benefits from it. But long years of careful study and observation have convinced me that since this Jehovah chose us we have had nothing but trouble, and it would have been far better if he had chosen some other tribe, or nation, or group, or whatever we are. Now, tell me, Soaper, from your knowledge of history, such as it is, can you see any tangible benefits we have received from being chosen?"

"Well, none come to mind right now," I said.

"And don't you admit that we've had far more than our share of trouble since we got chosen?"

"I think a case could be made out for that," I replied.

"A very good case, Soaper, a very good case, indeed. But let us return to our original problem: Why do I resent being called David? The original David, a slingshot artist who made good, had a friend of his named Uriah murdered so he could get his wife, Bath-sheba, with whom he had already slept. And I have to go through life named after an adulterous murderer, who, for reasons best known to Himself, was a favorite of this Jehovah, who chose us, without any invitation whatsoever. In addition this Jehovah is a chronic liar anyway, since for thousands of years He has promised us that we were going to live in a land of milk and honey, but has given us nothing but trouble."

"Well, Gromchik, I guess it's just as well that we have an alternate name for you, since that other one seems to bother you so much."

"*Seems* to bother me, Soaper? It *does* bother me."

"Very well, Gromchik, it *does* bother you."

"Yes," he said, and lapsed into silence.

"Gromchik," I said after a minute, "would it offend you if I made an observation about your personality?"

"That depends on what the observation is. It may or may not offend me. But go ahead and make your observation; that's what my father is paying you for. I wouldn't want him to waste his money. What *is* your observation, Soaper?"

"Gromchik, you have a lot of hostility locked up inside you."

"Do you really think so, Soaper?"

"Yes, Gromchik, I do."

"And toward whom am I hostile?"

"Your parents."

"Oh, jolly good for you, Soaper. You are acute. You are a keen observer of men. You are right, Soaper. Not only do I have hostility toward them, I hate them."

"It's never quite as simple as that, Gromchik."

"If it were, you'd be out of a job, wouldn't you, Soaper?"

"There are others toward whom you are very hostile," I said.

"Name my enemies, Soaper, and I'll lay them low."

"One of them is quite close to you."

"*You*, Soaper! I never would have thought it."

"No.'

"Let me guess then. Who else is close to me right now? Why, there's only me!"

"You've got it," I said.

"I hate myself?"

"Precisely."

"Oh, insight! It's wonderful! I hate myself. I know that I hate myself. I'm cured! I can go back to the Berk and make straight A's. Soaper, you're a marvel. Cured me in one session. Send the bill to my father. He'll be delighted to pay it."

"Don't mention it," I said. "I pull this sort of thing off every day."

"Golly, bygosh, and geewhiz, Soaper, I'm glad I met you."

"I'm glad I met you," I said.

"Would you like to kiss me?" he asked.

"It's not done," I replied. "People might talk."

"They needn't know."

"Still, we'd better finesse it for now."

"Transference, countertransference, and all that, I suppose?" he said.

"Those are pretty big words for me," I said.

"Ah, Soaper, that modesty of yours coming out again. I really must do something about your inferiority complex."

Silence.

"Soaper," he said softly after a minute or so.

"Yes, Gromchik," I replied.

"Soaper, do you have a hemidryad?"

"A what?"

"A hemidryad."

"I don't think so. What exactly is a hemidryad, Gromchik?"

"Soaper, you don't know what a hemidryad is?"

"No, I don't."

"Really, Soaper, what did they teach you at Yale if you don't know what a hemidryad is?"

"How do you know I went to Yale?" I asked.

"I researched you," he replied.

"How did you do that?"

"I went down to the main public library and looked you up in the medical directory, a big blue book put out by your union, the American Medical Association. I also went over to the med school library on Hospital Hill and looked you up in the directory of that other union you belong to, the American Psychiatric Association. I read all about you."

"Was this after or before Dr. Wilner made this appointment for you?'

"Afterward, Soaper."

"Why did you research me?"

"Forewarned is forearmed, Soaper."

"Not too trusting of the species, eh, Gromchik?"

"Very cautious with them, Soaper."

"Well, what conclusions did you come to in your research, Gromchik?"

"Would you really like to know, Soaper?"

"Of course."

He leaned forward in his chair and whispered loudly, "Soaper, you have written one hell of a lot of crap."

He sat back.

"Did you look at some of it, Gromchik?"

"Yes. They stack it at the public library and even have a couple of samples of it at the med school. I've written a letter to my congressman protesting such a waste of public money. I've also founded a society called the Weed-Out-the- Crap-at-the-Public-Library Committee. Would you like to join? You'd be the second member. You'd be getting in on the ground floor of a good thing."

"I'll think it over, Gromchik."

"A good, safe reply. Well, let's get back to that other matter," he said.

"What other matter?"

"Oh, Soaper, where is that remarkable memory of yours today?"

"Oh. You mean the hemidryads."

"Yes."

"No, I learned nothing about hemidryads at Yale. You'll have to tell me all about them."

"Well," he said, "ancient Greece, as you undoubtedly know, was covered with forests. In each tree was a spirit called a hemidryad. With the passing of centuries the forests have all been cut down. Undoubtedly soil erosion, floods, and all that sort of thing have been the result, but that is not what concerns us at the moment."

"What concerns us at the moment?" I asked.

"What concerns us at the moment is: What happened to all the hemidryads when their trees were cut down? Hundreds of thousands, perhaps millions, of hemidryads were left with nowhere to go and nothing to do. For centuries their whereabouts were not even known. But they have recently been located."

"Really? Where are they?" I asked.

"They are on assignments," he answered.

"Assignments?"

"Yes."

"What kinds of assignments?"

"They are detailed," he replied, "to stay with specific individuals to help them out."

"What do they do?" I inquired.

"Well, suppose you have to get up at four o'clock in the morning to catch a bus and your alarm clock breaks down during the night, your hemidryad tickles your feet and wakes you up at four o'clock. Or maybe you're about to leave your dorm for an exam and you've forgotten your crib notes. Your hemidryad stuffs them in your pocket. Or suppose you can't think of anything to say to someone sitting next to you at a fancy dress ball. Your hemidryad whispers to you to say, 'My, what an interesting costume you have on.' Their usefulness is endless and continual."

"I see," I said. "They are somewhat like guardian angels."

"Exactly, Soaper. Now, coming back to my original question, do you have a hemidryad?"

"Not so far as I'm aware."

"I didn't think so," he said. "Do you know how I knew?"

"No. How did you know?'

"Well, Soaper, if you will study your trousers, you will note that about two inches below your belt and three inches to the left of your fly—your left, not mine—there is a small coffee stain."

"Tea," I said. "I rarely drink coffee. I'm a tea drinker."

"Well, tea then. A hemidryad would have known the difference. As a mere mortal I could hardly have been expected to know. Anyway, if you had a hemidryad, he would have prevented that tea splash from falling on your trousers. Also, your shoes need polishing, and there are a few specks of dandruff or something on your right shoulder, and that far corner of your desk is, in brief, a mess. Even a casual inspection of you reveals that you have no hemidryad, and you need one badly."

"What should we do about it?" I asked.

"Would you like me to get one for you?"

"Yes, why don't you do that?" I said.

"Have you any preferences?" he asked.

"No, I'll leave that up to you." I had an afterthought. "Are there both male and female hemidryads?"

"No," he said, "they are all male. The female equivalent of a hemidryad is a nymph. Sprites may be either male or female, but the terms hemidryad and nymph in themselves denote the sex."

"Well, arrange one for me, will you?"

"Yes," he said.

"I take it there's no cost."

"None at all," he replied. "There is just one problem."

"What is that?"

"You must be approved."

"And who does the approving?"

"That," he said, "is all done by the Hemidryad Placement Bureau. I'll see what I can work out."

"Thank you."

"Don't mention it, Soaper."

He picked up his book bag from the table beside him.

"I must be going, Soaper. When do we meet again?"

"How about Tuesday at four?"

"It's a bit soon, considering all I have to do in the meantime in arranging for a hemidryad to be assigned to you, but inasmuch as I am not otherwise occupied at the moment I think I can manage it. Until Tuesday at four, then."

"Until Tuesday at four," I repeated.

He rose and left.

On Tuesday at four Gromchik came into my office, threw himself into the sofa chair, and said, "Soaper, I've done it."

"Got me a hemidryad?"

"What else? It was a tough job, but I swung it. It so happens that I've met him before. That was a stroke of luck."

"Tell me all about it."

"I thought you'd say something hackneyed like that," he replied, "and so I typed out the details about how I met your hemidryad and so forth. Here."

He shoved a piece of paper at me, saying, "His name is Peydle."

On the paper he had typed the following:

How I came to know Peydle. I was sitting in an aisle seat on a plane from California, reading a badly written book, *Beyond Freedom and Dignity,* which my roommate had pressed on me; I often wished he wasn't majoring in psychology. When an old man lurched against me, I looked up, but he was already shuffling down the aisle, fumbling with his zipper: bladder trouble. His hemidryad, Peydle, had sat down next to me and, disregarding the fat woman across the aisle who had interrupted her meal of diet wafers to gape at us, we talked. Peydle had been with the old man for twenty years and hadn't yet figured out why he merited a guardian spirit. Still thinking about the old man's bladder, I said, "Wouldn't it be good if he were a fish, maybe a grouper, so that he could urinate without having to look for a toilet." Peydle agreed. We decided that the old man would first turn into a bird, then into a reptile, then into an amphibian, and finally into a webbed and scaly fish.

Something about his personality. I found Peydle droll, rather easygoing, a braggart, terribly involved with the person he was currently guarding (this, however, is characteristic of most hemidryads), and interested in natural history and philosophy. He bragged that he had once been the hemidryad of an early Italian Renaissance Neoplatonist, Marsilio Ficino. But I don't know Peydle well, and you have the rest of your life to learn all about him.

How you happened to get him. After you said you'd like a hemidryad, I dropped in at the bureau, filled out the forms, and looked through the list of free spirits. I saw Peydle's name and immediately had him called. Peydle said he'd look you over. He showed up two days later and announced that he'd decided to attach himself to you on a probationary basis.

What he looks like. In California I had helped my aunt, for a lark, to shape cookie dough into crescents and balls; the consistency of the stuff interested me. Back home, in January, I tried to make out of flour, water, and salt a little statue of Peydle's old man turning into a solemn, unembarrassed grouper. Because I had hardly seen the old man, I substituted good old Peydle's face. I stained the statue nearly the natural color of Peydle's skin. The face therefore is a good likeness of Peydle's, even if the rest of the statue proved an unsuccessful attempt to record a reversion to the piscine state. The finished piece reminded me of a mildly obscene passage concerning my old headmaster, Goodwood Beechheart, in a book titled *Gromchik's Squat Day;* thus, I called the statue "Goodwood Beechheart's Change of Life." Since January Peydle's statue has dried out and cracked badly. I was going to throw it away, but now I suppose I'll pass it on to you.

After reading it I looked up at him.

"Well," he said.

"Well, thank you," I replied.

"No, no, Soaper, I want to know what you think of Peydle. Are you satisfied?"

"Yes."

"Good. I'm glad. I thought the two of you would hit it off."

"When does he arrive to take up his duties?" I asked.

"Arrive? Ye gods and little fishes, Soaper, he's been with you for the last three days. There he is, right now, sitting on your desk." He pointed at the center of my desk. "And I can tell you, by the look on his face, he's not too happy that you haven't noticed him yet, or are pretending not to. I didn't know you were a snob, Soaper."

I looked at my desk. He was so insistent and convincing that I had slight doubts about whether he was joking or really saw Peydle there.

"Tell him I'm sorry," I said. "I've been very busy. I appreciate him."

"*Me* tell him! Why don't *you* tell him! In fact, you'd better tell him right now. As you can see by the look on his face he's about to walk off in a rage, and if he turns in a bad report on you to the Hemidryad Placement Bureau, I shall never be able to get you another one."

I was uncertain what to do.

"Soaper," he cried, "for God's sake talk to Peydle and tell him you're sorry. He's about to go."

I turned to the desk and said, "Peydle, I'm sorry. As you know, I've been very busy."

"Oh Lord, Soaper, you *are* an idiot. Ask him to stay. Ask him to stay, right now."

"Peydle," I said, looking at my desk top, "please stay. You must learn to forgive my lapses and weaknesses."

I turned to Gromchik, who was staring earnestly at my desk. Then Gromchik sank back into his chair, and a placid look came over his face.

"As you heard him say, he's decided to remain," Gromchik said. "He's made his commitment."

"That's good," I said.

"That's very good," he retorted. "I don't think you realize how good it is. Do you know what is meant by the word 'commitment,' when used by a hemidryad?"

"I'm not sure," I replied.

"When a hemidryad makes a formal commitment to a charge, which is the word they use in referring to us humans, it means that he will stay with you for the rest of your life. You are very lucky to have got Peydle."

"We'll get along quite well, I'm sure," I said.

"You're not sure at all, Soaper. You're just saying that because you were really scared when Peydle threatened to leave. But it will work out. Peydle will meet you more than halfway."

"May I keep this typed sheet on Peydle?" I asked.

"Certainly. I wrote it for your enlightenment."

"In your description of Peydle," I said, "you mention something about a statue or statuette of him."

"Oh, yes, I'm glad you reminded me of that," he said. He thrust his hand into the book bag on the floor beside his chair and drew out a cardboard box. He set it on his lap and untied the string that bound it. He opened the box and drew out a small figurine. It was about five inches high and at its base was three inches from front to back. It was light tan in color and resembled a wrinkled, bald, gnomelike man; from the waist down the figure spread into a lumpy mass.

"It looks just like him, doesn't it?" he asked, smiling at the figure.

"Yes," I said. I felt he was joking, but I was not completely sure.

"Soaper," he said.

"Yes, Gromchik."

"Will you tell me something honestly?"

"I'll try, Gromchik.'

"I can't ask more than that." He paused. "Soaper, can you really see Peydle?"

"You mean the real Peydle, not the statue?"

"Yes."

"No, Gromchik, I honestly can't see him."

"I didn't think you could."

"Well, you were right," I said.

"Do you want to know why you can't see Peydle?"

"Yes, I would like to know why you feel that I can't see Pey-dle."

"I noticed how you reworded my question, Soaper, but I'll overlook that. The reason you can't see Peydle is because you're over the age of forty. Only people who acquire their hemidryads before forty can see them."

"Well," I said, "I hope Peydle understands that."

"He does now. The trouble dawned on me during our crisis, in which Peydle almost walked out. You see, when I filled out your request card down at the Hemidryad Placement Bureau, I wasn't exactly honest. I wanted you to get a young, vigorous hemidryad who could really do you some good; Peydle may not seem young to you, but for a hemidryad he's in the prime of life. So, I put your age down as thirty-four. That way, I figured the bureau would take more interest in you. Peydle had, of course, read your request card and consequently thought you were thirty-four. I told him you looked old for your age. Hence, he naturally assumed you could see him, and when you payed no attention to him, he thought you were snubbing him. It's lucky I realized this error and shouted to him that you were really over forty just as he was about to leave. Then he realized that you couldn't see him, and that squared things away. You heard me shout to him that you were over forty, didn't you?"

"In the midst of all the confusion I guess I didn't hear that," I said.

"Soaper, you're not really as observant as you think you are.'

"Well, maybe not."

He lolled in his chair and looked at my desk top complacently.

"Gromchik," I said, holding in my hand the paper he had typed, "this is rather well written. You have talent."

"Well, Soaper, having looked at some of the crap you've

written, I frankly don't think you know enough to judge. However, you meant well. If you really think I write well, you may want to take a look at this." He lifted his book bag off the floor onto his lap and began to rummage through it. He took out one book after another and opened their front covers, looking for something. Soon five or six books were piled on the table beside him. He finally found what he was looking for, and handed me an eight-by-eleven-inch piece of typing paper, in the center of which was typed:

> Thinking of Blanchert, he strategically shrieked and ran the other way. In vain. I, mangled in a wheat bin: "Where, mangler, go ye?" SALAMANDERS WILL EAT LETTUCE IF GIVEN THE OPPORTUNITY.

"Well," he said, as I looked up after reading it, "what do you think of that?"

"I think it's very good," I replied.

"Well, Soaper, thank you. However, as you know, I can't accept your opinion about writing as worth much, for reasons we've already discussed. Out of consideration for your feelings, I shall not dwell on this subject. Your guilt feelings about it are probably strong enough anyway, and I don't want to make them worse.'

"Thank you," I said.

"There's more."

"More what?" I asked.

"More about Blanchert," he replied.

"Do you have it with you?"

"Yes. Would you like to see it?"

"I should very much like to see it," I replied.

He turned over the book from which he had taken the first sheet, lifted up its back cover, and took out another sheet. On it the following was typed:

> Blanchert is the mangler. The other man, of indeterminate age, and the pallor of an underdone biscuit, comes along after the mangling has occurred. Hearing

the noise of someone's efforts to breathe despite a mouth-
ful of blood, he peers into the wheat bin and gazes fascinated at the body (whose most widely spilled and scattered blood has already begun to coagulate). After a
while the body stops trying to breathe. The enraptured
spectator realizes that Blanchert has most certainly done
the mangling, and a fine job of it. He strategically shrieks,
and flees.

I read it and looked up at him.

"Well, Soaper, from the psychiatric point of view, what do
you make of it? For reasons we've already mentioned, we
shall not discuss your opinions of its literary qualities. We
shall stick to psychiatry, under the assumption that you know
something about that."

"First of all, Gromchik, did you write this?"

"I wrote it."

"Is it the product of several drafts, or did you just sit down
at a typewriter and pound it out?"

"It is of the pound out variety."

"It is quite remarkable then," I said.

"From the psychiatric point of view," he added.

"From any point of view."

"I'll overlook that. What do you make of it from the psychiatric point of view?"

"Gromchik, I shall tell you what I think in the same spontaneous way in which you wrote it, and I shall talk on the
assumption that you are revealing yourself in it."

"Do that," he said.

"All right," I replied. "The themes here are violence, terror, and helplessness. You see yourself as the victim of violence, mangled in a wheat bin; you feel yourself painfully
trapped in a situation from which you cannot escape. A
wheat bin is a food-giving, life-sustaining container, which
has here been perverted into a place of meaningless horror
and suffering. That is how you see the world and your situation in it. Suffering in this place, you want to know what
more torture and violence will be inflicted on you.

"Who are the others?" I continued. "Who is Blanchert? Who is the pale man of indeterminate age? Who are the salamanders? They are all you.

"You are Blanchert, the mangler, as well as the victim, the mangled. Thinking of yourself, you shrink in terror and run the other way.

"Against this is the dream, written in large, hopeful words. The salamanders, if freed and given the opportunity, will live in comfortable liberty and will do as they wish. They will nourish themselves on what they need, lettuce. It is a desperate plea, a call; *lettuce* is *let us*.

"You are also the one who is fascinated by all these things. However, you fear self-destruction, and hence you strategically shriek. Why strategically? Because you want help, but feel it is obtainable only by devious strategies, about whose success you are pessimistic."

I stopped.

He stared at me.

"Well?" I asked.

"You have possibilities, Soaper. Like I said, another twenty years at this and you may develop into a halfway competent psychiatrist.'

He silently studied his hands for a minute and then looked up and said, "Will I make it, Soaper?"

"I think so, Gromchik."

"You're not really sure though, are you, Soaper?"

"We're never completely sure."

"What exactly do you sell here, Soaper?"

I hesitated.

"Don't tell me the crap, Soaper. I can spot it a mile off. Tell me the truth."

"Hope," I said. "Hope is what we sell."

"Thank you, Soaper."

I remained silent.

He slowly put his books into the book bag.

"You can keep those, Soaper," he said, pointing to the two sheets of paper in my hand. "Put them in my chart. I'm sure you must have a chart on me."

"I'll do that," I replied.

"When do we meet again, Soaper?"

"You've only used up half your time, Gromchik."

"We've done enough for today," he responded.

"Friday at four?" I asked.

"Friday at four," he said, and left.

When Gromchik next came, he inquired how Peydle was: I told him we were getting along well, and he said he was glad.

"We're supposed to talk about my parents here, aren't we, Soaper?"

"We discuss whatever you can talk about with reasonable comfort," I replied.

"'Reasonable comfort,'" he repeated. "That sounds like something from an advertisement for cheap mattresses."

"That's rather clever, Gromchik."

He reached into his book bag and pulled out a book, from which he took a sheet on which he had typed the following:

> For Soaper:
> I also have another code name for myself: The Pie Machine.
>
> My mother has no faith in psychiatrists. I think she regards them as excuses for weak people who haven't the courage to go it on their own. If I had been caught sleeping with my paternal grandmother or if I had knifed Stella Smith, it would be different; that is, I would really be "disturbed." But I'm not. What is wrong with me could be remedied if only I would face the facts and do something about them. My mother's idea of "doing something" seems to be doing everything I dislike or am afraid of again and again until I no longer fear or dislike it and yet retain my sensitivity, imagination, originality, sense of humor, and sanity. I consider her plan of action neither adequate nor realistic. My mother regards you as a luxury to be borne for the sake of my readmittance to Berkeley. When I return from a session with you, her unvarying query is: "Well, do you have to go back?"
>
> My mother says the reason I'm impatient with my father is that I'm very like him. She often points out my

likeness to my father, as do others, and I long ago stopped liking it. Others see my similarity to my father in such things as the shape of our faces, an ear for music, manual dexterity, omnivorous interests and an experimental bent. My mother, while recognizing and confirming these likenesses, seems to emphasize particularly the faults she thinks my father and I share. She seems to want to represent me, both the good and the bad of me, as my father's son. I feel my mother identifies herself much more with Phil, and especially Howie, than with me. I know she loves my father and me, but it's a different thing. She also feels a great bitterness toward my father, the reasons for which I can perhaps explain verbally. She is bitter about me, too, and has been for several years. Perhaps I'd better talk about it rather than try to write it down. After all, it's verbal communication you're supposed to promote, isn't it?

When I write that my mother "feels" this or "thinks" that, I am usually saying what I think she thinks or what I feel she feels. It doesn't matter too much whether or not my assumptions are correct, as long as I think they are.

Talking with you has been great fun, but has it accomplished anything?

After reading this I placed it in my lap and waited for him to talk.

"Well, Soaper," he said, "what's the verdict? What exactly is the state of my Oedipus complex and how do we mend the difficulty? In what nice ways must the relationships of my superego, my ego, and my id be adjusted to each other? Where are the exact points into which drops of oil must be placed to get everything humming smoothly again?"

"I'm not a Freudian," I said.

"I wouldn't admit that if I were you," he said. "It's not fashionable. Besides that, they might throw you out of the union, and without a union card where would you be? You might have to get out of the chitchat business and start yanking out kiddies' tonsils or setting bones. Well, maybe you are a behavior theory enthusiast and are going to recondition all my loused-up conditioned reflexes."

"I'm also not a behavior theory advocate," I said.

"Goodness, Soaper, what are you then? Are you an organicist? Are you going to give me shots to straighten out the fouled-up biochemistry of my brain? That would seem unlikely since so far we've been engaged in the chitchat line."

"Not that either," I said.

"Then you must be a devotee of one of the more esoteric approaches. Are you one of the little band who daily worship at the shrine of the mahatma of the Alps, the late, unlamented Carl Jung? Or maybe you toss incense on the altar of that deviant Freudian, the lost sheep Karen Horney. Or perhaps you are a lonely keeper of the flame for Adler or Rank; however, I hope not, since they're rather passé."

"For a mere stripling of twenty, you seem to know a fair amount about psychiatry, Gromchik."

"It's because of the one big mistake of my life," he said. "When I was six, I learned to read."

"And you've never been the same since?"

"Utterly smashed," he replied.

"And that's how you happened to read so much psychiatry?"

"Yes."

"Looking for answers?"

"Of course," he replied.

"Have you found any?"

"I've found dozens of them, hundreds of them, thousands of them, Soaper. Unfortunately, if I may be permitted to employ a technical term, they are all one big pile of crap."

"Really," I said.

"Is that all you have to say, Soaper? I had expected some thing better out of you."

Silence.

"Soaper," he said, "I'm curious. What particular line of psychiatric gunk do you peddle?"

"I peddle what is known as the interpersonal line, to the extent that I peddle anything. Our gurus are Adolf Meyer and Harry Stack Sullivan."

"I've never heard of the Meyer chap," he said, "but I've

heard of Sullivan. He was that fag from Baltimore, as I remember."

"Something like that."

"A trifle on the queer side," he added.

"I don't think that's relevant to his psychiatric theories."

"Ah, Soaper, perhaps I've found another of your little
weaknesses. You're irritated with me. You don't like me to
say that your guru went around sticking his dong into other
fellows' rectums. You don't like to think about that, do you,
Soaper?"

"We all have our problems, Gromchik."

"But doesn't that take a little of the starch out of a psychiatrist's theories? 'Physician, heal thyself,' and all that. How can
you see straight through crooked glasses?"

"It *is* an uncomfortable problem for people who feel that
Sullivan made significant contributions."

"Is that why you're so annoyed with me right now, Soaper?"

"You're very observant, Gromchik."

"Thank you. But let's keep that old countertransference
under control, Soaper. No feelings toward the patient, you
know. Be a mirror unto him, and all that. Understand him,
but don't react to him. Eh what, Soaper?"

"That's a difficult goal, Gromchik. None of us ever quite
reaches it."

"Well, at least *you* have not quite reached it," he replied.
Turning his eyes toward my desk top, he said, "Peydle,
soothe him down. He's a bit upset."

Arching his neck slightly, he rested his head against the
back of the chair and regarded me with a complacent smile.

"Now that you're calmed down and more comfortable," he
said, "perhaps we should return to my manuscript. What do
you make of it, Soaper?"

I looked it over again.

"The Pie Machine," I said. "Do you make pies or eat
them?"

"Both," he answered.

"Well, would you like to hear me free associate to that?"

"Love to," he said.

"You destroy what you build," I· said. "You devour what you create. You fear destruction of even yourself, by yourself."

"Very good, Soaper. All wrong, of course, but very good, nevertheless. You're earning your money, and that's what we're here for. We wouldn't want it all to be in vain, would we?"

"No."

"By the way, Soaper, why is it you always do the free associating? I thought I was supposed to do that."

"You are, but I don't think you would," I replied. "If I asked you to, you'd simply balk or talk flippantly in riddles. Then again, you might panic. And if you once panicked, I don't think you'd ever come back. You don't panic at the things I say because you can always dismiss them as not yours, or erroneous, or irrelevant." After a pause, I said, "Panic. Is that what happened with the other four psychiatrists?"

"Perhaps," he said.

"What were they like?"

"They were the strong, silent type," he replied, "not the gabby, stab-in-the-dark kind, like you. However, I suppose that by now you've phoned my father and he's sent over all their reports."

"No, I haven't."

"But you'll do that pretty soon?"

"I don't think so," I answered.

"Really, Soaper. Why not?"

"It might destroy the precarious relationship we have. It also might deaden my ability to deal with you on the level we're on. You would notice any change in my manner immediately, and if I read those records, you might trust me even less than you do."

"Is our relationship that fragile, Soaper? I thought we had the beginnings of a beautiful friendship."

"We've kept it going so far, which I consider somewhat of an accomplishment," I responded.

"Put three gold stars by Soaper's name," he cried, "and give him the psychiatrist-of-the-month award. Now, let's get back to my manuscript. Perform, Soaper."

"The second paragraph deals with the seeping hostility your mother feels toward you; in fact, there seems to be a good deal of hostility on both sides in this relationship."

"Exactly, Soaper. Our relationship is one of complete mutual understanding. We hate each other's guts."

"Do you have any speculations about why?" I asked.

"Yes. She has halitosis, which I can't stand, and my finger nails are always dirty, which she can't stand."

I went on. "Apparently, the hostility between you and your mother rarely comes out openly; it filters out slowly, perhaps continually. I doubt that you and she ever deal with it frankly."

"That is correct, Soaper. We are a courteous, well-bred family. Hence, we do not discuss such things. It would not be polite. I never mention her halitosis, and she never mentions my dirty fingernails."

"There's a good deal in the second paragraph," I said.

"Yes, I agree," he replied. "It is very pithily written. Lean, sparse prose with no unnecessary words. It shows the influence of my many years of reading the Kansas City telephone directory."

I could not suppress a slight smile.

"Do I amuse you, Soaper?"

"At times."

"Good," he said. "I'm glad somebody's getting something out of these sessions. However, go on in your discussion of the second paragraph. I'm all ears."

"It deals with your mother's hostility toward both you and your father. As you see it, she divides the family into two camps. She, Phil, and Howie are on one side; you and your father are on the other. However, though she may or may not be truly affectionate to Phil and Howie, you and your father are not really close to each other. The distance between you and your father is as great as that between you and your mother, but it is created by coldness and indifference rather than frank irritability."

"You're coming right along, Soaper. You're one of my most promising psychiatrists."

"Thank you, Gromchik. Incidentally, I take it Phil and Howie are boys."

"Yes, Soaper. You're really brilliant today. These two fellows with boys' names are boys."

"It's good to be sure," I said, somewhat defensively. "Phil could be short for Phyllis or Felice, and Howie could be a nickname for Holly. It's embarrassing suddenly to find out in the eighteenth interview that someone who you thought was a boy is a girl, or vice versa. I saw it happen once in a child guidance clinic."

"That's what I like about you, Soaper. You're scientific; you take nothing for granted and check out every detail. Incidentally, our dog is male and his name is Monty."

"How old are Phil and Howie?"

"Phil is eighteen and Howie is fifteen. We are a well-spaced, model family."

"What are Phil and Howie like?"

"Well, Soaper, despite my mother's preference for them, they are a couple of slobs. I might correct that statement and say that *because* of my mother's preference for them they are a couple of slobs. They are spoiled rotten. They make mediocre grades in school, are complete voids in athletics and have no noticeable talent in any of the arts; they are lazy and conceited, and spend money like it grew on the oft-cited trees. They also belch at the table occasionally. Howie has a motorcycle on which, with a little luck, he may kill himself within a year or two, and Phil has a car with which he may accomplish the same objective. They chase girls and boast of their copulative abilities in ways which, prude that I am, I find repulsive. My mother clucks over them with tender solicitude, and my father says that someday they will find their niches."

"Do you have any idea, Gromchik, about why your mother feels so differently toward you and your brothers?"

"None at all."

"Have you ever wondered about it?"

"I long ago discovered that I was happiest when I thought

as little as possible about my family. I view them as I view the drapes and carpets at home. Every home has drapes, carpets, and a family. Ours is no exception."

"Some psychiatrists might consider that a somewhat unhealthy attitude, Gromchik."

"That is a profound observation, Soaper, and I thank you for it. Would you care to comment on the last sentence on the page?'

"I am hopeful, Gromchik, that talking with me will have usefulness for you, but I cannot guarantee it."

"That's what I like about you, Soaper. You're such a humble toiler in the vineyards of mental health."

"I do my best," I said.

"And look back on every day with a feeling of satisfaction for jobs well done," he added.

"Not always."

"No? Well, I guess you can't win 'em all. Anyway, I think we've exhausted that page. I must be going."

"You have more time at your disposal in this session, Gromchik."

"I have pressing things to do, Soaper, and I can't spend the best years of my life talking with psychiatrists. When is our next encounter?"

We set the time and he left.

At the beginning of the next session he drew a sheet of eight-by-eleven-inch unlined paper from his book bag and handed it to me, saying, "Tell me what you think about this."

It was folded into quarters. I unfolded it and smoothed out the creases. On it he had typed the following:

TWO EXAMPLES OF HOW SAFE SUBJECTS SUDDENLY
DEVELOP SHARP EDGES, OR WHY I FIND IT INADVISABLE
TO TALK WITH MY MOTHER

The dog was scratching at one of the doors that divide the back of the house from the front. Mother went downstairs to let him outdoors. She returned in a few minutes and reported:

"He doesn't want to go out; he just stands in the middle of the kitchen and looks at me. He just doesn't want to be left alone in that part of the house. My God, a gregarious dog! The only normal one in the family, the only well-adjusted one. *He's gregarious!*"

"Mom, there's nothing wrong with not being gregarious. I mean, it's not abnormal."

"Well, you don't have to be gregarious, but you can't run away from everything and everybody."

My mother and I were in the kitchen.

"Hey, Mom, I almost forgot to tell you: Chuck Norris got turned down at K. U. medical school! They said he was too old. He's twenty-six, you know."

"Too old! He's just a senior, isn't he?"

"Yeah, but he's still twenty-six. He said that even though the age limit is officially twenty-eight, if they have a bunch of twenty-two-year-olds that are just as qualified as he is, they'll take them and turn him down. And that's what happened."

"I suppose they have a policy like that; after all, medical school takes such a long time. How come Chuck is only a senior in college?"

"Well, he was in the service, I think. . . ."

"Yes, but he didn't have to be!"

"I guess not, but, you see, he, ah, goofed around and failed a year or two at a university somewhere, but after that he really straightened out and—"

"Oh, I see!"

"But he's been doing wonderfully. Why, right now he's carrying fifteen hours of 'A'! I don't understand how they could turn down a fellow like that. And he was so sure he'd have no trouble getting in!"

"You see, that's what happens when people aren't where they belong in college, when they're older than they should be!"

After reading this sheet I said, "Would you like to proceed as we usually do?"

"By all means, Soaper."

"We'll take the first anecdote first," I said.

"Very logical, Soaper. I agree with you. The safe, prudent thing is to begin at the beginning."

"These two anecdotes are about communication; they deal with communication on two levels. On the first, obvious level the communication is about commonplace, simple things. On the second, deeper level, it is concerned with hostility and deprecation of you. Your mother is slashing at you because you are not the outgoing, socially comfortable, achieving person she wants you to be. Of course, no matter how conforming and achieving you were, I think she'd treat you much the same way; she has some deeper reason or set of reasons for despising you. Your performance of the last year or two has merely given her a better target."

I stopped and waited for him to say something.

"Don't look at me," he protested. "I'm not the psychiatrist. Go on to the second one."

"All right, Gromchik. The second one is largely the same as the first. The subject is more specific. Your mother is castigating you because you flunked out of Berkeley." After a pause I added, "She sounds like she can be quite a bitch."

"That's merely your opinion," he replied. "In the Jewish community of Kansas City she's considered to be a very fine lady. You may not be aware of it, but we are high society in Jewish social circles. We're old German Jewish stock; we came over in the eighteen hundred fifties. My father is the fourth generation of our family in his law firm. We're much more refined than all those Russian and Polish Jews who came over in the eighteen hundred and nineties. They have dreadful manners. My mother a bitch! How can you say such a thing?"

"And you're supposed to become a lawyer and be the fifth generation in this law firm?"

"Exactly."

"What were you studying at Berkeley?"

"General liberal arts."

"Pre-law?"

"Naturally."

"And you detested it?"

"No, I loved it. I detested where it was leading."

"To law school?'

"Yes."

"And then into your father's law firm?"

"Of course."

"And you felt that you couldn't do your own thing—do something different and lead your own life?"

"On the contrary, I arranged to do exactly that."

"In what way?"

"Oh, Soaper, you are in poor form today. It's obvious. I flunked out of Berkeley."

"I see."

"Billboards usually are easy to see," he replied.

"And that was your way of rebelling?"

"So I've been told by two psychiatrists. I considered the expression rather trite."

"Two of your former psychiatrists said you were rebelling. What did the other two say?"

"As I've said, they were the strong, silent type. They said 'Good morning' and 'Good-bye.'"

"Nothing more?"

"Sometimes they said 'Good afternoon' and 'Good-bye.' I once calculated that my father was paying them fifteen dollars a word."

"Do you agree that you were rebelling?"

"No."

"Then how do you figure it?"

"I don't figure it. If the patients figured it, it would put all the psychiatrists out of business, and the economic state of the nation is bad enough without that happening. I just sit back and let the psychiatrists figure it out."

"Could you give me your views about how you managed to flunk out of Berkeley?"

"I froze up."

"Could you elaborate on that a little?"

"I'm not inclined to."

"Would you mind if I tried to explore it a little?"

"Not at all, but I reserve the right to freeze up on you."

"When you froze up, Gromchik, where were you and what were you doing?"

"I froze up in various places while doing various things; however, the particular freezing up that caused all the trouble occurred during exams."

"All exams, or just some of them?"

"In the end, all of them."

"Do you know why you froze up?"

"Yes."

"Could you tell me?"

"I froze up because I sat there and just looked at the questions. I knew the answers, but my ballpoint pen wouldn't move. You may next ask why my ballpoint pen wouldn't move. It wouldn't move because my hand and arm wouldn't move. Beyond that I can't trace it."

"And how did you feel when your arm and hand couldn't move?"

"Very uncomfortable. Uncomfortable is a good word I learned from you, Soaper. It avoids using terms like 'scared shitless' and 'felt like puking.' You haven't done much for my psyche, Soaper, but you've contributed a few things to my vocabulary."

"How many times did you freeze up during exams?"

"Enough to get booted out of the Berk."

"And when you were booted out of the Berk, what did the dean, or the assistant dean, say to you?"

"The assistant dean said that I had problems. By this time I had seen two psychiatrists at the university health service, and that gave the assistant dean a clue."

"Did the assistant dean say anything else?"

"He said that if I solved my problems, I could be readmitted to the Berk."

"What did you say?"

"I thanked him most politely."

"And do you want to go back to the Berk?"

"It is the only thing I really want."

"No other college or university will do?"

"Hundreds of other colleges and universities will do, but I want to go back to the Berk. I loved the Berk."

"And how do your parents feel about you going back to Berkeley?"

"They feel I should study and be a credit to them and in time become a lawyer. After that I should be on the boards of five civic organizations and marry a nice Jewish girl from the right kind of nice Jewish family and live happily ever after."

"Will any college or university that leads to this happy state of affairs do?"

"Not exactly. It must be a reasonably prestigious college or university. The University of Chicago, or Michigan, or any of the Ivy League schools will do. Others will not do. When my father's friends mention how well their sons are doing at Dartmouth or Yale or Cornell and they ask my father how his son Gromchik is doing, it would not do for him to reply that Gromchik, alias David, is studying at Podunk U. or Gopher Junction Tech, or Akron Subnormal."

"I see. And you are absolutely set on returning to the Berk?"

"Yes."

"And nowhere else?"

"Nowhere else."

"And how do you intend to get back into the Berk?"

"That, Soaper, is where you come in.'

"I presume I am to cure you, and then you go back to the Berk?"

"Oh no," he answered, "I don't expect the impossible."

"Then I am just to patch you up in adequate condition to get you back to the Berk?"

"You overestimate your capacities, Soaper. I don't even expect that."

"Well, Gromchik, what is it that you expect of me?"

"Now we're getting down to business, Soaper. What I want out of you is quite simple. All I want, when the time comes, is a letter that lists your credentials and states that you have duly treated me for X number of months; the letter will then say that I have improved greatly and am now ready to go back to the Berk and get along well there."

"Am I to send this letter to the dean?"

"No. I prefer that you give it to me; I shall enclose it with a letter of my own to the dean."

"This arrangement is to make sure that I say the right things in my letter?"

"Exactly, Soaper."

"When do you envision that this happy event is going to take place?"

"In about five months."

"May I inquire how you can so precisely set the date for your improvement, Gromchik?"

"I wasn't talking about improvement. I was talking about the deadline for filing for readmission to the Berk."

"Oh. And what happens if in five months I feel you're not ready to go back?"

"You'll write the letter anyway," he said.

"What makes you think that?" I asked.

"Peydle will arrange it for me. He is grateful to me for getting the two of you together; he says you're his most interesting assignment since Marsilio Ficino."

"Do you hear from Peydle occasionally?"

"Every day," he replied.

"Do you hear from anyone else?"

"Yes.'

"Who?"

"Other hemidryads. However, you don't know them."

"In what way do you hear from them?"

"You're getting too inquisitive, Soaper."

"That's my job."

"Well, they talk to me, and I talk to them."

"Where?"

"Anywhere," he said. "They whisper things to me. Sometimes they slur and I can't make out what they're saying, but a lot of the time I can understand them quite well."

"And what do they say?"

"They say, among other things, that you'll get me back into the Berk."

"What else do they say?"

"That is private business between them and me and does not concern you," he answered.

"You wouldn't want to give me some hints?"

"No."

"Are all the hemidryad voices male?"

"I've already told you that, Soaper. All hemidryads are male."

I looked steadily at him for a minute or more, while he gazed complacently back at me.

I returned to our previous subject. "Gromchik, I think you overestimate me."

"Not at all, Soaper, I consider you to be utterly incompetent."

"I think you overestimate me as a letter writer," I said.

"How so?"

"I doubt I shall write that letter; or at least I don't think I'll write it in that particular way and at that time."

He became more sober. "You may not be sure that you are going to write it in five months, but I consider it a foregone conclusion."

"You seem very sure of that," I said.

"I have ways of arranging it," he replied.

"What ways?"

"Well, there's Peydle, of course, and in a crisis he can call in other hemidryads to work on you. However, I have other resources."

"What kinds of resources?"

"Must I show you my hand?" he asked.

"It might be in your best interests," I replied.

"Well, Soaper, while you have been studying me, I have not been idle. I have been studying you."

"More library research?" I inquired.

"No. I've got beyond library research. This has been laboratory research."

"Oh. You mean our sessions here."

"Yes."

"And what discoveries have you made in your laboratory research?"

"You, Soaper, have your weaknesses, as we have briefly mentioned before. I know much more about them now."

"I see. And you plan to manipulate my weaknesses to get the letter out of me.'

"Exactly," he replied.

"In order that we may both know where we stand and make sure that neither of us misjudges the other, I think it would be wise for you to tell me what my weaknesses are and how you intend to manipulate them, Gromchik. People have misjudged me before, occasionally to their cost. I wouldn't want you to make that mistake."

He became more serious, though traces of his flippancy remained.

"All right. I think no harm can come of letting you see the picture more fully. First of all, Soaper, you view yourself as humanitarian. You consider yourself a do-gooder. As a corollary of this, it is important to you that you do not intentionally harm people. This is important to you; you get hung up on it at times." He stopped.

"Go on," I said.

"You, of course, view your humanitarianism as a virtue; it is not, but we need not go into that. Your anxiousness not to damage people is interesting; guilt chews at your liver now and then, Soaper. This aspect of you will be very useful to me." He paused again.

"You obviously have more to say, Gromchik."

"True," he replied. "Secondly, Soaper, you are vain. You are not vain in the ordinary sense of the word. In terms of houses, fancy automobiles, expensive clothing, fashionable country clubs and that sort of thing, you are not vain. Your office furnishings reveal that. Your vanity is more subtle. You think very highly of yourself intellectually and professionally. You would be quite upset for a few weeks if I were to put a big blotch on your professional reputation in the community. That would stab you hard."

"And how could you put a big blotch on my professional reputation?"

"By killing myself," he replied. "I'm not the ordinary run-of-the-mill patient. My family is well known in Kansas City, especially in business and professional circles. I am young and bright. I have, despite my recent bit of trouble at the Berk, a brilliant future ahead of me just as soon as I 'settle down,' as everyone is sure I will. My death would be tragic and much discussed. 'He was so young,' they would say, 'and had so much promise.' You get the picture. Also, Soaper, I would do the job in a quite conspicuous way and would leave a suicide note amply involving you; in it I would forgive you for refusing to see me for extra sessions in recent weeks despite my urgent pleas for help. I would see that you were thoroughly smeared."

He smiled sweetly at me.

"Are you blackmailing me, Gromchik?"

"That is a nasty word," he answered. "Let us merely say that I am boxing you into a corner."

We sat in silence for a few moments.

"Well, Soaper," he said, "will I get my letter? It's an easy way out for you. I go back to the Berk, time passes, and you're in the clear."

"And what if you don't make it back at the Berk?"

"That's my problem," he replied.

"What if you pull off this little caper at the Berk?"

"Ah, don't worry about that, Soaper. If I have trouble at the Berk they'll undoubtedly send me off to the university health service again, where I'll run through another couple of shrinks, and by the time I get around to bowing out of the picture you'll be completely in the clear. The responsibility for botching the job on me will rest on someone else's shoulders. You may rely on me, Soaper. When I make a deal I keep it."

"The Berk may not accept a letter from me as sufficient basis for admitting you again, Gromchik."

"Oh, but they will," he said. "I'll see that my letter, accompanying yours, mentions your high qualifications, your fecundity as a writer, and so forth. You'll do very nicely. That was apparent to me from the moment I concluded my library research on you before our first appointment.'

"If you kill yourself in Kansas City, Gromchik, you will never get back to the Berk."

"If I don't get back to the Berk, I'm not particularly interested in going on with this lousy television serial called life. So it all ends up the same way."

A long silence ensued.

"Well, Soaper, do we have a deal?"he asked.

"Gromchik, if this is not a bluff—and I don't think it is—you have misjudged me."

"No, Soaper, it is you who is bluffing; you'll write the letter. Let's look at it this way. If you don't write the letter, I bow out. If you write the letter, you at least give me the chance of life. Who knows? I may make it at the Berk; but if you don't write the letter, you condemn me without a chance. Even if your vanity and a touch of fear do not pull the letter out of you, your humanitarianism will." Looking at my desk top, he smiled and said, "He'll do it, won't he, Peydle?" Turning back to me, he added, "Peydle agrees that you'll write the letter."

"Gromchik," I said, "you are very shrewd, but you have misjudged me. I'll take my chances. I shall not write the letter. You see, I have a different scenario in mind.'

His eyes narrowed a bit, and the lines in his face deepened slightly. "What kind of different scenario?" he asked.

"I see it this way," I replied. "Next summer or perhaps next fall you enter the University of Missouri-Kansas City; you continue to see me while you attend classes there. If you get along all right for one or two semesters at UMKC, I then shall write a letter stating that I have treated you, that you have successfully completed one or two semesters at UMKC, and that you are now ready, in my opinion, to return to Berkeley. Whether or not Berkeley gives you full credits for the courses you take at UMKC is unimportant to both of us. Your sole object is to return to the Berk. With the kind of letter I shall write, and which I can deliver directly into your hands if you wish, I would estimate that you will have a nine ty percent chance of returning to Berkeley. That's the way I see it."

He sat motionless, staring at me, for a few moments.

"Well, Soaper, I *have* misjudged you a little. If I agree with your plan, who is to decide whether I spend one term or two at UMKC?"

"So long as you take four subjects and have a C average,

with no grades under a C, you may decide whether you go one semester or two."

He studied the carpet for a minute or so and then looked up and said, "You have a deal, Soaper."

"Fine."

He picked his book bag off the floor and said, "It's time to go."

"You still have fifteen minutes left," I replied.

"We won't solve the rest of my problems in fifteen minutes. I may as well be moving along."

We set the time for his next appointment.

"Gromchik, there's one other thing that perhaps is worth mentioning today.'

"What's that, Soaper?"

"You, Gromchik, end the session each time; you always terminate before the fifty minutes are up. I would guess that you do so in order to beat me to the punch. You don't want even the implied rejection of my telling you that the interview is over, and thus dismissing you. Even such a minor rejection would be somewhat painful for you."

"You've been reading too many books lately, Soaper."

He rose and left.

My sessions with Gromchik continued at the rate of two a week. Each time he brought something he had typed and we used it as the basis, or the starting point, for the interview.

Seven months after he began to see me he started to attend the University of Missouri-Kansas City. He chose courses in which he felt he would do well, but they formed a reasonable academic load.

One afternoon he brought me a skit:

A PLAY IN ONE ACT

Thursday, November 17: In the morning I freeze up on a biology test. In the afternoon I cut biology laboratory to avoid Davis. In the late afternoon I keep an appointment with Mr. Harper, area director of Advanced Speaking Skills, who wants me as a demonstrator; I fake a disastrous performance to persuade him to forget it. I return home at evening to encounter my mother, who thinks, of course, that I've had a routine day.

The scene: It is evening. My father is attending a professional organization dinner somewhere, and my brothers are not at home. I am eating dinner at the table in the breakfast room. The kitchen is to my right; the dining room is beyond an archway to my left. My mother is putting away dishes in the breakfast room.

ME (casually, cheerfully): Man, you should've seen Gary this morning! He'd been up since he got off work at two this morning, and a customer had been buying him drinks all evening. He hadn't even been home to change clothes.

MOTHER (thoughtfully): Now let's see. I don't know Gary, do I?

ME: Oh, sure you do; he's the little guy with the big glasses, you know, the part-time bartender, the guy you saw me talking to at Linda Hall Library.

MOTHER: Yes, yes, the little one. So small!

ME: That's right.

MOTHER (suddenly remembering, or pretending to): Didn't you have your test this morning?

ME (without expression): Yeah.

MOTHER: Was it what you expected?

ME (stalling): What do you mean, was it what I expected?

MOTHER: Was it the kind of test you thought he would give?

ME (rambling, as I do when I don't want to answer a question I have to answer): Well, as a matter of fact, it wasn't. Davis usually gives essay tests and everybody was surprised when this turned out not to be one.

MOTHER (in the kitchen): What?

ME: I said, HE USUALLY GIVES ESSAY TESTS, BUT HE DIDN'T THIS TIME.

MOTHER (coming back into the breakfast room): I wonder why.

ME: Easier to grade, I guess.

MOTHER: That's what I think. I know he put off the test because he had the flu and didn't feel up to grading it. Maybe he still doesn't feel up to it.

ME: I don't know. (Trying to change the subject) Y'know, we were kidding around in the lab the other day, talking about the test, and I told Murray that if I didn't know something, I'd write French instead. And Murray said that I'd better be careful not to write too much, because it's pretty hard to grade tests by the light of a television set.

MOTHER: That Murray is some character.

ME: Anyway, he tries to be. But you understand, don't you, that it's not Murray who'll grade the tests. (My mother disappears into the dining room; in a moment she returns to the breakfast room. Having finished my dinner, I take my plate into the kitchen.)

MOTHER (with ill-disguised cunning): Did you write much French on the test this morning?

ME (whining a little): I don't want to answer your questions about the test, but if you have to ask 'em, can't you come right out and ask me if there were things I didn't know?

MOTHER: I was only . . . You told Murray that if you didn't know something you'd write French, and I—

ME (nastily): I told that to Murray, not you. Ah, Mother, dear, I follow your train of thought quite well. You're so damn perceptive, so clever. You're so deep you're transparent. And I don't particularly care for it.

MOTHER (losing control, which is rare for her): You're obnoxious!

ME: Next time I'll be sure not to tell you when a test is due; then maybe you'll leave me alone.

MOTHER (bitterly): Oh, yes, we've been *so* demanding! We've never demanded anything of you. We've made it so easy for you! And now you're a bum! A real bum!

ME (in my usual, somewhat nonchalant manner): Say, Mom, where's something I can wipe off the breakfast room table with? This towel okay?

MOTHER (very ill at ease about having lost control of herself): I don't care. The towel's fine.

(I wipe off the table, hang up the towel, and go upstairs to my room, where I type this play in one act).

As on other occasions in recent weeks, I tried to get him to talk spontaneously about what he had typed, but he refused,

saying that we would continue to the end as we had begun:
He would type and I would comment.

"So, Soaper, what do think of me as a dramatist? Will I
push Shaw and Brecht to the wall?"

"Well," I answered, "it's a trifle short and the action is
somewhat limited, but it has possibilities."

"Stop the dillydallying and start analyzing, Soaper."

"Before that, could you tell me something about your
freezing up on the test?"

"There's not much to say. I just froze."

"Can you tell me how you felt when you froze?"

"Like puking.'

"And what else?"

"That's all. I just felt like puking."

"What you mean, Gromchik, is that you can put nothing
more into words.'

"If you know what I mean, Soaper, why do you ask me
what I mean? Why don't you just tell me what I mean?"

I took a deep breath and went on. "Did you freeze on the
whole test?"

"No."

"On how much of it?"

"About half of it."

"How many questions were there?"

"Forty."

"And how many did you answer?"

"Forty."

"Then you really didn't freeze on the test."

"On the contrary, Soaper, I did. For the first hour I just sat
there looking at the paper. Then I unthawed a little and put
something down for every question."

"So it's possible you passed?'

"It's possible."

"Even probable?"

"It's even probable."

"And when you were frozen, Gromchik, what did you
think about?"

"Would you really like to know, Soaper?"

"Yes."

"I kept thinking how I jacked off during an English exam at the Berk."

"What do you mean, 'jacked off'?" I asked.

"Jacked off, ejaculated," he said.

"I'm not with you," I said.

"I had an English exam at the Berk, and I didn't know the stuff. It was mainly on a novel by Jane Austen; I think it was *Emma*. I didn't have time to read it, and so I just read every other page, thinking I'd pick up enough to pass the test. It didn't work. I was scared. As I sat there during the exam I got an erection, and it wouldn't go away. I didn't do anything to get it; it just came, and I ejaculated right into my underwear and trousers. It made a wet spot on the front of my trousers, and gooey stuff ran down my thigh. When the exam was over, I held my book bag over the wet spot on my trousers while I went up to the front of the room and turned in a couple of blank test booklets. I went to the dorm, took a shower and changed my clothes. And that fiasco is what kept going through my head as I sat there frozen during this exam on Wednesday."

"Do you have any idea how you managed to unfreeze and complete this exam?"

"No."

"Not even the slightest idea?"

"Well, to be frank, I know to a certain extent."

"Could you tell me about it?"

"Soaper, this is going to be embarrassing."

"Go ahead anyway, Gromchik."

"I started thinking about you," he said.

"Me?"

"Yes, you," he replied.

"In what particular way did you think about me?" I asked.

"I just kept thinking," he said, "how lucky I am to have you for my psychiatrist, and how wonderful you are, and how you've helped me, and about all the money you've made, and what a peachy-keen, true-blue, honest-to-goodness, modest, down-to-earth person you are. And I said, 'How can I let ole Soaper down? If I flunk this test, ole Soaper will probably plunge right through his office window in sheer despair, and since it is only a second floor window he won't accomplish anything except break a few bones and cause congestion in the parking lot for half an hour while they gather him up and haul him away.' And so I pulled myself together and unfroze and put something down·for every question and probably squeezed through."

"That's what I call a really good patient-therapist relationship, Gromchik."

"I'm glad you think so, Soaper."

"And now, let's go back to your play."

"Let's do just that."

"It's interesting," I said.

"That's not the question, Soaper. What I want to know is: Is it commercial?"

"You make it hard for me sometimes, Gromchik."

"Life was not meant to be easy, Soaper."

"When you quote yourself in dialogue in anything you write for me, as in this play, you talk somewhat differently from the way you do when you are in this office," I said.

"How so, Soaper?"

"You're more flippant here."

"Why do you think that's so, Soaper?"

"I would like to think that it's because this is a unique situation in your life. You know that here and here alone in all your interpersonal relationships the other person will not react emotionally to what you say and do. He will not get angry or become oversolicitous or become panicky about anything you say; he will merely try to understand and to be helpful. That is what makes this situation unique in your life."

"No, Soaper. It is true that this is a unique situation, but those things have nothing to do with it."

"Well, what does make it unique then?"

"You, Soaper, are the *only* person who gets paid money to talk to me. *That* is what makes it unique."

"This play," I said, attempting to regain my balance, "deals with deception in interpersonal relationships."

"You fascinate me, Soaper. Go on."

"Your mother plays tricks on you, sneaky, dirty, little

tricks. She pries, not to understand, but to stab. She lures you into a verbal interchange on a seemingly harmless topic and then slashes at you once your defenses are down. When this happens many hundreds of times, perhaps thousands of times, throughout all the years of childhood and adolescence, the individual who has been so battered develops the feeling that closeness between people leads only to pain. Every interpersonal relationship is seen as a trap, a trap with sharp blades. To be uninvolved is to be safe."

"Your skill in stringing clichés together is truly impressive, Soaper."

"This play also shows," I went on, "how hostility and depreciation of you can erupt suddenly through the usual façade of politeness at home, and how the façade quickly closes over again, hiding the nastiness and coldness beneath."

"Continue, Soaper."

"The play further shows how you use your habitual nonchalance and flippancy to protect yourself. It's your way of saying that nothing matters, that nothing touches you, and that it's all a silly game. But, as we both know, the defense doesn't work very well; the pain comes through. You carry the same flippancy and nonchalance into your relationship with me, to avoid involvement and the possibility of pain. I suspect that you carry this same smart-alecky jauntiness and levity into many other kinds of relationships. It keeps everyone at arm's distance. You feel safer that way."

After a pause he said, "I don't like being called a smart aleck."

"I didn't mean it as a depreciatory term," I replied. "It's not the right term to describe the way you talk and act, but on the spur of the moment it's the best I could come up with. If I hurt you, I'm sorry."

"I know that I annoy a lot of people with my brand of chatter," he said.

"It isolates you."

"And what's wrong with that?"

"It's dangerous," I replied. "You lose your perspective when you cannot continually check and modify your feelings, ideas, and actions in the context of reasonably healthy relationships with people. Also, life without a certain amount of comfortable closeness with others tends to be a mechanical, pleasureless thing. The satisfaction you can get from books, music, and solitary intellectual pursuits is limited."

"Well, I think we've exhausted that," he said, waving his hand at the two sheets of paper I still held.

"By that you mean you're getting a little tense and don't want to talk more about this subject, Gromchik."

"Soaper, when you make love to your wife or to anyone else, do you still go on making psychiatric comments?"

"You're attacking me, Gromchik. I know it's the best defense, but I'm on your side.'

"Enough, Soaper, enough. You've earned your money for today. By the way, is my father more or less paid up to date?"

"He is exemplary in paying his bills," I replied.

"Good. But, Soaper, if he suddenly went broke and couldn't pay you anymore, would you go on seeing me?"

"I don't know," I said. "I *have* done it occasionally in the past."

"But has that sort of benevolence ever amounted to more than two or three percent of your practice, Soaper?"

"I'm afraid not."

"And tell me honestly, Soaper, would you go on seeing me twice a week?"

"Probably not."

"So money is really what keeps this going after all, isn't it, Soaper?"

Silence.

"I must be shoving off, Soaper. I have to see a man about a guitar."

We set the time for our next appointment and he left.

When he came for his next session, he said, "I've given up plays and have gone back to straight prose," and he handed me a sheet on which the following was typed:

My father says he is afraid that I'll "get like Larry Schoenfield's brother, who has this thing about people."

It seems to me that he chooses an illogical way of discouraging me from being a recluse. If, for instance, I am invited to a party, lose my courage, and refuse to go, I get hell. If I do go to the party, but behave badly (by saying somewhat original, but slightly sharp-edged things or by saying nothing at all or by talking about the weather in an unconvincing manner), as I sometimes do, I get hell. If I go to the party and acquit myself well, I get neither praise nor blame, for I am only behaving as I should. (I might mention here that the party itself is an ordeal.) From past experience I know that I have a greater chance of bungling the party in one way or another than of doing well, and that I am therefore much more likely to get hell than to escape unchastised. I also know that every new failure brings reminders of past failures and warnings of future ruination, illustrated with references to odd relatives stashed away in discretely run nursing homes. It seems to be a case of negative reinforcement all the way around. I have no reason to *want* to attend parties.

Despite my father's gloomy predictions, I don't think that I'll end up with a "thing about people." I do think, however, that I would have an easier time if my father would keep quiet. Shutting him up wouldn't really do it, though; the only thing to do, I suppose, is to eliminate either him or me. I confess rather shamefacedly that I have done more than contemplate the latter of the two possibilities.

"Well, Soaper, what do you think of today's contribution? Is it up to my usual level?'

"It is," I replied.

"Then analyze," he said.

"This one is about your father," I began.

He slapped himself on the forehead and cried, "Soaper, your powers of observation absolutely astound me at times."

I went on. "For reasons that are unclear, Gromchik, both your parents have been subtly hostile and depreciating to you throughout your formative years. If one had been irritable and the other had been affectionate, you might have come through your childhood and adolescence undamaged.

The healthy parent would have counteracted to a large extent the influence of the unhealthy one. Your father was emotionally more distant from you than your mother; however, he set goals for you that you could not, or would not, reach and then flailed you with the same irritable, debasing talk you got from your mother. Thus, each parent seemed to confirm the other, and to you, the child, they represented reality. You concluded, inarticulately and in ways that were beyond your awareness, that you *were* the inadequate, unlovable, despicable person they said or implied you were, and you emerged into middle and late adolescence expecting no more from the world than you got at home. Beneath this is fury. You are very angry, Gromchik, about how you were robbed of your self-respect and peace."

"Soaper," he said, "I feel that your literary style has improved distinctly as a result of your association with me."

"What has made this all the more painful to you," I added, "is that your younger brothers Phil and Howie have been treated differently. They were reared with affection and respect. In fact, they perhaps have been overindulged. We do not know why there was such a difference in your parents' treatment of you and your brothers."

He raised his right hand.

"You may speak, Gromchik," I said.

"Teacher, I think I know the answer to that one."

"Tell me, Gromchik."

"I was an unwanted baby. I was born four months after my parents' marriage and caused much embarrassment and inconvenience to my parents and all other relatives. They detested me at birth and the attitude has stuck.'

"A very good answer, Gromchik. There is only one difficulty in your solution to this problem."

"What is that, teacher?"

"There is no evidence to support it."

"May I take it on as a project, teacher?"

"Yes, Gromchik. Look into the matter and report to the class on Tuesday."

"And will I get extra points for this project, teacher?"

"Certainly, Gromchik. Pupils who show initiative are always given extra points.'

He went on: "Fade-out. Silence. Fade back to classroom scene. Noise of feet shuffling and children coughing in the background. Teacher's voice comes in, close to the mike."

I went along with the script: "You have your hand up, Gromchik. What is it?"

"I have the report on my research project, teacher."

"Very good, Gromchik. Come to the front of the class and give your report. Speak loudly and clearly so all the children can hear you. Susie Grimes, stop talking. Tommy Wilson, sit down. All right, Gromchik, give your report.'

"I was born a year and a half after my parents married. Therefore the unwanted-baby theory is shot to hell. End of report."

"Very good, Gromchik. Your report is somewhat short and reveals, in its choice of words, the influence of modern literature. However, it has clarity of expression and conciseness. You get five extra points."

"Thank you, teacher."

"You may return to your seat and sit down, Gromchik."

"Teacher?"

"Yes, Gromchik."

"I have another idea."

"What is your other idea?"

"My grandfather dabbled in politics. He arranged for my father to receive a three- or four-year appointment to serve on the staff of a Missouri senator in Washington about a year after my parents were married."

"So?'

"I remember my father saying years ago that he had to turn down the appointment and remain in Kansas City, hacking away in the old family law firm, because of my mother's pregnancy. I remember my mother saying that it was a shame that he couldn't accept the appointment because they would have met so many interesting people in Washington and would have made such good connections there. I suspect that both of them had vague political ambitions for my father, which the inconvenient fetus loused up."

"Go on, Gromchik.'

"So maybe I was unwanted, after all."

"Perhaps," I said.

"How do we find out?" he asked.

"We don't. That was a couple of decades ago, and the only informants are the aforesaid parents; their memories are dulled by time and falsified by their inability to face painful things."

"Then we shall never know," he said.

"We don't need to," I replied. "All we need to know is that for unknown reasons your parents have treated you in an unhealthy way, much different from the way they treated your brothers, and that this has had unfortunate effects on your view of yourself, your attitudes toward people, and your capacities for getting along with people. Moreover, it's always a bit more complicated than that; if your speculation is correct, why couldn't they flexibly change their feelings toward the baby during the early months and years of its life? Why didn't their attitudes toward you change? Why have their unhealthy attitudes persisted?"

"Teacher?"

"Yes, Gromchik."

"There's one other possible explanation."

"What is that, Gromchik?"

"Maybe I really am a slob and have been treated no better than I deserve."

"We don't accept that point of view here, Gromchik."

"Teacher?"

"Yes, Gromchik."

"You once said you sell hope here."

"So I did, Gromchik."

"Maybe it's not hope. Maybe it's just crap."

"We prefer not to think so, Gromchik.'

"Teacher, there's one other thing."

"Yes, Gromchik."

"That story about my father's appointment to Washington is not true. I just made it up."

"That was naughty of you, Gromchik."

"Do I still get my five extra points?"

"Yes."

With that he got up and left the room.

Later in the day he called my secretary to set the time for his next appointment. He told her he left his last interview abruptly because he had to rush to the airport to meet a sick friend who was arriving from Alaska.

Gromchik continued to see me twice a week; each time we used something he had typed as the basis, or the starting point, of the interview. He never stayed for the full fifty minutes.

He passed all his courses at the University of Missouri-Kansas City. In the spring he got a letter from me and, attaching it to his transcript from the University of Missouri-Kansas City, sent it to the dean of Berkeley. Four weeks later he received a letter readmitting him for the following fall term.

At the beginning of his last interview with me he gave me a sheet on which the following was typed.

A RIDDLE

On the last day of May I walked into my parents' bedroom. Debbie was playing on the floor near the dresser. My mother sat, reading the newspaper, in a chair near her bed. As I sat down on my father's bed, my mother looked up and said:

"David, you're so pale, you frighten me."

"Aw, Mom, don't be silly!"

"No, a person can't *be* that pale. There's something wrong!"

"Listen, Ma, I've been pale, entirely without color, since I was, ah . . ." I searched for a suitably innocuous age. "Since I was twelve."

"Oh?" Her voice seemed quiet and strange. "And what else has been wrong with you since you were twelve?"

Uneasy, I shrugged my shoulders and left the room.

THE RIDDLE: What was my mother trying to say?

CLUE: The mordant Bisinger of Hughie Menchin's painting is the black spot.

"Well, Soaper, let's see how good you are at riddles."

"Give me more clues, Gromchik."

"No. All the clues you need are right there on the paper."

I studied it for a minute and said, "The dialogue between you and your mother is similar to many we've examined. Under the pretense of interest in your physical health, as indicated by your alleged or actual pallor, she unleashed a little irritability and scorn toward you. She does it by a subtle question. There being no way to combat this, you flee."

"Go on, Soaper."

"The riddle is in the riddle, and the clue gives the answer."

"Elucidate, Soaper."

"Shall I let my fine Joycean imagination go to work on it?"

"By all means," he replied.

I went on. "The riddle lies in the wording of the riddle: 'What was my mother trying to say?' Your mother, in addition to being all the other things we've discussed, is also the source of your life. Whether she is Mrs. Arthur Ross of Kansas City or the Great Earth Mother goddess of Asia Minor, a mother is the symbol and the source of life. So we reword the riddle to read: 'What is life trying to say to me?'"

I stopped.

"And the answer, Soaper?"

"The answer," I said, "is in the clue. 'The mordant Bisinger of Hughie Menchin's painting is the black spot.' To answer the riddle we must examine each word of the clue. Mordant is from the Latin word for 'bite.' I'm not sure what Bisinger is, but it suggests the word 'stinger' to me. Hughie is like *who-ie*, or 'who he?' And Menchin is akin to the German word *menschen*, for men or mankind. A painting is a design, and here it represents the pattern or the nature of life itself. The black spot is death. Thus, we have the answer to the riddle: *The biting stinger of everyman's life is death.*"

He looked at me with a slight smile.

"Well," I said, "did I guess the riddle?"

"Ingenious, Soaper, very ingenious. However, you didn't get the riddle."

"Then you tell me the answer to the riddle," I said.

"No, Soaper, I'll leave it with you. On rainy days when patients don't keep their appointments and you have nothing else to do, turn to the riddle and work on it."

"Will I eventually figure out the riddle?" I asked.

"I don't know," he said. "That depends.'

"On what?"

"On things. Ask Peydle. He may help you. Oh, incidentally, Soaper, this is our last session. I'm going to spend the summer working at a camp in Colorado. In September, as you know, I return to the Berk." He rose. "I'm going now. Good-bye."

"It's been a rather short session, Gromchik."

"I have an appointment with Hughie Menchin. We have to settle a few things about Bisinger."

He moved toward the door.

"Well, good-bye, Gromchik. Drop me a line or give me a phone call once in a while."

"I may do that, Soaper."

He left.

In early September I received a telephone call from Gromchik. He said he was leaving for Berkeley the next day and was calling to find out how Peydle was. I told him Peydle was fine. He asked me to give Peydle his regards.

In mid-December I received a Christmas card at my office addressed to Peydle Hemidryad, c/o Dr. A. H. Chapman. It was signed, "Best wishes, Gromchik."

When, after making rounds at two hospitals, I arrived at my office late in the morning on a Tuesday early in the following March, I found the following letter on my desk among several items of correspondence that my secretary had opened and laid out.

March 3

Dear Soaper,

I had thought that I would have time to write a proper note, something to put in an anthology or to hang on the wall, a veritable swan song, but I suppose not. I don't know if I'm taking enough; the capsules are homemade, compounded of four different medicines—to baffle the doctors—and I didn't have a chance to look up the minimum lethal dosage in the poison guide. I'm also painting peculiar designs on my face with blue paint, for a touch of maniacal intensity. Hopefully, I'll either die or recover completely. In any case, I shall bring myself to the attention of the authorities.

I have been talking things over with a fellow named Dawson (Code name: Bridegroom of the Sabbath) at the university health service. After the first two psychiatrists I saw there this year, Dawson is pure gold. However, communication has been a difficult business.

I won't attempt to explain my motives, but I want you to understand that I know precisely what I am doing. Where I hope to go, there are no dreams.

I was going to leave you my bronze lizard, my fossil titanothere humerus, and my six-foot fake digital computer, but if I did, I would have to make other bequests, and besides, you'd have no use for them. I simply leave you, then, all my good wishes.

Gromchik, Corpse

I immediately put through a telephone call to Dr. Dawson, at the university health service, the University of California at Berkeley. It took the university operator two hours to find him; he was giving, or attending, a lecture. It was about two o'clock Kansas City time, twelve noon California time, when he returned my call.

"Dr. Dawson, my name is Harry Chapman. I'm a psychiatrist in Kansas City. I believe you have a patient named David Ross. It that right?"

"Yes."

"This boy is a former patient of mine. In this morning's mail I received a letter from him, dated yesterday. Dr. Dawson, please take what I say seriously. I've been in psychiatry a long time and I know an ominous suicidal note when I see one. This boy is very suicidal; he must be hospitalized at once. Don't be deceived by his nonchalance and flippancy; he means business. This is a good-bye letter; he talks of distributing his possessions and more or less apologizes for what he's doing. I'll send you a photocopy of his letter in this afternoon's mail to help you to justify hospitalization; I'll also call his parents and ask them to back you up."

"You must be Soaper," Dr. Dawson said.

"I am. That was his nickname for me."

"He told me about you, but he wouldn't give me your true name. The letter was dated yesterday, was it?"

"Yes. You have no time to lose. Find him and hospitalize him. Believe me, I know what I'm talking about."

"Last night," Dr. Dawson said, "he loaded himself up with a lot of pills of some sort and then jumped from a third-floor dormitory window. He put some weird markings all over his face with blue paint. He's in Mt. Zion Hospital in San Francisco right now. He's in coma and has multiple fractures of his right shoulder. They're doing a hemodialysis, but it's doubtful that he'll pull through. While he's in Mt. Zion, Dr. Leonard Breitstein will be taking care of him."

"I'm very, very sorry to hear all this," I said.

"Was it a long letter he wrote you?" Dr. Dawson asked.

"No, just four brief paragraphs."

"You must have had a very good patient-therapist relationship with him," Dr. Dawson said.

I pictured Dr. Dawson as a young man who was financing his analysis by working at the university health service.

"Dr. Dawson, if I had had a good patient-therapist relationship with him, he wouldn't be dying right now. I would very much appreciate a few lines or a call from you in two or three days to let me know what happens to him. My address is in the American Psychiatric Association directory, which they undoubtedly have at the health service."

He assured me he would let me know, and we said goodbye.

I then called Gromchik's father at his office. He said his wife had taken an early-morning plane to California and that he was flying there later in the day. They had received a call the evening before from Mt. Zion Hospital. I told him of the letter I had received and expressed my regret.

During the next six days I received no news of Gromchik; Dr. Dawson did not call or write. Each morning and evening when I saw the Kansas City *Star*, I turned first to the obituary column to see if David Ross' write-up were there. I called his parents' home twice and was told that Mr. and Mrs. Ross were out of town. I declined to leave my name.

On the seventh day I received a telephone call from California.

"Soaper?"

"Yes," I replied, "is that you, Gromchik?"

"Who else? Look, Soaper, I called about something else, but since you happened to be the one who answered the phone, I might as well apologize for that letter I sent you. It wasn't up to my usual literary level, and there were even errors in punctuation; I feel quite bad about it."

"That's all right, Gromchik. I'm sure you had other things on your mind."

"Anyway, don't worry about me, Soaper. I'm fine."

"I'm glad to hear that, Gromchik. Incidentally, where are you?"

"I'm on the psycho ward of Mt. Zion Hospital here in San Francisco."

"How did you manage to get permission to call me?"

"I made a deal with my psychiatrist."

"What kind of a deal, Gromchik?'

"I promised him that if he'd let me call you, I'd not taint his reputation by committing suicide while I was under his care. He's a nervous little man and I had no trouble getting him to agree, especially after some of the capers I've pulled off here."

"What kinds of capers, Gromchik?"

"As a starter, when I was coming out of the deep snooze from which these people so unkindly awakened me, and realized that I was still on this planet, I pulled a plastic needle out of my vein, through which I was receiving life-giving water and salt; I refused to take any more. Then I got hold of a hand mirror, broke it, and hacked away at my wrists. I wouldn't let them put sutures in. And yesterday they hauled me to the operating room and gave me a general anesthetic to get the job done. I naturally tore all the bandages off as soon as I could, and then proceeded to yank off this ridiculous cast they put on my shoulder and chest. I also tried to hang myself in a shower stall after getting rid of a mentally retarded aide who's supposed to keep me under constant vigilance."

"You've had a rather busy time of it the last few days, Gromchik."

"Anyway, after pulling off these stunts I had no trouble getting my nervous little psychiatrist to accept my deal."

"Where do you go from here, Gromchik?"

"They're sending me to a fancy psychiatric hospital on the East Coast, where I am to live in what is known as a therapeutic community and be analyzed into sanity and studiousness."

"Good luck, Gromchik."

"Thanks, Soaper. However, as I said, all this is not the reason I called you. I mentioned these things only because you happened to answer the phone."

"What *is* the main reason you called me, Gromchik?"

"I wanted to know how Peydle is getting along. Is he all right?"

"He is fine, Gromchik. He is just fine."

"Thanks, Soaper. That was all. Give him my regards."

"I'll do that, Gromchik."

"So long, Soaper."
"So long, Gromchik."

A little more than two years later I received the following note from Gromchik. The envelope had a Denver postmark, but there was no return address.

> Dear Dr. Chapman,
>   Relax: this isn't another suicidal note. I only want to apologize for said note and any other trouble I gave you a couple of years ago. Both the contents of my note and my use of your code name were inexcusable. I am terribly sorry.
>   I hope that Peydle is still looking after you.
>   The hemidryads aren't speaking to me anymore.
>
> Sincerely,
Gromchik

I have not heard from him, or about him, since then.

The Mind-Reading Horse

A⟙ a little before nine o'clock on a Wednesday night in mid-October, my wife handed me the telephone.

"It's Dr. Grant," she said.

I felt uncomfortable. Dr. Grant had been our pediatrician when the children were young. He called infrequently, and his patients were always difficult ones. However, because of our long association I couldn't tell him I was too busy and refer him on to another psychiatrist.

I have known Dr. Grant for more than forty years. As a child I played with his two children in their house and yard up the street from my parents' home. For eleven years I went through grade school and high school, class by class, with his son Tommy. Tommy now teaches orthopedics at a medical school in Cleveland. Dr. Grant is in his late seventies, but he still goes on house calls (one of the few Kansas City pediatricians who does) and makes daily rounds at two hospitals. He invariably attends church on Sundays. I have never seen him without a white shirt and a necktie, and only occasionally without a suitcoat.

Dr. Grant's referrals to me are usually adults.

Why does a pediatrician refer *adult* patients to a psychiatrist? The answer to that lies mainly in Dr. Grant's personality. When his former pediatric patients are in serious trouble, even though they may be in their thirties or forties, some of them call him rather than their internist or family physician; they trust him more. Moreover, Dr. Grant has continued contacts with some of these people because he takes care of their children. There are two or three families, whom he

73

mentions frequently, in which he is taking care of infants whose grandparents were his pediatric patients.

"Good evening, Dr. Grant." I put my hand over the mouthpiece of the telephone and asked my wife to turn down the television set. The younger of my teen-age sons, sitting cross-legged on the floor, made a wry face; his generation views loudness as the main criterion of quality.

"How is Mrs. Grant?" I asked. His wife has been a wheel-chair invalid for ten years.

"She is fine, thank you."

"What do you hear from Tommy?" I asked.

"He and his family will be down for Thanksgiving. The first week in December he's going to deliver a paper on a new type of prosthesis for hip fractures at a medical congress in London." Dr. Grant is proud of Tommy. Tommy has the kind of industrious mediocrity, occasionally tinged with originality, that is often characteristic of physicians who prefer the quiet waters of academic medicine to the turbulent swells and rolls of private practice.

Dr. Grant obviously did not call at nine at night to chat about Tommy, but I could not give him my usual "What's the problem, Al?" or "What can I do for you, Jack?" with which I bring other late-calling physicians to the point. I also could no more call him Henry, which is his name, than I could call the Chief Justice of the Supreme Court Bud or Chuck.

There was another reason why I did not quickly bring him to the point; his patients often are hard to treat. When a physician like Dr. Grant has been practicing in the same locality for nearly fifty years, his patients tend to have certain characteristics. By the slow process of trial, rejection, and selection of doctors by patients, the people who form the patient load of a long-practicing physician tend to conform to a pattern, and their personalities and customs often dovetail with his. On the whole, Dr. Grant's patients are from cold, reserved, well-to-do business- and professional-class families who find in Dr. Grant's stuffiness and obvious respectability just what they are looking for in a doctor.

However, these qualities make them difficult psychiatric

patients. They have much trouble looking critically at their parents, their marital partners, their children, and the society they live in. To rage against one's father, to recognize one's mother's weaknesses, to see one's children's vices, and to stare frankly at the brutalities and shams of our society are hard things for them. That doesn't give a psychiatrist much to work with, and unless superficial counseling or medication can pull them out of whatever crises they're in, they are sticky problems.

There are far more people like Dr. Grant and his patients than the sociologists know; for a sizable minority of the American people, the permissive society is a myth.

While he chatted about Tommy for a minute or so I reflected that when he called me at nine at night, something must have gone seriously wrong in one of his families. He abruptly came to the point.

"Harry, I'm calling about Martha Wilcox."

Wilcox. The name rang a bell in some distant corner of my memory.

"I'm at her mother's house now," he continued. "Her mother and brother-in-law are here. Her mother says she knew your father. They're the Wilcox stage equipment people."

I remembered. Since shortly after the turn of the century the Wilcoxes, father and son, for three generations, had operated a firm that sold stage draperies, lighting fixtures, and sound systems to high schools, colleges, and churches over a six-state area. They had survived competition from larger firms in Chicago and St. Louis for decades. I knew one of them, a bespectacled, tense boy, in high school; he had died in the Air Force during the Second World War.

"I took care of Martha, and I take care of her two children," Dr. Grant went on. "She never had any unusual diseases." He continued for another couple of minutes giving me a review of her childhood illnesses which, of course, had nothing to do with whatever he was calling me about. However, even when he was younger, Dr. Grant had been a meticulously verbose man in talking about patients. My mind wandered; a pretty girl was advertising deodorants on the low-tuned television set before me. People like Dr. Grant, I reflected, must have sex with their mates since they produce between two and four children in every generation, but it was hard to imagine Dr. Grant having sex without a white shirt and a necktie on. The silliness of my thoughts annoyed me.

Then, abruptly, in two short sentences he covered the matter at hand. "This afternoon, very suddenly, Martha became disturbed. Perhaps you could drop by and see her."

He meant that I should come immediately. I had been up since six that morning and working since seven, but he did not ask *if* I'd come. He politely indicated that I was expected to come. If he, in his late seventies, could go, it was clear that I could not refuse. I hoped it was not out in Raytown or in one of the farther suburbs of Johnson County.

I pulled a ballpoint pen from my shirt pocket and, with my hand over the mouthpiece, asked my wife to give me a pad of paper from the writing desk in the corner.

"Martha Wilcox," I wrote as he gave me the data. "1025 Pershing Lane, 555–5719." I was relieved. It was a ten-minute drive from my house.

I asked for a little more data. Husband, Charles. Address, 846 Pershing Lane. He was in the family business. His last name was Straker. So she was really Martha Straker, but to Dr. Grant, who had known her since infancy and viewed her as a little girl who got bigger, she was still Martha Wilcox.

"I'll be there in ten or fifteen minutes, Dr. Grant, but could you give me some idea of what her trouble is?"

"She's very upset. She's convinced that her husband is dead. But he's not, of course. You can see when you get here."

That was it.

Martha Wilcox Straker was convinced that her husband was dead, but he was not. This could be anything. She could be an immature woman who lived two blocks down the street from her overprotective mother and who, unable to cope with two children and the roles of mother and wife, had floundered into her mother's house in a dissociative hysterical trance. She could be an alcoholic whose drinking had long been a carefully guarded family secret, but who was now in delirium tremens or alcoholic hallucinosis. She could be a schizophrenic whose inner chaos had shattered her fragile defenses and had thrown her into a psychosis. She could have various other types of problems.

Moreover, I wondered, where was this husband whom she believed to be dead, but was not? Was he also at her mother's house or at home with the children two blocks away on Pershing Lane or at an evening business meeting? All this would soon be clear.

I hung up, told my wife where I was going, and got my narrow black briefcase from a shelf in the bookcase of my study. After a ten-minute drive through the cold, empty streets I arrived at 1025 Pershing Lane. The light over the front door was on. It was a big, three-story house, probably built in the early 1920's, with a few old trees in the large yard that lay in front and to one side of it. The lawn was neatly trimmed and the leaves had been raked. Two automobiles were parked in front of the house, and another one was in the driveway that ran alongside it to the garage in the rear.

There were no lights along the dark front walk to guide an unfamiliar guest, and, since the ground rose slightly from the sidewalk to the front of the house, I guessed that there were steps somewhere on it, easy to stumble over. So I decided to walk up the driveway, from which I could cut over on a narrow path to the front door. As I approached the automobile on the driveway, I saw that it was parked obliquely, half on the drive and half off it. It had been rammed into a low hedge and a waist-high stone wall that separated the Wilcox's property from the adjoining one. The door on the driver's side was wide open.

I stopped and looked at the car. The right fender and bumper and the right side of the hood were badly smashed, and the hedge had been crushed against the stone wall over a several-foot swath. I hesitated for a moment, undecided whether to close the door. I stepped over to shut it, and as I did, I saw that the front seat and the floorboard were strewn with crumpled paper, dirty rags, cigarette butts and other litter. The door of the glove compartment lay open flat, and the ashtray had been yanked from the dashboard and lay amid the trash. By the light from the front door of the house I could also see that the keys were in the ignition switch. I took out the keys, slipped them into my topcoat pocket and closed the door.

These things made me apprehensive. Cautious, property conscious people like the Wilcoxes do not smash a car on a driveway; to do the damage that this car had sustained would require a speed of at least thirty miles an hour, and it looked as though the car had been rammed two or three times into the hedge and wall. I glanced over the adjacent lawn and saw car tracks going back onto it. Moreover, people like the Wilcoxes don't leave a car door wide open, with the keys in the ignition switch and trash from the glove compartment and the ashtray scattered over the floorboard and the front seat.

I went across the narrow brick path from the driveway to the front door, mounted the one step to the small stoop and pressed the doorbell button. As I waited for someone to come, I glanced down the front walk that led to the sidewalk and the street. With the porch light above and behind me I could see several steps in the walk where the lawn bent downward in a gentle slope to the street level. Along the steps were three two-foot-high metal poles with lantern-enclosed lights in them, unlit. They had either not been turned on or were burned out. This too was not what one expected of the Wilcoxes. When they are expecting a physician who has never been to their house, they turn on the lights along a front walk to guide him up its dark steps; this is cautious, polite, and legally wise.

No one came to the door. After waiting long enough for a second ring not to be discourteous, I rang again.

Still, no one came.

I became increasingly uneasy about what I would find inside, when so many things outside were out of place and haphazard.

Finally the door opened, and a thin, pale, short man, balding in front, stared at me. Discounting a few years, since early baldness would tend to make him seem older than he was, I guessed him to be in his early thirties.

I waited for him to say something and to ask me in, but he merely looked at me and said nothing.

"I'm Dr. Chapman," I said. "Dr. Grant called me. I'm expected."

"Oh, yes," the man said, as if starting out of a daydream. "Come in."

I walked into the front hall. A wide, carpeted stairs lay about fifteen feet in front of the door; it went up to a broad landing, where it turned right and then doubled back to go still higher to the second floor. To my right was a dark dining room with a long, polished table lined by heavy, carved wood chairs. Along one of the dining-room walls was an immense sideboard, behind whose glassed doors lay stacks of china and rows of glasses and crystal. A tea cart with an ornate silver tea set stood in one corner.

The living room was on my left. A large Persian rug covered most of the floor, and heavy, stuffed furniture formed a semicircle in front of a wide fireplace with a marble mantelpiece. Polished wood end tables and chairs formed groups in corners and occupied open spaces along the walls. Steam radiators, covered by brown metal casings, stood beneath the long rows of windows on two sides of the room, and the pipes to them were visible for a few inches as they rose from the floor and entered the metal casings. Beyond the living room, to the left of the fireplace, wide glass French doors opened onto a window-lined smaller room, a type of room often called a sunroom by older generations in the Midwest. The house was quiet and orderly; I had expected some kind of genteel chaos after seeing the smashed car and the unlit path lamps outside.

I turned to the young man, who had closed the door and was again staring silently at me. I found him annoying and puzzling. I wondered if he were the husband who was believed to be dead, but was not.

"I'm Dr. Chapman," I repeated, hoping he would tell me who he was, where Dr. Grant was, and where the patient was.

The thought skipped through my head that perhaps I had entered the wrong house. But he quickly eliminated that idea.

"Yes, Doctor, thank you for coming." But he said nothing more, and seemed uncertain what to do.

I began to take off my coat, after setting my hat on a side table in the hall. "Perhaps there's somewhere I can put this," I said.

"Certainly." He took my coat, picked up my hat, and put them in a small cloak closet beneath the stairs.

He came back and said, "They're all upstairs."

"Excuse me," I said, "but in my kind of work we often must evaluate a situation fairly quickly and decide what should be done. So it's good to know who everyone is and how he fits into the picture. Are you the patient's husband?"

"No, no. I'm her brother-in-law."

"In the rush I don't think you mentioned your name," I said.

"I'm sorry. I'm Fred Turner. I'm Martha's brother-in law. Or at least I was, until . . . Well, my wife, Martha's sister, died a month ago."

I looked steadily at him.

He stared back for a moment, and then his gaze turned to the side. "She shot herself. We have three kids."

I felt uncomfortable at getting so much tragic news in so few words. I felt as if I had jabbed my finger into an un-healed wound.

At that point Dr. Grant appeared on the landing of the stairs and, seeing me, came down.

"Harry, I'm glad you came right away. I've given Martha a shot, three grains of phenobarbital. It's all I had in my bag. I carry it for epileptics, whom we sometimes see in status. Of course, three grains is more than I'd give to a child in the first dose. It's two doses in fact. But Martha is an adult and she was so agitated that—"

I broke in; Dr. Grant, a taciturn man on most other sub-jects, had always been garrulous in talking about patients, and growing old had accentuated this.

"Maybe we could step into the living room," I said, "and get a little background information on the patient; then we can go upstairs and see her."

"Of course," Dr. Grant said. Then, turning to Mr. Turner, he added, "You've met Fred?"

I indicated that we'd just met.

"Very tragic," said Dr. Grant. "I took care of Anne, too. I took care of both the girls. Anne always had her illnesses harder than Martha. When they both had strep throats Anne was—"

Again I broke in, trying to get things straight. "Anne was Martha's sister, the late wife of Mr. Turner?"

"Yes, yes, of course," said Dr. Grant. "I suppose you know she took her life in September, this September, shortly after school started. She had been seeing Dr. Cantor for her prob lems. Depression. She shot herself in the head. It was dread- ful. Dr. Cantor was shocked. They called me when they found her in the bathroom after it occurred. They didn't have a regular family doctor or internist, and so they called me, since I take care of Anne's children, too. I called the cor- oner and Dr. Cantor. Dr. Cantor was very upset. He said he had no idea she was so depressed. He talked to me for fifteen minutes on the telephone, but he didn't come to the house." Dr. Grant plainly felt that it was Dr. Cantor's obligation to come to the house to see the bloody results of his error in judgment. Dr. Cantor had been practicing psychiatry in Kansas City for about ten years.

"Where do you live in Kansas City?" I asked Mr. Turner, still trying to piece the picture together.

"We live in Leawood Hills," he said. "Or at least we did. Since Anne's death we've been here with Mrs. Wilcox. I didn't know what to do, and Mrs. Wilcox insisted. I had no one to take care of the kids, and they couldn't stay in the same house where their mother died. The two older kids saw her. In fact, they were the first to reach her. She was, well, her head was . . . badly deformed." He groped for words to describe the hideous scene.

"The older girl has been having nightmares," Dr. Grant

said. "I've been prescribing Tribrium, one grain, at bed-time." He went on for another minute talking about some minor phobias in another of the Turner children since their mother's death.

Dr. Grant covered these details in his precise, neat manner. It was as if we were standing in a house that was about to crash on top of us and he was concerned with flakes of plaster on the carpet.

By then I felt that the Wilcox Straker-Turner family was in deep trouble and that Dr. Grant would be of no help whatever. I wished I were not there. I've struggled with enough families like this, and now that I'm middle-aged I almost always send such cases on to younger colleagues, saying that I "don't have time to do justice to the case."

As Dr. Grant talked on, I glanced back and forth between him, calm and medically dignified, and Mr. Turner, whose stomped-on look revealed the horror of his life for the past month. Despite my earlier suggestion that we should go into the living room, we were still standing in the front hall.

Dr. Grant's patter was broken by the appearance of a bright-eyed, thin woman on the stair landing above us. A short, middle-aged woman was behind her.

"Martha," said Dr. Grant, "I told you stay in bed." Though she was adult and psychotic, he treated her as if she were a placid six-year-old with the flu.

Martha, somewhat unsteady because of the phenobarbital, came clumsily down the stairs, clinging to the heavy handrail. She almost fell halfway down but regained her balance and made it to the first floor. The middle-aged woman, whom I assumed to be Mrs. Wilcox, followed her, chiding her constantly for coming down.

Martha became steadier once she got to the first floor. She ran at me, grabbed my right arm, and began to talk loudly and rapidly, close to my face.

"Dr. Chapman. You're Dr. Chapman, aren't you?"

I nodded slightly, indicating that I was.

She gave a boisterous laugh and shouted, "See, I knew he was Dr. Chapman. You took care of Arlene Stevenson. I

knew her. She was in my class in high school. They think I'm
crazy. I'm not. It's them. Look at him. He's washed out, shot.
No, it's his wife who's shot." Again she laughed loudly. "An
nie shot herself. She was crazy. Crazy to shoot herself when
she had a husband like Fred. Freddy, Teddy, weddy, Freddy
Teddy bear. He's a doll. I'm going to marry him. Tomorrow.
Tomorrow is my wedding day. Wedding bells will ring, for
Freddy and me," she sang off key. "For Freddy and me, and
baby makes three. Then we can do it legal. No more on the
sly. Right, Fred?" More raucous laughter. "Look at Mom.
Shocked. Oh, the Wilcoxes are shocked. The straitlaced, sober, Presbyterian Wilcoxes are shocked. But everybody does
it. Don't you?"

The last question was directed at me.

I said nothing, and she raced on. "Sure you do. How of
ten? Fred and I are going to do it all the time, aren't we,
Fred?"

Fred looked helplessly at her and then at me. His mouth
was slightly open and his hands trembled.

Mrs. Wilcox seized her daughter's arm and tried to drag
her toward the stairs, scolding her to go back to bed, but
Martha jerked her arm away.

"Fred and I can get married. Charles is dead."

Then her brittle gaiety shattered and she broke into sobs.
She clutched my arm and wailed, "He died, he died at two
fifteen this afternoon. He got bashed on the head and died.
Dead. Two children without a father, and me four months
pregnant." And she howled in an animal way and threw herself on my shoulder.

I looked over her head at Mrs. Wilcox and Dr. Grant.

"Let's go into the living room and decide what's to be
done," I said.

I led Martha, clinging to me and crying, into the living
room, and we sat on one of the sofas in the semicircle facing
the fireplace. After briefly introducing me to Mrs. Wilcox,
Dr. Grant sat on the edge of a chair facing us, and Fred
stood, aimless and anxious, behind him.

Mrs. Wilcox went to the mantel of the fireplace and, before

I grasped what she was doing, took a booklet of matches from a green jade box, stooped and lit the ends of newspapers sticking from under the carefully arranged logs. In a few moments fire was spreading beneath and behind the logs.

She rose and said quietly, "It's a cold night to get you out, Dr. Grant and Dr. Chapman. I'll make coffee. Or perhaps you'd prefer cocoa."

I protested that I wanted neither one, but she resolutely set off for the back of the house. She insisted on treating this urgent, painful situation as if it were a casual social visit. I increasingly felt that there was much bitchiness behind her politeness and propriety.

Martha had emerged from her brief despair and began to rattle on again.

"Cocoa. Just the thing for a cold night. But lots of other things warm you up better. Oh, look at stuffy old Dr. Grant. He doesn't like that. Pretend it doesn't happen. Immaculate conception, or something like that. Virgin birth. But there's no fun in that."

Dr. Grant in fact did not like that. He frowned at her severely.

"Martha," he said, "you should be ashamed of yourself."

"Oh, hell!" she shouted angrily. "I've had enough of that crap, and Mom's and Dad's, and everybody's. Call a spade a spade. The queen of spades, the king of spades, the jack of spades, and the ace of spades. Charles is dead. Dead, dead, dead. And I'll marry Fred. Fred, Fred, Fred. Tomorrow. 'Just Freddy and me, and baby makes three.'" She broke into the song, off key and disjointed, jamming in her own words for ones she couldn't remember.

Dr. Grant got up.

"Harry, I think I've done all I can. You can arrange what's best for Martha. I think I'll go."

I could not rise since Martha was clinging to my arm.

"All right, Dr. Grant. I'll see that the necessary steps are taken. Good-night."

Fred trailed after him to get his coat and see him to the

door. Before he left Dr. Grant came back to the living room
and said to me, "Tell Mrs. Wilcox that I had to go and
couldn't stay for coffee, and thank her." He turned to Fred,
said the same thing, and left.

"There goes Dr. Grant," Martha shouted after him. "He
never gets upset. 'The boy stood on the burning deck,/Eating
peanuts by the peck,/The flames came up and touched his
chin,/But still he stuffed the peanuts in.'"

She guffawed, released my arm, and clapped her hands
together with a loud smack. Then she doubled forward in
more laughter. Abruptly she sat upright, bent her elbows
akimbo with her hands in her lap, tossed her head backward,
and chanted, "Dr. Grant stood on the burning deck,/Swal-
lowing pills by the peck,/The flames came up and touched
his chin,/But still he stuffed the pillsies in."

She ranted on, singing, laughing, and shouting.

I turned to Fred, who was standing indecisively halfway
between us and the wide entrance that led from the living
room to the hallway. His lost look led me to order him about
as one would a submissive child.

"Fred, would you please get me my black briefcase. I think
I left it on the hall table by the door."

He brought it to me. I opened the briefcase, took out a
prescription pad, and scribbled prescriptions on two sheets
of it.

"Take these to the Margreen Drugstore at Sixty-third and
Brookside. They're the closest and they're still open. Tell the
pharmacist it's urgent and to fill them immediately. Then
bring the medication right back." He looked relieved that
someone had given him something to do, and he left the
room.

As he was going out, Mrs. Wilcox came in with a heavy silver tray lined with a fine, filigreed lace doily. On the tray
were cups and saucers, silver teaspoons, and an ornate,
heavy silver pot with a matching sugar bowl.

She saw Fred putting on his coat in the hallway and asked
him where he was going.

"I'm sending him out for some medication at the Margreen Drugstore," I said, hoping to avoid a discussion and to push things along. Martha continued to shout at all of us. She was no longer hanging onto my arm, and I was uneasy that, objecting to any medication, she would rise and try to intercept Fred before he reached the front door.

"I'll give you the money," Mrs. Wilcox said.

"That's not necessary," Fred replied.

"No," I confirmed. "It's rather pressing. Go ahead, Fred."

"No," said Mrs. Wilcox firmly, putting the tray down on a small table. "I'll give him the money. It's my responsibility until her husband returns."

She took a black cloth purse out of a drawer in the table and gave Fred a twenty-dollar bill. She turned to me and asked if twenty would be enough.

Above the racket of Martha's chanting, I said, "Yes, and make it as fast as you can, Fred."

I felt a vague irritability with Mrs. Wilcox, who seemed almost deliberately to ignore the urgent state of her psychotic daughter.

After Fred left, Mrs. Wilcox picked up the tray and brought it to the knee-high coffee table in the center of the semicircle of furniture before the fireplace, where a brisk fire now burned; the coffee table was about three feet in front of Martha and me.

Unsmiling but courteous, she said, "I thought cocoa would be better than coffee. Some people find that coffee keeps them awake at night. May I serve you, Doctor?"

I controlled my rising exasperation, but the question ran through my mind that if I felt so helplessly irritable with this cold but polite woman after being with her for twenty minutes, what would it be like to be reared by her? One of her daughters had committed suicide a month ago and the other was at my side in a manic psychosis.

However, Mrs. Wilcox did not have a chance to serve the cocoa. Martha barged in.

"Let me do the honors. It's the honorable thing. Honor thy father and mother. Mother, Daddy, honor and duty. Into the battle went the brave six hundred. Duty and honor. Cannon to the right of them, cannon to the left of them, cannon to the front of them, onward the brave six hundred. Theirs not to reason why, theirs but to do and die. Annie's dead and I'll serve the cocoa. One lump or two, Doctor? Take it or lump it, right?"

Mrs. Wilcox tried to intervene, but Martha pushed her aside.

"Let me do it. I'll serve the doctor. A drink for the shrink. The shrink drank the drink. Cocoa for the cuckoo. That's me, the cuckoo."

Talking constantly, she plopped four lumps of sugar into a cup, sloshed cocoa into it, and shoved it at me. But her hand jerked so quickly that the cup fell from the saucer onto the rug, splattering cocoa over my knee, the couch, and the rug.

"Oops," she cried, "a little mistake. It happens in the best of families. If at first you don't succeed, try, try again." She picked up the cup and dashed at the cocoa tray, where her hands met her mother's. In an instant the silver cocoa pot lay on its side with its spout over the edge of the tray and cocoa running across the table and onto the rug.

Mrs. Wilcox glared at her daughter furiously, jammed her lips together, and said nothing.

Martha set the cocoa pot upright on the tray, slopped what cocoa remained in it into the cup, and gave it to me.

"A drink for the shrink," she crowed. Then she put her hand to the side of her mouth, and behind it she said to me in a loud mock whisper, "Mommy's mad. Martha was a bad little girl. Spilled cocoa on the rug." She threw herself back against the sofa and shrieked with laughter. "Martha is a baddie. Mommy is a goodie. Cocoa, cocoa everywhere and not a drop to drink."

Then she grabbed the linen napkins that lay stacked on one corner of the tray and went down on her knees to mop up the cocoa, chattering continually.

Mrs. Wilcox, sitting upright on the edge of the sofa opposite me, with her hands clasped tightly in her lap, said, "I am aware that she is sick, Doctor, and this sort of thing must be accepted." Her face was rigid, not with concern or compassion but with silent anger.

Martha mopped the rug and tossed the cocoa-soaked napkins onto the table while she alternately ranted and giggled. In a vague way she perhaps grasped the fury that lay behind her mother's stiff façade, and dimly sensed that her psychotic illness enabled her to do endless things she had never done before. She was turning her mother slowly on a spit over a fire. The cutting reprimands, the guilt-laden harangues and the cold rebuffs with which her mother had controlled her for thirty years were now useless.

After I quickly drank my cocoa Mrs. Wilcox took the tray back to the kitchen, from which, at my request, she brought a plastic water bottle and a glass, which she laid on a side table. They were to use in giving Martha the medication that Fred would soon bring.

About five minutes later Fred arrived and gave me two medication bottles. Martha tried to grab them out of my hands, but I held them at arm's length on the side opposite her. As she hollered, "No pills for me, no bilge for me," and Mrs. Wilcox and Fred watched silently, I quickly checked the labels: chlorpromazine capsules, 300 milligrams, and chlorpromazine syrup, 10 milligrams to the teaspoon. With enough of this antipsychotic medication in her she would soon be drowsy and manageable, and later she would be asleep. Then I could get more information from Mrs. Wilcox and Fred, and make plans for hospitalizing her.

I took five of the capsules from one of the bottles and dropped them into my right coat pocket. It was a heavy dose, but it was better to give too much than too little, since a patient with a manic disorder sometimes requires a sizable amount to calm him. Moreover, an excessive dose of chlorpromazine does no harm; the patient merely sleeps for a day or two. In addition a patient does not get sensuous feelings from chlorpromazine that might lead him to abuse it once he has experienced it; it is not possible to become physically addicted to it.

"Not for me," Martha shouted as she saw me put the capsules into my pocket. She gave me a strong shove on the shoulder and moved away from me on the sofa. "No shrink pills for me. Annie took shrink pills, and had shrink talk, and look what happened to her. Not me. Annie, nannie, quite the dandie, how does your garden grow? With psycho pills and talk that kills, and kiddies all in a row."

The rantings of an intelligent, well-educated manic patient may be montages of incoherence and startling insight, and their craftiness with words is at times uncanny. When I look at *Ulysses* or *Finnegans Wake* I sometimes wonder if James Joyce had a thread of mania or schizophrenia in him.

Martha clanged on. "Annie, Annie, pandie nannie, wasn't contrary enough. She talked, not balked; and Dr. Cantor, with his banter, was a can't-er, not a doer, and his pills were bilge and his talk was squawk. Squawkie-talkie and bilgey pills. Walkie-talkie and willy-nilly. So Annie, nannie, sister mine and sister thine, put a popgun in her ear, let it off loud and clear, and now she lies five fathoms deep, for keeps."

I told Fred to pour a glass of water from the water bottle on the side table into the glass beside it, and to bring it to me.

"Not for me," Martha hollered. "Water, water everywhere, but not a drop to drink. Good for washing babies' asses, not for drinking out of glasses. Five fathoms deep, sound asleep." She burst out laughing and then sputtered into a fit of coughing; she was gettting hoarse from continual ranting. She stared at me, flush-faced and bulge-eyed.

To get five capsules down a patient like this requires a bit of skill, but I've been at it for almost three decades, and I usually can pull it off.

"Martha," I said firmly and slowly, "you're tense. You're on a jag. You need something to calm you down so you can sleep a little. These capsules will not harm you. Now, here's the first one and some water. Take it. It's good for what ails you."

"Give it to her," she said, waving at her mother, "or him," pointing to Fred. "I won't take any pills. No pills, no swills for me. If anyone's crazy, it's her or him. Or you take it. Physician, heal thyself. The shrink-doc wants me to take pills so the nice dockie can go home and go to bed. Not on your life."

I held the capsule out in my left palm, and I held the water in my right hand, a little farther back, so that if she tried to slap the glass onto the floor I could quickly pull it out of her reach.

"Martha," I said quietly, "*take* the capsule."

She did nothing, and I repeated, "Martha, *take* the capsule."

She stared at me, motionless for a moment. Then she darted out her hand, picked up the capsule and tossed it into her mouth. She took the glass of water and swallowed the capsule with a small gulp.

"Another," I said, holding out a second one that I had fished from my pocket.

"Oh, no," she croaked hoarsely, "one is enough. Give it to them or take it yourself."

"*Take* it," I said firmly, never letting my eyes leave her face. She took it and swallowed it, and within a minute or so had taken all five of them. For another twenty minutes she clattered on while the rest of us watched her; I occasionally made a short comment, and I had silenced her mother and Fred with a gesture. Then she became drowsy and her speech began to slur.

"It's the pills," I said. "You need some sleep, Martha. Mrs. Wilcox, perhaps you might help her upstairs to bed; and perhaps you might help, Fred. She may be a little wobbly on her feet. Tomorrow, when you wake up, you'll be calmer, Martha."

"*Where* will I wake up?" she asked.

"I don't know," I said.

"Yes, you do, you liar," she shot back. "In some damn hospital probably. A psycho ward."

"I don't lie to patients," I replied quietly. "They find out, and when they do, you're finished. I really don't know where you'll be tomorrow. I haven't had a chance to talk with your mother, Fred, and your husband."

"My husband is dead," she said groggily. "He died at two fifteen this afternoon. He was hit on the head."

"I think you'll see it differently when you feel better," I replied. "Your mother and Fred will help you upstairs to bed." Turning to them, I said, "She'll soon be asleep. I'll wait for you here. Then we can settle things."

"Settle me, you mean," Martha said in speech that was becoming garbled. "But you can't settle me. I'm already settled. The Wilcoxes were some of the first settlers in this cow town. Settled all over the place. And the Ramseys, too. Mom's people. Old settlers on all sides. Everybody's all settled down, down, down."

After Fred and Mrs. Wilcox helped her to her feet it was clear that she was so unsteady that my aid would be necessary to get her upstairs. When we had made it up the flight of stairs and were on the second-floor landing, I stepped back and watched Mrs. Wilcox and Fred guide her to a bedroom door. After they went in I looked for a moment down each of the corridors that led away from the landing. Behind closed doors children were in bed. I wondered if the older ones were asleep or if beneath their blankets they were listening to distant, frightening sounds.

I went downstairs and waited.

I was no longer annoyed that Dr. Grant had called me; this would be an interesting tangle to try to unravel. Martha had spewed out a lot of riddles. I settled onto a couch in the living room, looked at the fire briefly, and then drew from my black leather briefcase a couple of sheets of patient record paper to make preliminary notes on Martha. I had filled a page and a half with data before Mrs. Wilcox and Fred came downstairs and joined me.

Mrs. Wilcox sat down on a sofa opposite me, calm and businesslike. Fred sat in a chair halfway between us, at the center of the semicircle of furniture before the fireplace; he gazed at the fire, his lips slightly apart, and I doubted that he listened to most of what Mrs. Wilcox and I said.

"Mrs. Wilcox, it's late, but there are a few things I should know, and we should make plans for Martha's care."

"Any definite steps should be arranged with her husband," she replied. "We've put in calls for him. I'm surprised we've not heard from him yet."

"Where is Charles?" I asked.

"He's out of town. We're in the stage and auditorium equipment business. We have salesmen and installation crews who handle most of the out-of-town jobs. However, when we have large out-of-town orders and difficult installations, Charles occasionally leaves the city for a few days to check on the work. He left early yesterday for Des Moines, where we are outfitting a university auditorium; today he went on to Council Bluffs and then to Omaha, where we have high school auditorium contracts. He was scheduled to come back by way of Lincoln and Hastings. However, he will have to cut the trip short and return to Kansas City at once. When my husband was alive, he did most of the traveling, but Charles does it now."

"How long has Mr. Wilcox been dead?" I asked.

"He died six years ago last June, quite suddenly, of a heart attack. He was sixty-four."

All her information was neat and exact. Such precision is useful in business, but I suspected that she dealt with her husband and children in the same manner.

I jotted down this data in the record I had begun on Martha, using my briefcase as a writing lapboard. Note-taking under these circumstances rarely bothers patients and their relatives; in fact, they wonder how a psychiatrist can keep his patients straight if he does not make notes.

"From your familiarity with these details," I said, "I take it you are in the business."

"For twenty-seven years I have handled most of the paperwork. I have four girls who help me. Since Mr. Wilcox's death I have more or less run the firm."

I had sketched on a third sheet of notepaper the outline of the family structure shown below; I proceeded to get the information I needed to fill it in and to get relationships and time sequences clear.

"I take it Martha is in her early thirties?"

"She was thirty last May."

"And Charles?"

"He's thirty-one."

"Let me just cover the other people involved so I can have a clear idea of Martha's background."

"Of course, doctor.

"I take it Martha has two children?"

"Yes. A boy who is six and a girl who is four."

"And how old was Anne when she died?"

She breathed a bit more deeply and said, "Thirty-two."

"You and Mr. Wilcox had just the two children?"

"We had a son; he died in the Second World War, in the Air Force," she replied.

"How old is Fred?" He did not seem to notice we were talking about him.

"He is thirty-two also."

"And Anne had three children?"

"Yes. Two girls, aged eight and six, and a boy, aged three."

"How old are you, Mrs. Wilcox?"

"I am sixty-four."

"I take it both you and Mr. Wilcox were brought up in Kansas City or near here."

"Both of us have lived here all our lives."

"And do both of you have brothers or sisters in the Kansas City area?"

"I have a sister who lives in Raytown. Mr. Wilcox had a brother, but he died in childhood of polio."

"Thank you. That gives me a good outline of the family structure."

"Of course." However, Mrs. Wilcox was getting a little restless. She did not like this probing into her family life. She wanted to get down to the immediate matter at hand, Martha's illness. However, there were other things I needed to know.

"How long has Charles been in the business?"

"About eight and a half years. He and Martha married immediately after their graduation from Oberlin. They were in the same class. Mr. Wilcox invited Charles to join us in the business, and so he did, of course. It was a good opportunity for him; he will take it over one day.'

"Then Fred is not in the business?"

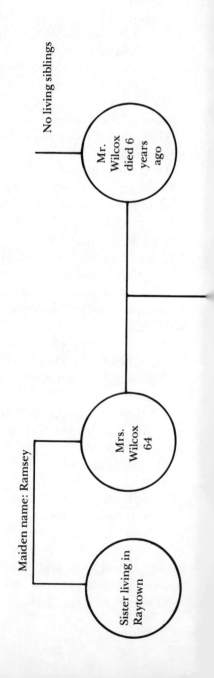

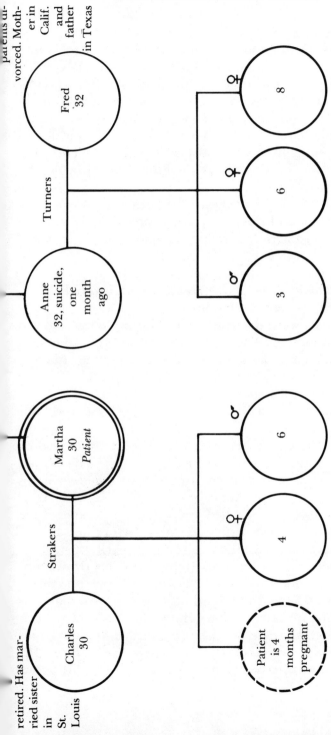

parents di-
vorced. Moth-
er in Calif.
and father
in Texas

Fred
32

Turners

Anne
32, suicide,
one month
ago

♀
8

♀
6

♂
3

Martha
30
Patient

Strakers

Charles
30

retired. Has mar-
ried sister in
St. Louis

♂
6

♀
4

Patient
is 4
months
pregnant

"No," she replied. "Mr. Wilcox invited him to come into the business when he and Anne married, two years before Martha and Charles married. But he declined. He's an architect and preferred to go his own way. Mr. Wilcox and I felt that his training as an architect would be a good background for our business, and he would have come in, had it not been for Anne. She objected. She thought he should work independently. Anne was headstrong." She corrected herself, for one does not speak so of the dead. "I mean, she had firm ideas on things."

"Where do Charles' parents live?" I asked.

"They live in Redbridge. His father is retired. He was with the Robertson-Davis Insurance Company here for many years."

"Does Charles have any brothers or sisters?"

"He has a married sister in St. Louis," she answered.

"And Fred's parents?" I inquired.

"His parents were divorced when he was young. He was raised by his mother. She has remarried and lives in San Diego now. His father lives in Texas. We rarely see either of them, or hear from them. Fred is an only child." She thus blocked a question about his siblings.

My outline of Martha's immediate interpersonal world was complete.

"I take it," I said, "that, given some distortions caused by her state of mind, Martha's account of her sister's illness and death is more or less accurate. It checks with the few things Dr. Grant told me about Anne."

"Yes," Mrs. Wilcox replied unblinkingly. "I knew little about it until she died. Until a few days before her death I was not even aware that she was seeing a psychiatrist. I was not consulted. I don't know anything about this Dr. Cantor, but it seems to me that proper measures to protect Anne's life were not taken. Anne did things on her own, independently. I think it would not have ended this way if I had been consulted and her care had been planned differently. This Dr. Cantor was not recommended by Dr. Grant or by Dr. Matthews, our internist. Anne heard of him through a neighbor of hers out in Leawood. I think it is unwise to put one's life and welfare into the hands of unknown, untried people. However, as I said, I was not consulted."

I looked at her in silence for a moment. This woman's bitchiness was finely honed and thoroughly respectable.

Before asking for details about the onset of Martha's illness, I felt I should find out exactly where her husband was. Perhaps he could be reached by telephone, and with his verbal authorization and a promise that he would arrive in Kansas City the next morning, I could hospitalize her at once or let her sleep overnight on the sedation and arrange hospitalization early the next day.

"Where is Charles now?" I asked. "Is he in Des Moines or Omaha? Where can we reach him?"

She frowned slightly. "I don't know. Late this afternoon, even before I telephoned Dr. Grant, I put in a call for him at the hotel where he always stays in Omaha. He had a reservation there. I always make reservations for our men when they travel. Charles has not returned my call. At eight thirty I called the hotel again. He had not arrived yet, but they were still holding his reservation. I again left a message for him to call me as soon as he came in, and emphasized to the room clerk that there was sudden illness in the family. It's strange he has not called. I thought that maybe he had been held over a day in Des Moines, and so I called his hotel there shortly before nine, a little before Dr. Grant called you. They said he had stayed there last night and had checked out at eight this morning. It's a little less than one hundred and fifty miles from Des Moines to Omaha, and even if he spent time inspecting our jobs in Des Moines and Council Bluffs, he should have arrived in Omaha by now. Perhaps the room clerk neglected to give him the message in spite of my urgent instructions."

She turned to Fred.

"Fred, telephone the hotel in Omaha and ask if Charles has arrived. The number is on the pad by the phone. Call me when you get him."

Fred rose and went to the phone, which apparently was in

an alcove at the rear of the entrance hall, beneath the first landing of the stairs.

"Perhaps he had car trouble," I suggested, "and has stopped overnight in some small town while his car is being repaired.'

"That's unlikely," Mrs. Wilcox said. "He's driving a company car. The company cars are never more than two years old, and I always have them checked at the garage where we park them before any of the men take them out of town. Moreover, Charles would call to let us know where he was if that happened. There often are messages from customers or instructions from the office."

Her use of the word "instructions" annoyed me; I had the feeling that she was the one who gave the instructions.

Fred soon returned. "He hasn't arrived at the hotel, and they've had no word from him. They say there's been a light snow and there's ice on some of the roads up there; it's early for snow, but it turned cold last night. Maybe he decided to stay overnight at a motel on the highway."

"Well, that's probably it," said Mrs. Wilcox. "Still, it's unusual he hasn't called. But we'll hear from him early tomorrow. By midday at the latest, he'll call the office."

"There are some other things to cover briefly," I said. "I know it's late, but a few things should be arranged for managing Martha here overnight, and I need to know a little more about her illness. I can get more information about her background in an office visit with Charles in a day or two."

Hands in her lap and her small body erect on the edge of the sofa, Mrs. Wilcox watched me coldly. I had the feeling she thought I already had enough "background" information about Martha.

I think she and I more or less understood each other. Though we were about fifteen years different in age, my background was similar to hers. My father had had business dealings with them; by now I had recalled hearing my father talk of "Dick Wilcox, in the stage equipment line."

"We can manage Martha at home here until midday tomorrow," I said. "Take this bottle of capsules and give her three of them at eight or so tomorrow morning. It's not important whether she eats, but make sure she gets a reasonable amount of fluid. Orange juice, water, soft drinks, anything she wants, will do. She will be fairly groggy and perhaps sleep much of the time until tomorrow afternoon. I think you should call a nurses exchange and get a practical nurse to stay with her tomorrow morning from seven o'clock onward. Someone must be with her constantly to accompany her to the bathroom, to prevent her from trying to come downstairs, and so forth; she might fall."

"Charlotte, our maid, comes in tomorrow. She's been with us for eighteen years. She's reliable," Mrs. Wilcox replied.

"Well," I said, "she'll be fairly busy with the children, and I think a practical nurse is necessary."

"Very well, Doctor."

"There are a few things more I must know, and then I'll go," I said. "Exactly when and how did Martha's illness begin?"

Mrs. Wilcox shifted her position slightly and began: "She seemed quite all right until early this afternoon. Since Charles was out of town she and her children were spending the day with me. They live just two blocks down the street, and I don't go to the office on Wednesdays or Saturdays now. After lunch she lay down to rest. When she's pregnant, she often does that. Dr. Latham says it's advisable, since she's had two miscarriages in the last couple of years. She fell asleep; I noticed she was sleeping when I went upstairs to put some linen away. At a little past two I heard her screaming. I went upstairs at once. I thought something must have happened to one of the children; they were playing in the playroom on the second floor. As I went up I saw her at the top of the stairs. She was very agitated. She screamed that Charles was dead and that he had died of a blow to the head. Apparently she had waked up screaming. I thought she had had a nightmare; she had them as a child."

Mrs. Wilcox paused and glanced toward the stairs; a slight wave of tenseness passed over her face. Perhaps behind her cold reserve and self-control lay more anxiousness than one would suspect.

She held the edge of her upper lip between her teeth for a

moment and then went on. "No matter what I did, I couldn't calm her down. She ranted on and on, talking of Charles. Her speech grew more confused as the afternoon wore on, until after a couple of hours she was, well, she was as you saw her. I had Charlotte spend most of the afternoon with her, and I gave her a couple of sedative tablets that I had left over from a prescription Dr. Matthews had given me when Mr. Wilcox died. I only took one or two, and they've been in the medicine cabinet ever since then. I put in a call for Dr. Grant at six, but he was at a hospital meeting and didn't call me until about seven thirty. He got here a little after eight thirty, and when he saw the state she was in, he called you." She stopped for a moment. "Before Charlotte left I had her go down the street to Martha's house and bring the children's pajamas and other clothing. I sent them to bed early. I expected to hear from Charles by now."

"Has she ever been like this before?" I asked.

"No, never."

"Has she ever seen a psychiatrist for any reason?"

"No." She amended her statement. "Not so far as I'm aware."

"With the exception of her sister's illness and her treatment by Dr. Cantor, has anyone in your family ever seen a psychiatrist?" This was a tactful way of asking if she or Mr. Wilcox or any of the children or any other close person had had psychiatric difficulties and treatment.

"No."

Fred looked up, first at her and then at me, but said nothing. Apparently he was paying more attention than I thought.

"Well," I said, "I shall outline to you briefly what is wrong with Martha and what we can do about it. She has a manic disorder, or a manic psychosis, as it is sometimes called. We see them fairly often in our work. It is more or less the opposite of a depression, which is perhaps what Anne had. A manic patient is physically overactive, talks constantly, flits in a helter skelter way from one topic to another, darts from one task to the next in a disorganized way, and sometimes is delusional. The treatment for this kind of difficulty is good. In almost all cases, with medication and a good psychiatric hospital environmental program, a manic patient is much better in from three to four weeks and recovers in from six to eight weeks. He continues to take a small daily maintenance dose of medication for three or four months after he leaves the hospital. If the patient will engage in it, we often try to do psychotherapy, that is, interview treatment, during the convalescent period and afterward, to help the patient understand and resolve the inner turmoil that led to his illness. The prognosis is, as I said, very good."

"And you feel that hospitalization is absolutely necessary?" Mrs. Wilcox asked.

"Yes," I answered, "it is absolutely necessary." I had the feeling she thought that Martha might "snap out of it" after a good night's rest.

"Well," she said, "you can settle all that with Charles tomorrow. As soon as I hear from him, I'll tell him to call you; by tomorrow afternoon at the latest he will be in Kansas City."

"Hospitalization should not be put off," I said. "If there is any delay in hearing from Charles, we should hospitalize Martha on your authorization. If the husband is unavailable in an urgent situation like this, you, as her mother, can sign the hospital admission papers and Charles will also sign them when he arrives."

"No," she said firmly. "Any decision about hospitalization is Charles' responsibility. Many things in this country would not be as they are if everyone accepted his responsibilities."

I looked at her in silence for a moment. This was a cast-iron woman, unrusted and unbending.

She and Fred saw me to the door.

"Thank you for coming, Doctor," she said.

Fred muttered his thanks.

As she looked from the door into the night, she noticed that the lights along the front walk to the street were not lit, and she apologized; in the turmoil of the evening's events she had forgotten. She flicked a switch by the door that turned them on, and she asked Fred to accompany me to my car.

The word "car" reminded me of the smashed car in the driveway.

"I noticed as I was coming in," I said, "that the car in the driveway had been driven into the hedge and the wall. The door on the driver's side was open and the keys were still in the ignition switch. I took the liberty of removing the keys and shutting the door." I felt my right overcoat pocket, took out the keys, and handed them to her. "I thought it unwise to leave the keys in the car."

"Thank you, Doctor. We've had a difficult day, as you know. That is Martha's car; she parked it there when she and the children came this morning to spend the day. Early this evening Martha tried to leave, but she couldn't get her car down the drive. Three or four times she backed it off onto the lawn and ran into the hedge and wall each time she tried to get onto the driveway again. The last time she must have damaged the motor; it won't start. Tomorrow morning I'll have the man who takes care of our company cars send out a tow truck to pick it up."

We said good-night.

I told Fred I could find my way without difficulty, but he insisted on seeing me to my car.

When we got to the car he said, "Doctor, there are some things you ought to know, things I couldn't tell you in front of Mrs. Wilcox."

I waited for him to go on.

"It will take a little time, maybe fifteen or twenty minutes."

"Well, call my office early tomorrow and make an appointment," I said. "Tell my secretary who you are, and tell her that I said to work you in."

He demurred.

"I wouldn't want Mrs. Wilcox to know I saw you," he said.

"She need not know," I replied. "As she herself has carefully pointed out, she is not the responsible relative in this situation."

"Could I catch you somewhere early tomorrow morning, at a hospital or some other place, and talk to you for fifteen minutes?"

This frightened, perplexed man obviously had something pressing to tell me.

"If you want," I said, "you can wait for me in the small visitors' waiting room at the entrance to the psychiatric ward of St. Catharine's Hospital. I go through there every morning between nine and nine thirty. There are some conference rooms on the ward where we can talk privately."

"I'll be there," he said.

We parted and I went home.

That night I slept badly. Nameless, troubling things wandered through my sleep; at six, my usual hour, I awoke, uneasy and vaguely irritable. However, by seven I was on the psychiatric ward at Mt. Sinai, and the problems of the day quickly put the Wilcoxes out of my mind. A little before nine I finished at Mt. Sinai, and shortly afterward I arrived at St. Catharine's. Fred was waiting for me in the small waiting room, made by a widening of the corridor, outside the entrance to the psychiatric ward.

He stared at me like a scared schoolboy. I wondered if his wife had dominated him and whether she had been protecting and affectionate or exploitive and abrasive in her dominance. I suspected that he had nothing really important to tell me and that perhaps he was in a way looking for treatment for himself or maybe simply for someone to tell him what to do.

I asked him if they had heard from Charles yet.

He looked at me blankly; apparently he had been preoccupied with other things.

"No, no," he replied, "but he'll call this morning. By noon at the latest. Mrs. Wilcox says he has to check with the office about whether a public address system is ready for delivery and installation in Omaha next week."

He pawed his hat, looked apprehensively at the other people in the waiting room, and said nothing. I watched him for a few moments, during which he started twice to say something, but couldn't speak.

Finally he said, "Is there somewhere we can talk?"

"Yes. There are interview rooms on the ward. It's this way."

I walked out of the waiting room and a dozen paces farther down the corridor to the door of the psychiatric ward, with Fred trailing behind me. I pressed a button beside the door, and from a small speaker flush with the wall I heard the ward secretary, from her desk in the nurses' station at the end of the ward, say, "May I help you, please?"

"It's Dr. Chapman, Mary," I replied.

Immediately there was a whirring noise, indicating that Mary had pushed the button beside her desk which unlocked the door. I pulled the large, heavy door open and motioned for Fred to go in. I went in behind him.

"The conference rooms are on this side," I said, and I led him to a small interview room and closed the door behind us. I sat down on a wooden chair behind a small table, while he sat, hat in hand and with his topcoat on, on another chair against the wall a few feet away. As in every room of St. Catharine's, a crucifix was on the wall. Other than two metal ashtrays on the desk and a couple of polished wooden chairs along the wall opposite Fred, there was nothing else in the room. The frugal nuns of St. Catharine's do not buy unnecessary furniture.

After glancing at me briefly and looking about the room, Fred settled his gaze on the floor and said nothing. He seemed relieved to be there. After a minute or so, I shifted impatiently from one ham to the other; I had little time to talk with him. This was not a scheduled therapeutic session; it was a brief interview, requested by a nonblood relative, presumably to tell me a few minor things he thought I ought to know.

Since he remained silent, I began.

"How is Martha this morning?" I asked.

"Oh, she's all right," he answered, with a slight start. He obviously had been thinking of other things.

A silly reply, I thought to myself. Martha was not "all right." She was psychotic.

There was another half-minute of silence.

"Well, Mr. Turner, what was it you wanted to talk to me about?"

He stared at me and said nothing.

I felt impatient with him. Like many middle-aged people who passed their formative years in the 1920's and 1930's, when life was simpler and harder, I have a tendency to become annoyed with some of the aimless products of the affluent society. It is a weakness that I recognize and work to control in myself.

I folded my hands on the desk, sat back in my chair, and softened my voice as I said, "Fred, you must excuse me if I try to come to the point. Our main problem just now is Martha's illness, although there may be other problems involved; perhaps you have something to tell me that you feel has a bearing on Martha's illness."

"Yes," he said, but he did not go on.

"Well, could you begin to tell me about it?"

"I was married to Martha's sister. However, I guess you already know that."

"Yes," I said. After a pause I went on. "And I know that a lot of very disturbing things have happened in your life lately."

"Anne committed suicide a month ago, a month and four days," he said.

"It must have been a devastating experience for all of you."

He could not continue.

"What was Anne's trouble?" I asked. My interest in him was beginning to push aside my impatience. The clinician in me was taking over. "I assume she was depressed," I said. "Did she seem so to you, and what did Dr. Cantor say?"

"Yes, she was depressed, very depressed. Dr. Cantor said

she was depressed. He gave her antidepressant medication
and talked with her."

"And did you have any conferences with Dr. Cantor?"

"Twice."

"What did he say?"

"He told me she was depressed, but that she was not so depressed that she needed to go to the hospital, and that with
the medication and the psychotherapy she ought to be much
better in a month or two.'

"Was that all he said?"

"He asked me if I knew of anything that might be causing
her depression or playing a role in it."

"And what did you say?"

"I said that I didn't." He stalled and then plunged. "That's
why I wanted to see you. If I had told Dr. Cantor everything,
maybe Anne wouldn't have died."

After a pause I asked, "What was it you felt you should
have told Dr. Cantor and now want to tell me?"

"Well, you see, Anne and I and Charles and Martha have
known each other since college. We were all at Oberlin at
about the same time. Anne and I were in the same class, two
years ahead of Martha and Charles. We were all friends. I
dated Anne, and Charles dated Martha. Sometimes we went
out together."

He stopped and could not go on without a question.

"And then?"

"In our last year at college, Anne's and mine, Martha and
Charles broke up. Martha is very strong-willed. She likes to
have things her own way. Charles is strong-willed, too. They
fought and made up a lot of times. Every time they broke up
Martha became sweet again, and so they were soon back
together."

Once more he stalled.

"And how did you and Anne get along?"

"Oh, we never had any trouble."

"Was Anne strong-willed too?"

"Yes, I guess so."

"Would it be fair to say that all of them—Mrs. Wilcox, Anne, and Martha—are rather strong-willed?"

"Yes, I suppose so."

I altered the focus for a few moments. "Did Mrs. Wilcox dominate her husband?"

"Yes."

"Did she more or less run things, both at home and at the office?"

"Yes. He was a good salesman. Everybody liked him. However, in the office she ran things, and at home, too."

"How did Mr. Wilcox accept this? Did he and Mrs. Wilcox get along peacefully, so to speak?"

"Yes, they never fought. At least so far as I know. No, I'm sure they never fought."

I shifted back to our former point of attention. "And you and Anne—did she usually make the plans and settle things?"

"Yes. She was very well organized, a good manager."

"She sort of ran things at home, and you ran things in your professional business?"

"That was more or less it," he replied.

I shifted our attention back to Charles and Martha. "After they were married, how did Charles and Martha get along?"

"The same as before. It's not a good marriage. They fight a lot."

"Each one of them struggling always for the dominance that the other one will not concede," I suggested.

"Yes, that's about it." He looked up at me, perhaps a little surprised and puzzled at the rapidity with which the pieces were being fitted together. It wasn't clear whether this relieved or frightened him.

Fred and I were now in that timeless, placeless world where past and present cease to exist; in psychotherapy the boundaries that divide time and place are crossed and recrossed from moment to moment.

Although the main threads of the interpersonal web of this family had been traced out, we had not approached whatever it was that he wished to tell me—the things he felt might have saved his wife's life had he told them to Dr. Cantor.

He sank into silence again. I preferred that he spontaneously tell me what he had to say, but it was clear that without systematic questioning he could not go on. Moreover, it was probable that unless he told me what he wished to say in the next fifteen to twenty minutes, he would never do so. I had several patients to see on the ward at St. Catharine's, and I had to be in my office by noon. I was expecting at any time to hear from Charles, and once I had spoken with Charles, Fred would recede into the role of a distant, nonblood relative, an ex-brother-in-law of the patient. A psychiatrist cannot push a husband and a mother aside and deal confidentially with a patient's ex-brother-in-law. This would probably be my last contact with Fred.

I began to ask questions.

"Fred, the thing or things you want to tell me, are they things that happened recently, or are they things that happened some time ago?"

He mumbled, "Both."

"Do these things go back, to any extent, to the time when you were all in college together?"

"Yes."

I was somewhat taken aback. I had assumed he wanted to talk about recent events. I had asked a question about the earlier period only to eliminate it from our attention and to narrow the time span we would cover.

"Let me understand this clearly," I said. "These things either occurred while you were all at Oberlin or began there?"

"Yes."

"This would be ten or twelve years ago," I said.

"Yes."

"What happened then?"

With his eyes on the floor, his elbows on his knees, and his hands clasped before him, he began to talk. "It was during the last year Anne and I were in college, in the fall. Martha and Charles were two years behind us. They had had a particularly bad fight and had decided to break up for good; they didn't date for a month or so. About a week after they broke up I got a call at my dorm from Martha. She said she wanted to talk to me. She said she was upset about breaking up with Charles and had to talk to somebody. But she said she didn't want Anne to know about it. I felt uneasy about that; Anne and I were engaged and were going to get married right after graduation. I told Martha that I didn't think it was a good idea for me to get mixed up in her troubles with Charles, but she insisted and started to cry, and I gave in. I had a car. We agreed that I'd pick her up on a corner near the administration building at eight that night. And I did."

He stopped talking.

"Where did you go?"

"She asked me to drive out into the country, where we could talk alone. I didn't want to. I told her Anne wouldn't like it, but she said that what Anne didn't know wouldn't hurt her. She insisted, and so finally we drove out and stopped at a state park campsite off the road. There were no other cars around."

"And what did she talk about?"

He did not reply, and I repeated my question.

"She said that Anne didn't know how lucky she was to have an understanding man like me to talk to and to be with and so on. She said a lot more things. I told her I wanted to go back to town, but she took the keys from the ignition switch and slid them down between her seat and the door on her side."

He stopped talking.

"What else did you talk about?"

He looked steadily at the floor, motionless and mute.

"What else happened?"

He couldn't go on. Guilt padlocked his jaws.

Using my intuition, I began to probe.

"Did she touch you?"

"Yes."

"Where?"

"On the arm, at first."

"After a while did she kiss you?"

"Yes."

After a pause I asked quietly, "Did you have sex?"

"No."

"She didn't want it?"

"No, she wanted it."

"But you refused?"

"Yes."

"Did she push you on it?"

"Yes, and then she got mad. She got mad even while she was, well, playing with me."

I was puzzled; how could so passive a man refuse the aggressive seduction of a domineering, attractive woman, even though she was his fiancée's sister?

"*Why* did you refuse her, Fred?"

"I didn't have a rubber with me, and she wasn't on pills."

"And without a condom, the fear of her becoming pregnant held you back? And because of this you were able to refuse her?"

"I guess so."

"So you went home?"

"Yes. But it was late when we got back."

"And was that the end of it?"

"No."

"Did you go out with Martha again?"

"She had made me promise that I would go out with her again before she had given me the keys to the car."

"And when did you next go out?"

"The next night."

"And what happened?"

After a long pause he said, "I guess you might say we had an affair."

"How long did it go on?"

"About two weeks."

"And then it broke up?"

"Yes."

"Who broke it off, you or Martha?"

"Anne found out."

I looked at him in silence for a minute, and thought of the hatred and suspiciousness that must always afterward have existed between these two sisters, one of whom had died by suicide a month ago and the other of whom was now psychotic.

I was no longer keeping track of time or thinking of my morning's schedule.

"How did she find out?" I asked.

"She began to wonder why I was seeing less of her in the evenings. I told her I was having trouble in a couple of courses and was studying more. Then she called the dorm a few times at night to see if I was there; she caught me in a couple of lies. She accused me of going out with another girl."

"And then?"

"Then one night she followed my car, somehow or other, and saw me pick up Martha. She was waiting for me in front of the dorm when I got in that night. She made an awful scene. Fellows stuck their heads out the dorm windows to see what was going on. She insisted that I go with her, then and there, to talk it out. She took me to a bench on the other side of the campus. It was dark there. She pumped me and got it all out of me."

"What did she do?"

"She hit me, slapped me, twice."

"And then?"

"I promised her I'd never go out with Martha again. So she let me go back to the dorm. She just sat on the bench and watched me go off."

"What happened between her and Martha?"

"I don't know, but it must have been terrible. Anyway, after a couple of weeks everything was back the way it had been. Martha made up with Charles, and Anne and I went on as before. At the end of the year, after graduation, Anne and I got married. Charles and Martha had two years more to go. After graduation they got married, too."

I slumped back in my chair, watching him steadily. "And after all this settled down, did Martha and Anne get along all right again?"

"On the surface, yes, but underneath, no. Anne never really forgave Martha and never trusted her after that."

Silence.

"Is that all?" I asked.

"No."

I had a vague apprehensiveness about what was to come.

I waited for him to proceed, but he did not; he looked at the floor and clenched his hands together.

"There was more?" I asked.

"Yes."

"When?"

"Last summer."

"How did it happen?"

He began to talk in a low, expressionless, tired voice.

"July and August are busy months for the Wilcox company; high schools and universities want their auditoriums ready for the beginning of the school year. During those months Charles is out of town a lot. Charles and Martha were having a rough time; they fought constantly. They talked about divorce, but Mrs. Wilcox wouldn't hear of it. She got into it, and it was awful. All this was hidden from outsiders; even people in the firm didn't know what was going on.

"Then, one day at my office, about three months ago, I got a call from Martha. She said she had to talk to someone about her and Charles. She wanted me to meet her for lunch. That sounded all right to me. So I agreed to meet her at Reinert's, on the Plaza. She said that was okay. But she said her car was in the garage being fixed and asked me to pick her up at noon in front of Wallman's at the Sixty-third Street shopping center, near where they lived. So I did. After she got into the car she said that Reinert's would be too crowded, and that we couldn't talk there. She said she knew a small restaurant out on Highway Forty-six. It was only fifteen or twenty minutes away, and so we went there."

He stopped and couldn't go on without a question.

"You had lunch there?"

"Yes."

"And what did you talk about?"

"About her trouble with Charles. At first."

"And then?"

"About how it might have been, as she put it."

"How might it have been?" I said.

"She wished, she said, that she had married me, that she hadn't given me up when she and Anne fought over me at college, that I was an understanding man and that Charles was, well, she said he was a bastard. That's the word she used. They must have had a bad fight a day or two before that. She was very bitter toward him."

"And what did you say?"

"I don't know. I was pretty mixed up by all this."

Silence.

"What happened then?"

"She was sitting beside me, in a booth. We were in the back of the restaurant, and there were only a few people there. She put her arm through mine, leaned over, and kissed me, on the neck. I told her not to do it and tried to move away. But she was sitting on the outside seat of the booth, and I was next to the wall. I couldn't get away. She laughed, moved closer to me, and kissed me again. And she patted my leg." He breathed shallowly with his lips apart.

His left elbow was on his thigh, and his forehead pressed downward on the rump of the palm of his hand. His right arm hung limp, and his hat lay where he had let it fall on the floor. His eyes were closed.

I felt I knew the rest, but he had to tell me. After that I had to tell him the reassuring lies he needed to hear.

"Then?" I asked.

"There was a motel attached to the restaurant. We went there."

"And had sex?"

I was dissecting it out. After many years at this kind of work one becomes inured to patients' anguish, but a certain sadness always hangs over it.

"Yes, we had sex."

"Was that the only time?"

"No."

"Several times?"

"More or less."

"During July and August of this year?"

"Yes."

"When did it end?"

"About the middle of August or maybe a little later."

I calculated silently. A little more than sixty days ago.

"*Why* did it end?"

"Because she told Charles about it."

That stunned me. My preconceived picture fell to the floor and smashed.

"*Told Charles about it?*"

"Yes."

"*Why?*"

"I don't know. I think they were having a fight, and she just blurted it out. Threw it in his face. Told him that she was having an affair with me. Told him he was cuckolded. That was her word. She called him a eunuch. He got wild. He threatened to kill her, kill us all, kill himself. I think he scared her. But in time he calmed down. He told her that if she ever saw me again, in that way, he would kill her. She was frightened. Charles is not a weak man. I don't think he'd really do it, but with him it's possible."

"How do you know all this?"

"The next day he came to my office, shut the door behind him, and told me everything. Everything she said, and everything he said. Then, he asked me if it was all true, and said he'd beat it out of me if I didn't tell him."

He stopped talking.

"And what did you say?"

"I said it was true. And then I cried." He looked up at me, his face a grimace of pain. "I know it sounds corny, but I cried, and I asked him to forgive me. Not out of fear. At least I don't think I asked him out of fear. I felt awful."

"Guilty," I said, supplying the clinical word.

"Yes, guilty. Oh, God, I was stupid."

"And what did Charles say?"

"He said, '*Then she didn't just make it all up to hurt me,*' and he walked out of my office."

After a moment's pause I asked, "This was in about the third week in August?" I was trying to work out time sequences.

"Yes, about then."

"And when did your wife become sick? When did her depression begin?"

"A little later, a week or two before Labor Day."

"The connection is very close," I said. I was looking for a link between these things and the beginning of Anne's depression.

"*Charles told Anne,*" he said.

I leaned forward in my chair and stared hard at him. Just when I think that I've heard every story and brag to myself that given half the pieces of a jigsaw puzzle, I can predict what the other half is like, the patients teach me that I'm still a beginner.

"He *told* Anne about it?"

"Yes. He left my office, went straight to our home, and told her everything."

I sat mutely, without questions.

His body bent forward, staring at the floor, he went on.

"About an hour after he left my office he called me. He said he just wanted me to know that two could play this game, and that he had told Anne everything. He said he was then going to tell Martha what he had done."

He paused. I no longer probed, but only waited.

He began again. "I expected Anne to be furious at me. Maybe to throw me out of the house and divorce me. I thought maybe Charles and Martha would divorce, and that it would all be a horrible mess. But nothing happened. When I went home that night, Anne just looked at me. She had a sort of blank look. We ate dinner. She did everything just like she always did, but she walked around like she was in a daze or something. I could hear her that night, wandering

around the house until two or three o'clock. Afterward—
that's the way it went on, day after day. She didn't leave the
house much. She would stay up half the night ironing or arranging drawers, which she didn't have to do; we had a woman who always came in to do that. Then, in September, shortly after school started, she went to see Dr. Cantor. She saw
him a few times. Then she died."

"And she never said anything about your affair with Martha?"

"No."

"And you never mentioned it in any way?"

"No."

"And did Charles and Martha go on as before?"

"Yes, so far as I could see."

He paused and then said, "There's something more.
Anne's death disturbed Charles a lot. A week after she died
he came to my office. He was very upset. Depressed, I guess
you'd say. He said he felt like he was the one who had killed
Anne, just as if he'd put the revolver to her head and had
pulled the trigger. He said that if there was ever anything he
could do to help me and the kids, money or anything, to let
him know."

As he was saying this, I abruptly realized that Charles,
Martha, and Fred had been seeing a lot of each other since
Anne's death a month before. Fred had no one to look after
the children, and they could not go on using the same bathroom in which their mother had died so gruesomely; hence,
they all had been living with Mrs. Wilcox, whose house was
less than two blocks from Charles' and Martha's house. From
once to several times a day Charles, Martha, and Fred had
probably come together, the three of them sharing the grim
secrets they hid from everyone else, and each of them knowing that in his own way he had contributed to Anne's death.

"Has Charles continued to be depressed?" I asked.

"Yes, but he goes on working."

"Does Mrs. Wilcox know any of this? Does she know anything except that her daughter Anne committed suicide a

month ago and her daughter Martha became psychiatrically ill yesterday?"

"No. She doesn't know anything."

A family of strangers.

"I felt I had to tell you this," he said. "I feel that if I'd told all this to Dr. Cantor, Anne might still be alive."

He had come to the end of his story.

I watched him in silence for a minute or so and then began to talk. "Fred, it's clear that you feel very upset about these things. You feel very guilty, and your guilt feelings are unjustified. The causes of the illnesses of Anne and Martha are more complicated than this. They are caused by multiple long-term unhealthy relationships with people, and by many accumulated stresses. What you have told me is no more than a small cause, at most. Many women and men go through experiences like these, and very few of them commit suicide and become psychiatrically ill. It takes more than this, a lot more. The causes stretch back through all the years of a person's life, through childhood and adolescence. These recent happenings could play only a tiny role in the troubles of Anne and Martha."

I was telling him what he had to hear; he had three children to rear, a job to do every day, and forty years of life ahead of him.

"If you want to talk out these these painful feelings with a professional person who can help you see them in their proper perspectives, I can recommend someone to you. I cannot do it myself; in our kind of work we don't deal intimately with more than one member of a family."

"I'll be all right," he said. "I just felt it was my responsibility to tell you this."

He picked up his hat from the floor, rose, and smoothed out a few wrinkles from his topcoat.

"If there's a bill for this, send it to me at my office," he said. "I'm in the phone book."

I said there was none. I accompanied him to the door of the psychiatric ward, where I waved to the ward secretary behind her glass partition at the end of the hall; she pressed the button that released the door's lock, and he left.

By late afternoon, having heard nothing from Mrs. Wilcox, I called her home. A woman, who upon my inquiry identified herself as a practical nurse, answered the phone. She said that Mrs. Wilcox was at her office at the Wilcox Company. I asked if the children and the day maid were in the house, and the nurse said that the children had been sent to spend the afternoon and night at the home of a sister of Mrs. Wilcox, a Mrs. Stewart in Raytown.

They had left a psychotic person alone with a practical nurse whom they had never met until she appeared for duty that morning.

I asked the nurse if they had heard from the patient's husband. She answered that they were expecting a call from him, but, so far as she knew, he had not yet called.

I asked her how Martha was. She said she had taken her chlorpromazine medication that morning, as I had ordered, and was sleeping. I asked if there had been any difficulty in getting Martha to accept the medication; the nurse replied that she had refused to accept it from her mother, but with some coaxing she, the nurse, had got Martha to take it. In reply to further questions the nurse said that Martha had taken fluids well, had eaten a light breakfast and lunch, and except for trips to the bathroom had remained in bed all day; she had been drowsy or sleeping most of the time.

I asked the nurse if she were speaking to me from a telephone on the first or second floor. She replied that she was talking to me from the telephone on the table on the second-floor landing. That explained how the nurse could be keeping a close eye on the patient and yet answer the phone so promptly. I had not noticed the extension telephone on the second-floor landing when I was there the preceding evening. I have an unpleasant, but useful, habit of double-checking people.

It was past the usual hour for a day-shift practical nurse to leave, and I asked her if Mrs. Wilcox had arranged for another practical nurse to come on duty; she said that she and Mrs. Wilcox had talked by phone and that she had offered to stay on into the evening and could even spend the night on a cot in the patient's room, if need be. Practical nurses earn several dollars more per shift for psychiatric cases, and Martha was not a troublesome patient; it made sense.

She then said that she was Mrs. Vaughn and that she had taken care of my patient Mrs. Alpers at Mt. Sinai about six months before. I remembered her well. She was a tall, lean, capable black woman. I felt relieved.

I told her to give Martha two more of the 300-milligram chlorpromazine long-release capsules at seven and covered a few other points with her. I asked if she could stay on constantly at the Wilcox home a day or two more, if necessary; she said she could. I thanked her, gave her my office and home telephone numbers in case she needed me at any time, and we said good-bye.

After my interview with Fred I was not surprised that we not yet heard from Charles. He could be stone drunk in a motel in Council Bluffs or groggily slumped over the counter of a bar in Omaha or simply too depressed to bother making his routine calls to the home office. However, with Mrs. Vaughn in the house I could hold the situation for another couple of days. The next day was Friday, and Charles would undoubtedly arrive in Kansas City late that day or by midday Saturday.

At eight that night Mrs. Wilcox called me at my home, saying that she had not yet heard from Charles. There had been no sign of him anywhere on his scheduled travel route after he had checked out of the hotel in Des Moines the preceding morning. She had talked with the reception clerks at the hotels in Omaha and Lincoln where he had reservations, and she had spoken with the Wilcox Company's installation men in Des Moines, Council Bluffs, Omaha, and Lincoln. She said she was becoming a little worried. I reassured her, saying that I was confident we would soon hear from Charles and that something unusual had probably delayed him on the road. I added that with Mrs. Vaughn in the house we could hold Martha there for another thirty-six hours, if necessary.

I asked her how Martha was. She said she had been upset earlier in the evening; for a short time she had sobbed and moaned that Charles was dead. However, she was now drowsily watching television in the upstairs sitting room with the nurse. I told Mrs. Wilcox that I would drop by the house briefly between eleven and twelve the next morning, while on the way from St. Catharine's Hospital to my office. I told her that I would like her to be home when I came by. It's unwise to make a house call on a young psychotic woman without a relative in the house, even though a nurse is present.

Mrs. Wilcox was annoyed by my request; she said that Friday was a busy day at the office but that she would be home when I got there. However, by the next morning, she added, we certainly should have heard from Charles. I asked her if Fred were there. No, she replied, he was working late at his office. I was struck by the ironic fact that he and Martha were under the same roof while her husband was out of town.

The next morning I arrived at the Wilcox home at a little past eleven. An elderly woman whom I did not know met me at the door. I indicated that I was Dr. Chapman and she introduced herself as Mrs. Stewart, Mrs. Wilcox's sister, and she added that she lived in Raytown. I said that she must be the one with whom the five children had been staying since the preceding morning, and she said that that was so.

Mrs. Stewart talked continually as she took my coat and hat and hung them in the cloak closet. "Such a tragic business. One awful, unexpected thing after another. It's the poor children I'm most concerned about. They're no trouble at all, of course. We have room enough, and I have two married daughters who live near me in Raytown. And Mr. Stewart is retired. Forty-three years with the Union Pacific Railroad, in the accounting department, and he likes children. But who will take care of them? In the long run, I mean, after all these tragic things. I marvel how Kate holds up under it all, and carries on. A husband dead six years ago, a daughter dead by her own hand scarcely more than a month ago, and now all this."

I asked if Mrs. Wilcox was upstairs with Martha and the practical nurse.

"Yes, she's upstairs, along with Fred and a couple of men from the office."

"The office?" I inquired.

"Yes, the Wilcox Company office. They were the ones who got the news first. They came straight here to tell Kate, and they called Fred, that is, Mr. Turner. Fortunately, the nurse was able to get Martha to take some extra sedation, and she's asleep. She doesn't know, poor girl. We're all crushed by it. Kate just sits and says nothing, and poor Fred seems utterly bewildered. Poor man, he's been through so much and he—"

I interrupted her. "What news are you referring to?"

"Why, about Charles. Don't you know? Didn't someone call you? Someone from the office was supposed to call you after Mr. Hatfield and Mr. Gardner told Mrs. Wilcox and Mr. Turner. It's a blessing poor Martha doesn't know, seeing the condition she's in. And, of course, the poor children don't know. I'm sure I can't see who's going to—"

"What news?" I repeated. "Where is Charles? Has he arrived?"

"Oh, dear Lord, you don't know? Why, he's dead. He's been dead for almost two days. His car ran off an embankment on Wednesday while he was driving from Des Moines to Omaha. It was hidden by trees and underbrush, and it wasn't found until early today by a couple of boys who were hunting. The highway patrol went through his wallet and called the office, since his credit cards and driver's license list the office as his Kansas City address. And Mr. Hatfield and Mr. Gardner were the ones who first got the news, and they arranged for an ambulance to be sent up from Kansas City to bring the body, and someone from the office went along in the ambulance to identify Charles, and then they came here. Mr. Gardner called me and I came right over."

I went quickly up the stairs with Mrs. Stewart behind me.

When we arrived on the second floor, Mrs. Stewart said, "They're all in the sitting room at the end of the hall."

We went to the end of the hall and entered a large room with rows of windows on three sides. Mrs. Wilcox sat silent, motionless, and alone in a wicker chair at one end of the room, and Fred sat quietly in another wicker chair at the opposite end. Two men whom I did not know, presumably Mr. Hatfield and Mr. Gardner, stood in front of me with their backs to windows, talking softly to each other.

I went to Mrs. Wilcox.

"Mrs. Stewart has informed about what happened to Charles. I'm sorry, very sorry."

She looked at me, dry-eyed but stunned.

"Thank you, Doctor," she said.

I looked at her for a moment and then went across the room to Fred, as Mrs. Stewart sat down beside Mrs. Wilcox.

"I'm sorry, Fred. I know this has hit you very hard."

He gazed up at me, his mouth slightly open and his face gaunt; he said nothing.

I walked to where Mr. Hatfield and Mr. Gardner were; we quietly introduced ourselves, exchanged a few comments, and stood in silence for a few minutes, our backs to the line of windows that formed the long side of the room.

Mrs. Wilcox looked toward me.

"Doctor," she said, "do what is necessary for Martha."

I nodded, and in a few sentences it was agreed that I would arrange for Martha to be admitted that day to the psychiatric service of either Mt. Sinai or St. Catharine's, and that Mr. Hatfield or Mr. Gardner would bring the hospital admission papers to Mrs. Wilcox for her signature.

I noticed Mrs. Vaughn, the practical nurse, at the door.

Excusing myself, I left the room and went with Mrs. Vaughn to the bedroom in which Martha lay sleeping. Mrs. Vaughn agreed to accompany Martha until she had been admitted to a psychiatric service. I thanked her, gave her a few instructions, and told her to leave her bill with either Mr. Hatfield or Mr. Gardner.

As I was leaving Martha's room, Mr. Hatfield was walking down the corridor, and I asked him to go to the first floor to talk with me for a few minutes. We went to the dining room, where I pulled back a couple of the heavy wooden chairs and motioned to him to sit down.

I asked him who received the news of Charles' death at the company office.

"Mr. Gardner and I. Mr. Gardner took the call, and when he learned that it was from the Iowa State Highway Patrol, he asked me to get on an extension phone with a pen and pad to write down any information—addresses, telephone numbers, and that sort of thing. We had been expecting to hear from Mr. Straker for two days, and we'd begun to get worried. It wasn't like him not to check in by phone every day. However, we didn't expect anything like this."

"*When* did the crash occur?" I asked.

But he didn't tell me *when;* he told me *how.*

"Apparently Mr. Straker missed a curve and went over an embankment. The highway patrol say that the car must have been going at least one hundred and twenty miles an hour, and it fell into a wooded gully about one hundred and fifty feet beyond the highway. But I think they must be mistaken about the speed. Charles, Mr. Straker, that is, was a careful driver. I just can't understand it."

He paused. "Maybe he was delayed by car trouble or by something else on the road and was trying to make up for lost time. We have a couple of big jobs in Omaha, and maybe he was trying to get there that afternoon to see how both of them were going. Still, it's hard to imagine him doing one hundred and twenty miles an hour or more. He just wasn't like that. Anyway, the car crashed into the woods and was covered by tree limbs, underbrush and a light snow. A couple of kids out hunting rabbits found it. He'd been dead for almost forty-eight hours."

"But exactly *when* did this occur?" I asked.

Mr. Hatfield grew uneasy.

"Well, as to the day, it's clear that it occurred on Wednesday. From the snow on the car and the state of Charles' body, they agree on that. As to the hour . . ." He stopped and frowned at the dark, polished dining room table. "Well, his wristwatch was stopped at one thirty-five, and the clock on the car dashboard was stopped at almost the same time; the car clock could have been a few minutes wrong."

"That's very strange," I said.

Mr. Hatfield moved restlessly in his chair for a moment, and did not look at me as he talked on.

"Yes. When we told Mrs. Wilcox the time the accident occurred, she just stared at us for a minute or so. It seemed to stun her more than anything else. She said that that was exactly what Martha had said. Mr. Gardner is blunter than I am; I'd never ask Mrs. Wilcox such a thing, but he asked her what she meant. And she said that Martha's illness began at about a quarter past two; she was taking a nap and she woke up screaming that Charles was dead. She kept saying that he had died of a blow to the head. All of us—Mrs. Wilcox, Mr. Gardner, and I—were struck by the coincidence."

"The time difference is only about forty minutes," I said.

Mr. Gardner chewed his upper lip slightly for half a minute and made a small circle with his finger in the fine layer of dust on the table.

"It may be less than that," he said quietly. "The highway patrol say that he probably did not die immediately after the crash. The car door on his side was not badly damaged, and his body was about fourteen feet from the car. There was a lot of blood in the car, and between it and the spot where they found Charles. They say that apparently, even though he was badly injured and bleeding heavily from the face and neck, he dragged himself outside the car and died within an hour after the accident. They have experts who determine these things."

A few days later I wrote the Iowa State Highway Patrol for a copy of their final report on the accident, and a couple of months afterward received a photocopy of it. They put the cause of death as head injury and subsequent loss of blood from lacerations of the scalp, face, and neck, and they placed the time of death at a little past two in the afternoon.

On a Sunday morning in the following February I went to

the downtown office of the Kansas City *Star* and carefully read the reports of the accident in the newspapers of the preceding October. The accounts in the *Star* and the data in the highway patrol's report agreed on all important points.

The facts, at least in psychiatry, are always capable of more than one interpretation.

There are three ways of explaining the fact that Martha's illness began, almost to the minute, at the time of her husband's death 180 miles away and that she identified the time and cause of his death, a head injury, with uncanny accuracy.

First, these facts could be the result of coincidence. Blind chance. An odd quirk of fate.

Second, in ways of which she was not consciously aware, Martha may have sensed in Charles a deep despair, tinged with violence, that could turn itself inward on himself. He was very depressed when he left Kansas City, and he had threatened violence against his wife, his sister-in law, his brother-in-law, and himself within a short period before he started his trip. Perhaps there was something in the way he said good-bye to her and the children or in the manner in which he made preparations for the trip or in the way he settled certain personal affairs before setting off or in other things too small and vague to be consciously defined but evident to perceiving but uncomprehending eyes that told her he was going to commit suicide on the trip and probably would do it in such a way that it would look like an accident.

Moreover, perhaps in earlier years she had been with him on business trips on these oft-traveled routes and knew enough of his schedule and the general terrain to have unconscious glimmerings of where and when such an act might occur. In other words, *she may unconsciously have surmised that he was going to commit suicide on the trip and she may have had a vague premonition about how and when it would occur. In addition the anguish and guilt of knowing that her conduct was an important contributing cause to his death may have been a crucial precipitating factor in the psychotic illness she developed at the moment he died.*

Third, these facts can be explained by *extrasensory percep-*

tion. The theory of extrasensory perception (ESP) proposes that without the use of such senses as sight, hearing, and touch, some individuals, especially at times of special emotional turmoil and sensitivity, can receive communications from other people or can perceive events in distant places by means that are not yet understood scientifically. For example, it has been suggested that such *extrasensory* (that is, beyond the usual *senses* of sight, hearing, and touch) *perception* could be by means of electromagnetic messages traveling from one person to another, even over long distances. Thus, electrochemical discharges of brain tissue, which are crudely detectable by electroencephalograms (brain-wave tracings), could conceivably be transmitted from one brain to another without the transmitter's or the recipient's being aware of how the information was sent and received. Proponents of the theory of extrasensory perception have accumulated a great deal of data and have advanced many theories on this subject.

The founders of the modern study of extrasensory perception are J. B. Rhine and L. E. Rhine; most current activity in this field springs directly or indirectly from their lifelong work on this subject. In the late 1920's these two psychologists, husband and wife, were driving through the countryside of a southern state when they noticed a sign advertising a mind-reading horse. They stopped and went in to see the beast. After carefully observing the horse, whose name was Lady, they came to the conclusion that the horse could receive telepathic (extrasensory) messages from nearby people, including themselves. The horse demonstrated these abilities by picking out various wooden blocks on which the humans were concentrating.

The Rhines reported this horse in a scientific journal. Two years later they returned and examined Lady again. They found that for unknown reasons this horse had lost its telepathic abilities. They reported this in the *Journal of Abnormal and Social Psychology,* volume 24 (1930), page 287, in an article titled "Second Report on Lady, the 'Mind-Reading' Horse." In the concluding paragraphs of this article the

Rhines assured their readers that they intended to look further into extrasensory capacities in both animals and humans.

Although the facts recorded in this case could be explained on the basis of extrasensory perception, some people find it difficult to take seriously a field of investigation that began with the study of a mind-reading horse.

Oedipus Milkman

THREE o'clock. The patient for this hour is new. She is Deborah Adams, a married woman referred by Dr. Martin Sawyer, an internist in Prairie Village, a Kansas City suburb, who made the appointment a week ago with my secretary Marie. Marie took the patient's name, address, and telephone number, and her husband's first name and telephone number at work. There is no work telephone number for the patient, and so I surmise that she does not work outside the home.

This information is typed in the upper right-hand corner of an eight-by-eleven-inch sheet of unlined medical record paper. The patient's name is on the left-hand side of the sheet, three inches from the top and one inch from the left edge; the day's date is below the patient's name. This sheet, with several other blank record sheets beneath it, is attached to a clipboard. A ballpoint pen lies on top of this as yet blank record, and both are on top of my desk.

In most cases I take notes while interviewing a patient. The exceptions include highly upset patients, paranoid patients (who fear to have "their words written down"), adolescents, children, and other special kinds of patients. A psychiatrist with a busy consultative and therapeutic practice cannot keep his patients straight and have all relevant data available for review and retrospective organization if he does not keep good notes. Like most physicians, I write in a scrawl that approximates a personal shorthand, with many abbreviations that I have developed over the years. For example, PR_x means psychotherapy, R_x means therapy or treatment other than psychotherapy, ć means with, fa is father, ' means inside or within, and so forth; I use about 300 such abbreviations for common words and phrases. I can take notes while paying close attention to the patient.

My note-taking is, of course, selective and to some extent is timed to occur during pauses and periods of lesser emotional intensity during the interview. I spend at least eighty percent of the time looking at the patient. Moreover, the notes vary a good deal from patient to patient and from session to session. Some patients talk pithily, whereas others spend much time saying little or repeating previously covered material. In my opinion note-taking does not detract from the quality of interviews if the therapist's attention is focused continually and intently on the patient. After I have been seeing a patient for some time, or when sessions are supportive or brief, I may make notes only at the end of each interview.

Attached to the clipboard is a small piece of paper on which Marie has written, "Dr. Sawyer says that the patient functions pretty well but is nervous." When I am dictator, I shall have the word "nervous" eliminated from the language. It can mean anything from schizophrenia to thumb-sucking. Sometimes it merely indicates that the referring physician is tired of the patient and wants someone to take him off his hands.

However, Martin Sawyer has been referring patients to me for more than ten years. If a patient is psychotic and requires hospitalization, he talks to me directly; but if the patient has a neurotic disturbance or a situational-adjustment difficulty or some other kind of problem that can be handled on an outpatient basis, he makes an appointment with Marie and gives her a one-sentence reason for the referral. Martin is an endocrinologist, but there's not enough endocrinology in Prairie Village to keep him busy, and so he spends seventy percent of his time doing general medical work.

I go out the door of my consultation room and down a short corridor to the waiting room. That short corridor is important. There is, in my opinion, no such thing as a soundproof door; no matter how thick the padding and how elaborate the locking gadgets are, vague noises come through a door at times. Thuds, squeaks, and vague vocal sounds from the waiting room make both the patient and the psychiatrist uneasy, for it would seem logical that if noises can get in, they can get out.

A well-carpeted, acoustic-ceilinged corridor between the consultation room and the waiting room reduces such noises greatly and has even greater psychological value. Both patient and therapist often feel uncomfortable if only two inches of wood or metal, no matter how well padded and sealed, separate them from a receptionist and waiting patients outside. The corridor symbolizes privacy and security, enabling the patient to talk about things he can discuss in no other room.

The corridor leads into the waiting room through a doorless archway. Marie is seated at her glass-topped, dark wood desk on my left, typing letters. She looks up briefly as I enter the waiting room.

Marie is in her late fifties, and she's been with me for fourteen years. Before that I had younger women for secretaries, but they invariably got married and pregnant or tired of the job or restless to see what life in California was like and never lasted more than a year or two. So, when the physician for whom Marie worked for many years died suddenly, I indecently called her on the day of his funeral and hired her. Marie is single; she has never been married. I call her Marie and she calls me Doctor. We understand each other pretty well.

The waiting room is conservatively furnished; some might say it is old-fashioned. It has a large dark rug that covers most of the floor; a maroon leather sofa and two matching chairs occupy the far end. Four high-backed, carved wooden chairs line the walls; and there are four end tables, separating the chairs and the sofa, with lamps and ashtrays on them. Off-gray venetian blinds let in sunlight during the afternoons and paler light during the mornings. The three pictures on the walls are time-dulled oil landscape paintings.

The patient is a woman in her late thirties, sitting tensely on a chair near Marie. I step into the waiting room, introduce myself, and by a motion of my hand indicate the way to my office. She goes down the corridor and enters my consultation room through the open door; I follow her and shut the door behind us. I make a gesture toward the upholstered chair and invite her to sit down. She is dressed in a well-tailored, tan suit and has left her fur-trimmed coat in the waiting room. Well-to-do patients usually leave their coats and parcels on the sofa or on one of the tables or chairs in the waiting room, whereas working-class patients usually bring them with them; there are two coat hooks and a small rectangular table on one side of my office for these things.

Mrs. Adams places her purse in her lap, and I sit down in the padded swivel chair before my desk, about twelve feet in front of her chair. The room is simply furnished. My desk, a large, heavy, time-scarred, wooden one, which was my father's before he died, occupies the corner in which I sit. On the wall above the desk are two framed medical certificates and a framed photograph of my father, taken when he was about fifty, standing beside a cherry tree in the backyard of the house in which I was reared and in which my mother has now lived for more than half a century.

A dark brown rug covers most of the floor, and there is nothing between me and the patient. Cream-colored venetian blinds prevent strong light from entering the two windows. There is a low fluorescent lamp on my desk; two floor lamps, which can be turned on and off by switches beside my desk, stand in the two corners of the room behind the patient's chair. Two high-backed, cushion-seated wooden chairs line the wall to the rear of the patient, for occasional use when I interview more than one person, as in a conference with relatives. There are three framed, lithographed pen sketches of university buildings on the walls, and there are no drapes.

Mrs. Adams asks if she may smoke, and I reply that she may. Most patients do not ask; they note the ashtray on the table beside the chair and begin.

She lights her cigarette and relaxes a little.

I pick up the clipboard from my desk and lean back slightly in my swivel chair. Although my body is turned halfway between the patient on my right and the desk on my left, my head and shoulders are turned toward her.

"Mrs. Adams, perhaps you might begin wherever is comfortable or convenient in telling me about whatever difficulties bring you to see me."

This was merely a broad invitation to talk.

"Perhaps Dr. Sawyer told you about my problems," she replied.

I covered for Dr. Sawyer. "Dr. Sawyer outlined your problems briefly, but I'd like you to tell me in your own words how you see the difficulties or situations that bring you to see me."

"I'm nervous. Very tense, I guess you'd say."

She did not go on.

"Perhaps you could tell me what you mean by 'nervous' and 'tense,'" I said. "People use those words in many different ways to describe uncomfortable things they feel or difficult situations in which they live."

"I worry about things," she said. "Things that I really shouldn't worry about. I'm upset, tense, a lot of the time. And there are some things I'm afraid of. Silly things. Things that ought not to bother me."

She stalled again.

I wait for her to go on, but she could not.

It was clear that she would need a lot of help if she was to explore her problems. Free-flowing talk, whether on a couch or in a face-to-face position, probably accounts for no more than five percent of all psychotherapy done in the United States. In the vast majority of cases the therapist must be fairly active in an ongoing dialogue of exploration and explanation. The therapist is, as Harry Stack Sullivan phrased it, a *participant observer;* he actively *participates* in a therapeutic venture in which he is also an alert *observer.*

"Perhaps you might tell me about some of the specific things you worry about," I said.

With a slightly awkward smile she said, "I worry about my health. Dr. Sawyer has checked me over two or three times and says I'm fine, but I still worry about diseases. Lung cancer, leukemia, and a lot of others."

She stopped.

"Do you worry about these illnesses most of the time? Are they persistent worries that won't go away?" I asked.

"More or less. Some days and weeks are better than others."

"Is there any particular kind of illness that *especially* worries you?"

She was silent.

"Heart disease?"

"No."

"Sudden death by some type of disease that begins abruptly?"

"Yes."

"What kind of disease?"

She was becoming visibly anxious, leaning forward in her chair with her palms pressed tightly together. "Various kinds," she replied.

"Perhaps you might tell me about one of the main ones," I said.

She was again silent. She sat back, opened her purse, and took out a handkerchief, which she began to roll, twist, and crumple. Her cigarette stub burned, untouched, tilted down into the ashtray.

"There are few things," I said slowly, "that cause sudden death. Since you do not fear heart disease, do you fear some other kind of vascular disease such as a brain hemorrhage?"

"No."

"Do you fear violence of some type?"

She pressed her lips together and twisted her handkerchief.

"Violence by others toward you?"

She shook her head quickly from side to side.

"Violence by your own hand?"

She hesitated and said, "Yes."

"Violence by your own hand directed at yourself?"

"Yes."

"Violence by your own hand toward other people also?"

She shook her head briefly from side to side and looked down at her lap.

I watched her in silence for a moment and then said, "This is a common thing people fear, and very few people who fear it actually do it.

"Now," I asked slowly and with emphasis, "do you *fear* suicide, or do you sometimes feel that you *want* it?"

"No, no," she said hastily, "I *fear* it."

This is an important point; both *fears* of suicide and *urges* to commit it are common in psychiatric patients, and a psychiatrist frequently must distinguish between them.

"There's a significant difference," I said. "People who *fear* suicide rarely do it. People who *want* death and find the idea of suicide attractive are the ones who give us our big problems."

I was making her feelings more articulate to her, and I was giving her reassurances; both things were important at this stage.

I waited for her to go on, but she could not.

"Do you fear," I asked, "that before committing suicide, you will become mentally ill in some severe, weird way?"

Staring hard at me, she nodded her head up and down quickly.

"It's obviously difficult," I said, "and perhaps very frightening, for you to put these things into words."

"Yes."

"Sometimes," I went on, "people fear that by putting such thoughts and speculations into words they may actually hurry them along and precipitate such disasters. They fear that talking about them breaks barriers and brings them closer to occurrence. Do you feel that way?"

"Yes." She eyed me steadily and her hands were, for the moment, motionless.

I smiled encouragingly and inquired, "Does it seem as though I am reading your mind a little? That is, putting into words the things you fear but cannot say, before you actually tell me about them?"

She gave an abrupt, short laugh, the expression of both anxiety and relief, and said, "Yes, I suppose so."

"No. We don't read people's minds. We're not that good. However, after spending many years sitting in a corner of a room listening to people talk, one is able to make shrewd guesses about what many persons are afraid of."

I waited once more for her to talk, but fear held her back.

"Well," I said, summarizing what she had so far revealed, "You are afraid that you will develop a severe psychiatric illness—that you will become insane—and that while in that state you will kill yourself. And you fear that this can happen to you suddenly and at any time."

"Yes." She was obviously somewhat relieved by the fact that we had put these things into words and I did not seem worried about them.

"Do you have this particular fear every day?"

"Yes."

"In varying degrees, is it with you from one to several hours every day?"

"More or less."

"Have you ever told anyone about this fear before?"

"No."

"Not even your husband?"

"No."

"Nor any physician or friend?"

"No. Never."

"And how long have you had this fear?"

"A couple of years. No, more than that. Maybe three or four years."

"That's a very heavy burden to carry around alone for so long," I said.

"Yes."

"Why didn't you tell anyone?"

"I was afraid they'd think that anyone who had such ideas was . . ." She stopped.

I completed her sentence. "Insane, crazy, very sick psychiatrically?"

"Yes," she replied.

"And would be quickly packed off to the nearest psychiatric ward," I added.

She smiled apprehensively and said, "Yes."

"We've been talking for only a very short time," I said, "but from what I've seen so far I think there's very little chance of your ever becoming psychotic—that is, insane. You probably have no more chance of becoming psychotic, insane, than the average person walking the street outside."

Her face relaxed somewhat.

"Is that good news?"

"Yes." She forced a weak smile.

"Of course, I am aware that my saying that will not eliminate your fear. However, it may give you hope that in time it can be eliminated. At least my reassurances may take the edge off your fearfulness somewhat."

I shifted the focus of our attention. "Have you ever seen a psychiatrist for any reason before?"

"I've seen Dr. Branson."

"Dr. Edward Branson on Sixty-third Street?"

"Yes."

"When was that?"

"About two years ago."

"How many appointments did you have with him?"

"Two."

"Why did you stop?"

"He didn't say very much. And I couldn't talk. And, well, I just didn't go anymore."

"Did you tell him about your fears?"

"No. I just couldn't talk about them."

"Have you ever seen any other kind of counselor—a clinical psychologist, a marriage counselor, a clergyman, or any other kind of adviser or therapist?"

"No."

"Do you have any other fears or worries that are as persistent and painful as this one—that is, that you will become abruptly insane and kill yourself?"

"No."

"Then your worries about leukemia, cancer, and other diseases are much smaller?"

"Yes, they come and go, but they don't bother me nearly as much as, well, the other one."

"Now, you mentioned earlier that you are to some extent afraid of various *things*. Did you mean by that that you have fears of any specific objects or situations, such as dogs or the dark or small rooms or other things?"

"Sometimes I feel afraid to leave the house, but that's not a big problem; I can overcome it when I have to, and I don't have it all the time. And I don't like small rooms and elevators, especially if they're crowded, but I can stay in them if I have to. And I've been afraid of the dark for as long as I can remember. I think it goes all the way back to my childhood. Even now I always leave on the bathroom light and the hall light outside the bedroom at night."

During the next twenty minutes I systematically inquired about other kinds of emotional problems and found that her symptoms consisted essentially of those listed above.

On a line by itself, in the notes I was jotting down, I wrote, "Mixed psychoneurosis, with obsessive, phobic, and anxious features." Diagnoses don't help patients, but they are necessary for insurance forms, correspondence with physicians, and occasional other administrative purposes. In the left-hand margin beside the diagnosis I drew a small star so that Marie could find the diagnosis easily if she ever flipped through the record looking for it.

So far we had talked about symptoms.

I now shifted my attention to who she was. Deborah Adams, a name with twelve letters, would gradually assume the form of a person—a complex, skillful animal with an intricate past and present.

"Mrs. Adams, we've more or less defined the specific discomforts that bring you to see me. Perhaps we may now begin to sketch out your current life situation, your background, and the interpersonal world in which you live and have lived. To begin with, how old are you?"

"Thirty-eight."

"And you're married?"

"Yes."

"Have you been married more than once?"

She smiled and replied, "No. This is my only marriage." She was more relaxed now; we were, temporarily, dealing with routine, factual material.

"We always ask that," I said. "Divorce is common, and unless we ask specifically, some people don't mention a previous marriage. How old is your husband?"

"He's thirty-nine."

Turning my sheet of note paper over and looking at the information typed in the upper right-hand corner of the first page, I said, "His name is Thomas, I believe."

"Yes."

"Do you call him that, or is it Tom?"

"It's Tom."

"What kind of work does he do?"

"He's an accountant."

"A company accountant or a certified public accountant?"

"He's a CPA."

"Does he work for himself or for a firm?"

"He and a partner have their own firm."

"I take it he does pretty well at it?"

"Yes."

"Then you have no pressing financial problems?"

"No."

"That helps. Financial pressures don't cause psychiatric problems, but they can complicate them."

In a conversational way we were surveying patient's general life situation.

"Do you have children?"

"Yes, one. She's fourteen."

"What is her name?"

"Sharon."

"You and your husband didn't want more children?"

"We intended to have more, but I had a gynecologic condition—endomeritosis, or something like that."

"Endometriosis?"

"Yes, that's it. I had to have an operation, and after that we couldn't have more children. We thought of adopting one, but we decided not to."

"And how is Sharon getting along?"

She smiled tensely. "She's fine. I don't think I've damaged her with all my fussing and worrying. Everyone says she's a fine girl. She's popular, and she makes good grades in school."

"Have you worried that you might have damaged her?"

"Well, yes. The child-rearing books all say that if a mother is not relaxed with her children, they may grow up tense and a little neurotic."

"Life is more complicated than that," I said. "An anxious mother may be a conscientious, excellent one, and a relaxed mother may be a negligent one who causes her children a lot of trouble. There are no valid general rules. Anyway, I take it that Sharon is getting along all right?"

"Yes."

"Do you fear that you may have had an untoward effect on anyone else?"

"No."

"On your husband?"

"No," she laughed, "nothing bothers him."

"You must have a somewhat low opinion of yourself if you feel you're the kind of person who may damage people."

"I suppose I have a sort of inferiority complex."

"Do you feel less capable and less worthwhile than most other people, a pygmy in a forest of giants?"

"Yes, I've felt that way since childhood."

"Perhaps in time we can help you see yourself in a different light," I said.

She managed a slight smile but said nothing.

"How do you and Tom get along?" I asked.

"Fine."

"He's a pretty good husband?"

"A very good husband. That part of my life is fine, thank God."

I silently noted the "thank God"; other parts of her life, apparently, were not, or had not been, so good.

During the next fifteen minutes we sketched the outlines of her current life situation. Before marriage she had worked as a secretary and had helped her husband in his office at times during the first few years of marriage. However, she had not done any secretarial work for the past twelve years. She was moderately active in the neighborhood Methodist church they attended and served on a committee at the country club to which they belonged. She stated she had no particular stresses in her relationships with people. They had the usual comforts and luxuries of a successful professional-class life. She described her husband and daughter as well-adjusted, bright, outgoing people. She reemphasized that there were no problems in her marital adjustment; she only occasionally had an orgasm in sexual intercourse, but what she lacked in passion she covered with feigned excitement, and this was a small secret she kept from her husband.

"I take it you're the kind of person who always tries to please people?" I asked.

"How do you mean?"

"You go out of your way to avoid arguments, friction, and conflicts with others."

"Yes."

"Do you often get angry?"

"No."

"Do you *ever* get angry?"

"No, practically never."

"If you find yourself on the verge of getting angry or if someone gets angry at you, does it make you uncomfortable?"

"It makes me nervous."

"By nervous, you mean tense, anxious, a little upset?"

"Yes."

"When it's necessary, can you stand up for yourself, or do you tend to let people take advantage of you?"

She stumbled a bit. "Well, I guess they do tend to take

advantage of me. I have a hard time being firm with people."

"Is your husband the same way?"

"Oh, no." She laughed slightly. "Nobody pushes him around."

"And I take it you find some comfort in that. Is he the one who stands up for the two of you when it's necessary?"

"Yes, I guess so."

"Is he the one who takes things back to stores and demands your money back and handles little problems with neighbors and relatives when need be?"

"Yes, he does all that. He says I'm too soft and that I let them run all over us."

"Does he boss you around at times?"

"No, not really. He's very good to me. He makes the decisions, but he's considerate."

"No women's lib here, I take it?" I asked with a smile.

She laughed. "No. I agree with them, but, well, I'm just not that type."

She was a passive, frightened, submissive woman, I reflected, who, in the lottery of marriage, had been lucky. She got a dominant but affectionate husband. If she had married a dominant but harsh or negligent man and had not sufficient assertiveness to free herself from him, she would have become a more miserable, and probably much sicker, person.

We then began to trace out other areas of her life.

"Are your parents both living?"

"Yes."

"How old is your mother?"

She thought for a moment. "Sixty-one."

"And your father?"

"Sixty-four."

"Do they live in Kansas City?"

"No."

"Where do they live?"

"They're divorced. My father lives in Milwaukee. My mother is in Fulton."

"Fulton?" I asked.

"Yes." She hesitated a moment. "She's in the state hospital there."

"How long has she been there?"

"About twenty-four years.'

I paused. "When was she last out?"

"She's never been really discharged since she entered. During the first year or two she came home a few times on short leaves, but she soon went back. She couldn't make it outside the hospital."

The state hospital at Fulton is one of the major state psychiatric institutions in Missouri. Patients from Kansas City go either to the state hospital at Nevada, Missouri, or to the one at Fulton.

I went on, phrasing my questions carefully about what was probably a painful area.

"What do the doctors say is wrong with her?"

"They say she has schizophrenia."

Despite the vast improvement in the treatment of schizophrenia during the past three decades a minority of schizophrenics still become chronically institutionalized.

"Your mother's illness," I said, "has probably bothered you a good deal at times, especially since it apparently began in your early adolescence or late childhood. This can be quite upsetting to a child or adolescent; it may be related in some way to the specific kinds of fears you have. We shall probably deal at length with this area in future sessions."

I put a small check in the margin by my notes at this point; in this way I mark things that merit careful investigation later.

"Were you reared in the Kansas City area?"

"Yes."

"Where?"

"In Brookside. It's an old district, a small one, between Brookside and Troost, from Fifty-fifth Street to about Fifty-ninth Street."

"Yes, I'm familiar with it," I replied. I was reared a few blocks from there, and I reflected that she probably attended the same schools I did, a decade or so later.

"Do you have brothers or sisters?"

"No. I was an only child."

"And when were your parents divorced?"

"When I was nineteen."

"Your mother, then, had been sick for a number of years when the divorce occurred?"

"Yes. About six years, or more."

"I take it your father was the one who sought the divorce?"

"Yes."

"Did he remarry?"

"Yes."

"When?"

"About two months after the divorce."

"And when did your father move to Milwaukee?"

"About eight months after the divorce, six months after his remarriage."

"What kind of work does he do?"

"When I was small, he had a milk route. He was a milkman for the Sure-Way Company. Later on, when people began to buy their milk at supermarkets, he became a salesman for Sure-Way, and then a sales supervisor. When he was transferred to Milwaukee, he became district manager for a three-state area. He still is. I guess he'll retire in another year or two."

"Did you receive all your education in Kansas City?"

"Yes. After high school I attended the University of Missouri here for two years, and after that I had six months of business school. Then I worked."

"And with whom did you live after your father moved to Milwaukee?"

"I lived in an apartment near the Plaza with three other girls."

In the next few minutes we outlined how, during a three-year period, she worked for a time, met her husband, and married.

"Are your husband's parents and family in Kansas City?"

"No. He was brought up in Springfield, but he's been in Kansas City since he started college at UMKC. His father is a lawyer in Springfield, and he has a married sister there. I get along fine with his family; they're wonderful to me."

"I take it that they more or less constitute your family now."

"Yes."

"Have you seen much of your father since he moved to Milwaukee?"

"Not much. He's dropped by a few times when he and his family went through Kansas City on their way west, on vacations, and he and his wife came down for my wedding. But it's been at least three years since I last saw him."

"How old is his wife?"

"I don't know," she replied, "but she's at least ten or fifteen years younger than him. My father looks younger than he is. I guess you'd call him a good-looking man, for his age."

"Does he have children by his second marriage?"

"Two. I think he really didn't want them, but his wife did."

I placed my clipboard, with its three pages of notes, on my desk and said, "Well, I believe we've come to about the end of this session, Mrs. Adams."

As is my custom, I proceeded to summarize briefly the material we had covered. "We've defined your symptoms—your fearful thoughts and speculations—and some patients find that this in itself has some usefulness. It gets your problems out on the table, so to speak, where we can take a good look at them. And sometimes, after that, they're not quite so frightening as they previously seemed. Also, we've tried to put your fears in their proper perspective. They are apprehensive thoughts and speculations and no more; they are not signs of serious mental illness or impending disasters, though they cause you a great deal of discomfort.

"With the information I have now," I continued, "I can give you a ninety-five percent assurance that you have no more chance of becoming psychotic—that is, of becoming insane or losing control and running amok—than anyone else in the general population. Also, your chances of ever attempting to harm yourself are no greater than those of the average person in the street. After we've had another couple of sessions I shall probably be able to raise that figure to ninety nine percent; and better than that, we can do for no one."

I paused to allow her to ask questions or make comments, but, though she looked somewhat relieved, she said nothing. I therefore went on.

"These fearful thoughts and speculations and the other fears or phobias you have are very miserable to live with. My reassurances will help only to a limited extent; they will do no more than take the edge off your terror. Thus, our main job is to discover and resolve the things that have happened in your life that have created in you the emotional turbulence that comes to the surface in the form of these fears. As a rule, there is no one cause of such fears. There usually are various causes, or many causes, rising out of many kinds of stressful interpersonal relationships and events during childhood and adolescence, and perhaps also adulthood. The causes of this kind of emotional problem are like the roots of a tree; some roots are large and some are small, but they all contribute to the tree. Our job is to expose the roots and examine them. We rarely uncover all the roots, but we uncover enough of them to allow you to live a much more comfortable life."

She watched me attentively, bent slightly forward in her chair.

I went on, explaining what the treatment would be like. "Some people can, without much trouble, talk spontaneously about their experiences and feelings. This is the best way, if the patient can do it. Hence, the more freely you can talk, without inhibitions and with relatively few questions from me, the better. However, in many cases the patient has much difficulty in talking freely; he needs a lot of help. In these cases therapy becomes a dialogue in which the therapist talks a fair amount. We work as we can."

I then covered a few routine things that many patients wonder about, and which should be clarified. I indicated that medication would not help her significantly and that hospital treatment of any kind was irrelevant to her problems. I said that I did not need to see her husband, but that if he wished to see me, he could come with her to her next interview or one of the following ones. If he came, I stated, the three of us would talk together; with a patient who feared severe mental illness as strongly as she did, I explained, I rarely saw relatives without the patient present, for if I did, the patient often worried that I gave the relatives a grim outlook while offering a reassuring view to the patient. We covered the frequency of her visits, the specific days and times she would come, the fees, and other details. I also mentioned that if she found spontaneous talking difficult and wanted to make a few notes to bring with her to each session, she could do so, since some patients found this helpful.

We rose and parted.

As she talked, I had sketched the diagram below, which in future sessions would at a glance summarize to me the interpersonal environments of both her current and past life situations.

I then dicated a brief letter to Dr. Sawyer, which Marie would type the next morning. Physicians are annoyed if they don't receive reports on the patients they refer. They don't want long reports; they want the main facts in fifteen to twenty typewritten lines.

Dear Marty,

    I today saw in her first interview Mrs. Deborah (Thomas) Adams, a thirty-eight-year old housewife from Prairie Village. For three or four years she has had various kinds of obsessive fears; she also has had some minor phobias and free-floating anxiety. Some emotional traumas during her childhood and adolescence are at once apparent in a brief survey of her formative years. Her mother became psychotic during the patient's early adolescence and has been almost continuously hospitalized at the state psychiatric hospital at Fulton for about twenty-four years. The patient's current life situation, including her marriage and general social adjustment, seems reasonably sound. Medication will not help her significantly. I think she is a good candidate to improve with psychotherapy, the length and depth of which will depend to a large extent on how well she can participate in it. I think she was somewhat relieved by my initial explanations and reassurances. Thank you for referring this interesting patient.

Best wishes
Harry Chapman

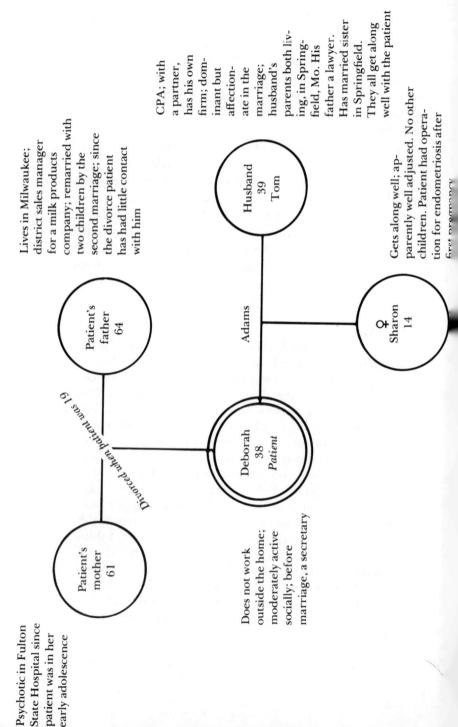

At the beginning of the fourth interview I focused our attention on the patient's relationship with her mother. I asked her to tell me all she could about her mother's personality and the kind of interpersonal adjustment she had with her.

"My mother was always somewhat nervous. She was easily upset by things, by almost anything. Once I dropped a jar of jelly on the kitchen floor; it didn't break, and only a little spilled out, but she slapped me and yelled at me for an hour or more. She was a very tense person."

"When she was angry at you, what did she say?"

"She bawled me out. I guess you'd say she was, well, very critical of me."

"In what kinds of ways?" I inquired.

"She would say that I was no good, that I did things on purpose just to upset her, and that her nervousness was all because of the way I acted. She said I never did anything right. No matter what I did, it was wrong; I couldn't please her in any way."

"Was she like this often or only once in a while?"

"A lot of the time. I remember her being angry at me or someone else much of the time. I guess she wasn't, but that's the way I remember her, angry and working. She worked all the time."

"What kind of work?"

"She was very particular about everything around the house. She was continually cleaning everything and putting everything in its place. She couldn't stand dirt or anything out of place. She would spend hours cleaning the kitchen or the bathroom or the porches or one or two rooms of the house. Everything had to be just right all the time. She couldn't stand a dirty ashtray; she emptied it, wiped it out with a wet rag, and put it back in its place. If she saw a spot on the rug, she got cleaning fluid, went down on her hands and knees, and rubbed it out. The towels and washcloths in the bathroom had to be on their proper racks and hooks; if I put a towel or a washcloth on the wrong rack or hook, she would scream at me and make me come into the bathroom at once and put it in its place. If the curtains and drapes didn't hang just right, she worked at them until she had them the way she felt felt they ought to be. She'd put them up, then take them down and iron them, and put them up again. She would do it as many as four or five times until she felt she had them just right. Everything in the house had to be spick and span. She couldn't leave dirty dishes in the sink; right after a meal she washed them all, dried them, and put them away. Then she polished the sink and cleaned and dried the drainboard. She was like that about everything."

"Did she offer reasons for this constant cleaning and arranging?"

"She just said it was the way things ought to be."

"Nothing more?"

"She had little sayings: 'A place for everything, and everything in its place.' 'If a thing's worth doing, it's worth doing well.' 'Cleanliness is next to godliness.' And she had others."

"Was she religious?" I asked.

"No, not much. She went to church once in a while, but she said it made her nervous to sit through the services. She wasn't a member."

"What church did she go to?"

"A Presbyterian church not far from where we lived."

"Did she make you go?" I asked.

"Only a few times."

"Did she make you help her in her endless cleaning and arranging?"

"Not much. Once in a while she'd tell me to do something, but then she'd always say that I hadn't done it right. I could never please her. She'd say that she had to do it over again herself and that it was more work for her to get me to do something than to do it herself."

"Did you clean your own room, make your bed, and put away your clothing in your dresser and closet?"

She smiled slightly, in a mixture of embarrassment and tension. "That was a constant hassle. She hammered at me continually that it was my responsibility to take care of my room, to make my own bed in the morning, to put my clothes and shoes in exactly the right places in the dresser drawers and closet, to keep my schoolbooks in the proper places in the bookcase, and to keep my desk tidy. But no matter how hard I tried it was never good enough. She'd come into my room and complain that the bedspread was crooked, that there was dust on my desk, that the wastebasket had trash in it, that things on my dresser top were out of place, and so on, and then she'd go to work to set it all straight. Sometimes she'd tell me to get out of the room while she did it, and other times she'd lecture me the whole time she was doing it. If I tried to help, she pushed me aside."

"That must have been a very uncomfortable way to live," I said.

"I guess so. But she couldn't help it. She was nervous. I guess she was sick even then. She had a hard childhood."

"Did she talk much about her childhood?"

"Yes, a lot."

"What did she say?"

"Her parents had come over from somewhere in Central Europe, I think it was Czechoslovakia, before she was born. Her father worked in a bakery, six days a week, from before daybreak until late in the afternoon, and her mother worked in a company that made venetian blinds, the Volker Company. My mother was the oldest of four children. One of them died in childhood, and another was killed in the Second World War. The other one lives in Texas, near Houston, but I haven't seen or heard from her for many years. My mother more or less raised the other children, since her parents worked all the time. On weekends her father drank a lot. They lived in the old North End. Both her parents died by the time she was twenty-five. I don't remember either of them. But my mother talked about them and about her childhood a lot.

"She'd often talk about how hard a life she'd had and how easy a life I had. She harped continually that all her childhood she had nothing but poverty and hard work, and then she'd say that I was being raised in the lap of luxury and didn't appreciate it. She'd take out her dentures and wave them at me and pull back her gums to show me the sores her dentures made; she'd say that it was because she didn't have money to go to a dentist when she was growing up, and so all her teeth got rotten and had to come out, and that I was taken to the dentist every six months and then didn't brush my teeth properly. After I'd brushed my teeth she'd tell me that I didn't brush them long enough and send me back to brush them some more. And then she'd inspect them and put her finger into my mouth and scrape a little white stuff off one of my teeth with her fingernail and send me back to brush them more, saying that she did without things to give me the best of everything, but that I didn't give her any cooperation and ruined everything she tried to do for me."

She stared vacantly at the floor and became silent.

"All this must have left you feeling very guilty and worthless," I said.

"Yes, I suppose so," she replied.

"What other things of this kind did she say to you?"

"Oh, she told me many times how much she'd suffered in having me; she said she was sick and vomited bile most of the time she was pregnant with me, and became anemic and weak. She'd tell me how hard her labor with me was, because I was the first one, and that she almost died, and that I was a forceps baby. She said over and over that she never really regained her health and strength after she had me; one way or another, she said, she'd always been sick after that."

"Did you feel, when you were a child and perhaps long afterward, that you were the cause of all her suffering?"

"I guess I more or less did. She harped on it so much. And she said I had no gratitude for all she'd done for me, and all she'd suffered on my account, and she said that I aggravated her and made her sicker by the things I did."

"What sorts of things?" I asked.

"By not being as clean and orderly as she felt I should be, by not being exactly on time for things, by not getting grades in school as good as she thought I should, and many other things. If I got at all dirty while playing or didn't come right away when she called me or was late getting home from school or anywhere else, she yelled at me. She'd take some of her hair in her hand and ask if I saw those gray hairs and if I knew who was putting them there and who was making her sick all the time and who was driving her to an early grave. And she'd say it was all my fault."

"What kinds of sicknesses did she say she had?"

"She had bad stomach cramps and backaches and head-aches. I especially remember the headaches. She would go to bed with a wet washrag on her forehead and lie there for a couple of hours; sometimes she'd vomit with them. Then she'd get up and go to work again; no matter how bad she was she couldn't stay still very long. She never slept well. She'd work in the kitchen or do ironing or something else, half the night, and then go to bed. She took a lot of medicine, three or four different kinds at the same time. My father said we had a drugstore in our house; she kept all her bottles of medicine on a special shelf in a kitchen cabinet."

"Did she go to doctors much?"

"No. I think she was afraid of them. However, there was a doctor on Troost she went to once in a while. My father didn't think much of him, but my mother liked him; he didn't charge much and didn't do a lot of lab tests and pre-scribed medicines that weren't expensive. However, she mainly took the kinds of medicines you don't need a pre-scription to buy. She took medicines, sometimes two or three kinds, three or four times a day. If I was in the kitchen when she was taking them, she'd ask me if I saw what she was doing and say that she had to take all that medicine because of the way I continually upset her. And then she'd ask me if I were happy now that I'd made her like she was and say that she hoped I'd never suffer one one-hundredth what she suffered and that she hoped my children wouldn't do to me what I was doing to her."

"Until her major psychiatric illness began, when you were in your early adolescence, did she ever see a psychiatrist?" I asked.

"One, that I know of. She went to see Dr. B. Landis Elliot a couple of times. She thought he was a 'nerve doctor' and that somehow that was different from a psychiatrist. But when she found out that he was a psychiatrist, she was furious and quit. She said he was a quack and that all he was interested in was money and that that was the only thing all doctors were interested in. She said they exaggerated whatever was wrong with you to keep you coming and gave you shots you didn't need and did unnecessary operations and passed you around from one of them to another and split fees on operations and got kickbacks from the laboratories where they sent you for tests. The only doctor she trusted was this one on Troost. He just took her blood pressure and listened to her heart, and then told her she worked too hard and gave her a prescription. She got quite upset when he died; he died when I was about ten or so. I saw him a few times; she'd sometimes take me with her when she went to him. He was an old man. My father said he didn't know much about medicine but that it made you feel good just to go and see him. His office was on the second floor, over a used furniture store, in one of those old two-story buildings on Troost. His name was Dr. Revel. I haven't thought of him for many years."

"Did anyone else live in your home for any length of time during your childhood?" I asked, continuing my survey of her childhood interpersonal world.

"No."

"You mentioned you were reared in the Brookside district. Where in Brookside?"

"On Oak Street, between Fifty-seventh and Fifty-eighth streets."

I knew the street. My scoutmaster lived there when I was a boy. It was, and is, a street of small, neat bungalows with long, narrow backyards.

"Did your parents own your home?"

"Yes. They bought it on a fifteen-year mortgage; it was a little expensive for them, but they economized in other ways. We didn't have a car until I was ten. The house was near the Country Club streetcar line, and later the Country Club bus line. So my father could get to work that way and we got around town without any trouble."

"Did your mother have many friends, and did she sometimes invite people to the house?'

"No. No one ever came to the house. She knew the neighbors on both sides and behind us and a few other people on the block, but she didn't have any real friends. No one ever came in for coffee or a snack or anything like that."

Piece by piece, the pattern of an isolated, frightened, guilt-ridden childhood was emerging.

"Did anyone else play a significant role in your childhood, besides your father? We'll talk about him later. Were there any close friends or uncles or aunts or cousins or neighbors with whom you spent a lot of time? Did you, in short, have any close relationships with people in which you could develop a more hopeful, encouraging view of yourself?"

She gazed down at her hands for about a full minute. I don't think this question, an obvious one to a person in my kind of work, had ever occurred to her.

Finally she said, "I don't think so."

"Did you spend appreciable amounts of time playing in the homes of neighborhood children or visiting in the homes of school classmates?"

"No. My mother worried about me if I wasn't either at home or at school. She had to know where I was and what I was doing all the time. If I were ten or fifteen minutes late getting home from school, she'd want to know where I'd been and what I'd been doing, and she'd say she'd been worried sick about me and had imagined me dead, run over by a car or hurt in some other way. She told me how men lured little girls into cars by offering them candy and then molested them; she talked about the Chalmers case, and described how the little Chalmers girl had been lured into a car and then had been molested and beaten to death on a road out near Harrisonville. She'd say that I tortured her by dilly-dallying along the way home from school and arriving late. And I could play only in my own yard, and with children she approved of. If some child she didn't like came into our yard, she'd call me into the house; sometimes she'd tell other children that I had work to do or that I had to study or something else, and sometimes she told them to go home and play in their own yards."

"Did you ever go to summer camp or join a Brownie troop or belong to any other kind of organization?"

"No. I wanted to do some of those things, but she said that I'd associate with the wrong kind of children and pick up bad habits and get contagious diseases from them."

After a moment of silence I moved on to another area. "Did you ever resist your mother or talk back or rebel in any way?"

"No, but I guess I showed something, since she was always telling me, 'Get that sullen look off your face.' She'd say, 'I know you hate me, it shows on your face,' and I'd reply that I didn't hate her. And she'd say, 'And do you love me then?' and I'd say that I did. And then she'd say I was a liar and ungrateful.'

"Did she accuse you of other things?"

Anxiously fingering and rubbing the ends of the arms of the chair, she went on. "If something were missing, she'd say I took it; if she thought something had been taken from the refrigerator or if she felt that some cookies had been taken out of a package, she'd say I'd done it. She'd yell at me and shake me until I started crying, and she'd call me a thief, a cheat, and a tramp. A few times she shoved me so hard that I fell down, and then she'd accuse me of falling down on purpose, to get sympathy.'

She was becoming upset, and I felt it was best not to explore this area further at this time. "You must have had a lot of time on your hands during your childhood," I said, "since you rarely left the house and yard and, aside from school, saw few people."

"I played by myself in my room and listened to the radio a lot, and when we got a television set, I watched it."

"What else did you do?'

"I had my animal collection."

"What kinds of animals?" I asked.

"Toy animals, all kinds of them. Little stuffed cats, dogs,

lions, tigers, bears, skunks, foxes, ducks, and many others. I had a lot of china ones and a few wooden ones. There was a big bookcase in my room, and I kept them in it, lined up on the shelves. I played with them for hours and hours on end."

"And what did your mother think of them?"

"She didn't mind. She even approved of them; she said it taught me to take care of things.'

"Where did you get these toy animals?"

"I guess it began when I was little more than a baby. I had a stuffed giraffe, and when I began to walk, I carried it everywhere with me; that's what my father told me. So he and my mother gradually gave me more, for birthdays and at Christmas and at other times. When my father left his milk route and became a salesman, he went to out-of-town sales meetings a couple of times a year, and he'd usually bring me back a stuffed animal or a china one. They accumulated, and finally I had eighty-seven of them. They're now in Sharon's room in a special bookcase. Even now, when she's at school, I sometimes go to her room and sit on the floor and go over them, one by one, and call them by their names."

"Their names?"

She laughed in slight embarrassment. "They all have names, silly names, kid names."

"Such as?"

"Jerry the Giraffe, Stinkie the Skunk, Larry the Lion, and so on."

"The hours you spent with them," I said, "must have been some of the more comfortable times of your childhood."

"I guess so," she replied.

We were sketching the general outlines of a significant period of her life, perhaps the most important period in terms of the problems that brought her to see me; we would spend many subsequent hours exploring how she developed in it fears and insecurities that haunted her still. During these painful years she acquired ingrained feelings that the world was a threatening place, that relationships with people were more often painful than rewarding, and that she was a shabby, worthless, unlovable person.

I went on. "What were holidays like—Christmas, Thanksgiving, Easter, and others?"

"My mother went all out to give me a good Christmas, as she said. And at Thanksgiving she always made a big meal, with a turkey and all the trimmings. I believe that a couple of times her sister, who now lives in Texas, came with her husband and a baby, but I can't remember clearly. Right after Thanksgiving my mother would start decorating the house for Christmas. She put strings of Christmas lights on the bushes beside the front door and lit them for two or three hours every night. She put wreaths in the front windows, with red metal candles in them; they had red lights that she turned on every night when it got dark. She put pine branches and cones on the mantle and sprinkled artificial snow on them. And on a table in the living room she put a small white church, with a light inside it; it had a winder on the back and played 'Silent Night' for a couple of minutes when you wound it up. Beside the church she put a little manger scene with Mary, Joseph, Jesus, the shepherds, the wise men, and the cattle. In the corner of the living room there was always a large Christmas tree, full of lights and other decorations, with a star on top and the presents at the bottom."

"Was Christmas a happy time?" I asked.

She hesitated. "Well, not really. It was always sort of sad, I guess. My mother would cry and talk about her childhood, and then she'd get mad at me and say that I didn't appreciate all she'd done to give me a good Christmas. She'd compare it with the kinds of Christmases she'd had as a child. She'd say that I didn't appreciate my presents and talk about how much they cost."

"What did your father do at such times?"

"He listened to football games on the radio, and later, when coast-to-coast television came in, he watched them on TV."

The session was nearly over.

"Mrs. Adams," I said, "today we've talked about a lot of things that probably have much relevance to the causes of the problems that bring you to see me. However, we have not discussed the most important aspects of these things; we have covered events and relationships with people, but we have not dealt with how you felt about these events and relationships, and what their emotional impacts on you were. We have not explored the anxious daydreams, the frightened speculations, and the guilty feelings that these events and interpersonal relationships aroused in you. Also, underneath this we quite possibly may find much smoldering, inarticulate anger, and still more guilt about that anger. And within you there has long been a nameless terror that all this turmoil would someday erupt, with disastrous results for you.

"Equally important," I continued, "was the influence these things had on how you viewed yourself, on what kind of person you felt you were, and on your concepts of what intimate life with other people is all about. There is a lot to work on here. There is much turbulence inside you. By uncovering it gradually, seeing it realistically, and working through it gently, this turbulence can be resolved. This will enable you to become a more comfortable person and be rid of the fears that brought you to see me."

She studied my face carefully. She did not seem relieved or reassured by my words, but on the contrary seemed very apprehensive.

I smiled and said, "You look a little doubtful about it. Perhaps you fear the work will be too painful, or that I am too blandly optimistic about it."

"No, no," she said, and forced a smile.

We watched each other in uneasy silence for a moment, and then I said, "Well, we'll go on next time."

We rose and parted.

During the next three months much of the time in our twice-weekly sessions was spent exploring in detail Mrs. Adams' relationship with her mother, the dominant figure during her formative years. This relationship had a particularly significant impact on Mrs. Adams since, in addition to her engulfing control, her mother excluded her from close relationships with other people who might have helped her to develop healthier personality characteristics and sounder ways of viewing herself.

In psychotherapy the patient and the therapist repeatedly approach the same areas of the patient's life from different points of view, gradually enabling the patient to see his life in broader, healthier ways and to work through emotional turmoil arising out of both his past and current life experiences; this, when successful, gradually resolves the difficulties that are producing the patient's distress.

This process, which Harry Stack Sullivan called *consensual validation*, may, in a crude simile, be likened to the study of a statue. If a person sees a statue from one side only and in semidarkness, he has an imperfect and often distorted view of it. If he attempts to form opinions based on what he has seen, these opinions and any feelings and acts related to them are apt to be warped and unsound. If, on the other hand, he can in brighter light examine the statue from various points of view and can scrutinize its details with the aid of an informed observer and can pass his hands over it to feel its form and texture, he gradually develops a much clearer concept of the statue; his viewpoints and feelings about it are no longer distorted and confused.

In psychotherapy emotions and feelings are as a rule much more important than simple facts. The patient's feelings about the things that happened in his life, especially in his close relationships with people, are usually more significant than the events themselves. The variations of such features from patient to patient are endless. It is this that makes psychotherapy a fascinating adventure.

As we slowly explored Mrs. Adams' relationship with her mother, we rarely talked about her father. In time it became clear that this was not because there was little to say about him or because he did not play a significant role in her childhood; Mrs. Adams actively avoided more than superficial references to him. It was evident that an appraisal of him, and his impact on the patient, would not come out, at least for a long time, without deliberate inquiry. (This, incidentally, is one of the respects in which an *interpersonally* oriented psychiatrist, such as myself, differs from a *Freudian* psychiatrist; a strict Freudian would wait, even for months or years, until, directly or through dream analysis, the patient dealt spontaneously with this area.)

Early in an interview during the fifth month of treatment I said, "Mrs. Adams, we have never talked much about your father—about your relationship with him and his relationship with your mother and his general characteristics as a person. Perhaps we might examine this aspect of your life."

She became noticeably uneasy, but she began to talk about him. "He was a quiet man; he didn't talk very much. He liked sports. He and a few of the men he worked with went to baseball games and football games a lot. He also listened to them on the radio and watched them on TV. Until I was about twelve he was always home at night, but then he was promoted in his work and began to travel out of town; he would be gone for two or three days at a time. He covered towns in western Missouri and eastern Kansas."

She stopped talking. After a minute or so I said, "Can you tell me more about what kind of person he was and how he got along with your mother and you?"

"He and Mom got along all right, and he was good to me. But he really didn't spend much time with me."

She lapsed into silence again, and I began to poke and peer in random ways.

"Did he ever take you to baseball or football games?"

"No."

"Not even a few times?"

"No, he said that girls wouldn't like them."

"Many girls and women do," I said.

"I guess he was old-fashioned that way. He said that if he'd had a son, he would have taken him. But he really didn't seem to mind that he had no son."

"Did your mother ever go to these games with him?"

"No."

"Did they ever go anywhere together?"

"Every Friday night we went out to dinner. We usually

went to the same place, a small restaurant in Waldo. The manager—or maybe he was the owner—always came to our table and talked to us for a few minutes. My father knew him; his name was Frank. He would pat me on the head and ask 'how the little lady liked her dinner.' My mom and dad thought it was funny the way he always called me 'the little lady,' and in time we called it 'the little lady's restaurant. It's not there anymore. They tore it down when they expanded the parking lot of the supermarket in Waldo."

"Did he and your mother ever go anywhere else together?"

"They went to company parties a couple of times a year. His boss always gave a cocktail party and buffet dinner a week or two before Christmas for everybody in his department. My father said the company paid for it. And once in a while there were other company parties, especially when someone from the home office in Los Angeles was in town."

"And was that all?"

"Yes."

"And what did you do on vacations?"

"We took a few trips when I was little. One year we went to Daytona Beach in Florida; I still have a souvenir ashtray from there. We went to Yellowstone Park on a bus tour one summer, and another year we went to Washington, to see the White House, the Capitol, the Lincoln Memorial, Mt. Vernon, and all the other places; we went on to spend a few days in New York. But after I was about eight or nine we didn't go on vacations anymore. I don't know why. Dad went hunting or fishing for a week or two a couple of times a year with friends from the office; he used up his vacation time that way."

"And you and your mother stayed at home?"

"Yes."

"Did he and your mother get along well?"

"They got along all right," she replied.

"Did they argue much?"

"No. Not much."

"Your mother didn't try to dominate him in the same way she dominated you?"

"No. Maybe she did when they were first married, but never that I can remember."

Although she was answering my questions, she was resistant to examining this area of her life. I went on, but with no clear concepts about where we were going.

"But what was her attitude toward him? How did she seem to *feel* about him?" I asked.

She paused. "I think she was a little afraid of him."

"Afraid?'

"Maybe I'm wrong, but she seemed a little afraid of him."

"In what ways did she show her fear?'

"Oh, little things."

I waited for her to go on, but she did not. "What sorts of little things?" I asked.

She frowned slightly and looked downward. "She never bucked him. If she complained about something or started to nag, he'd say something sharp, and she'd stop."

"And then?"

"Nothing. She'd go back to her housework, and he'd go on with whatever he was doing. He had a little workshop in the back of the garage; he separated off a part of the garage for it. He had a lathe, a motor-driven saw, a drill, and a lot of other tools. He made all sorts of things—coffee tables, chairs, bookcases, and other things."

I returned to a previous point. "Your mother never persisted with him in trying to have her way about things?"

"Only a few times."

"And what happened on those occasions?"

She faltered a little. "Once or twice or maybe a few times, he hit her."

"How did he hit her?"

"In the face. He slapped her hard across the face. Then she'd stop talking and begin to cry, and he'd tell her to stop her blubbering, and he'd go to his workshop or turn on TV."

"You saw him hit her a few times?"

"Yes."

"It must have frightened you."

"I guess so."

"Did anything else ever happen?" This was a general question inviting her to go on.

"Once in a while they had big arguments. I remember one of them. It was on the back porch in the morning; it must have been a Saturday or a Sunday, since he was at home. He finally told her he'd had enough and that they only had one kid and that if she didn't get off his back, he'd pack up and leave."

"He threatened to divorce her?"

"Yes."

"Did he use that word?"

"I think so. Anyway, that's what he meant."

"How did your mother seem to feel about that?"

"I think it frightened her. She had had a hard childhood, and poverty terrified her. I believe my father knew that and used it to shut her up. I remember he once told her that she could just see what it would be like trying to live alone on a small alimony check and child support."

"Did he ever threaten anything else?"

She paused, and then said, "No."

"Are you sure?"

"Once he said that if it ever came to a divorce, he'd take me. He said she was crazy and that he could get reports from Dr. B. Landis Elliot and other psychiatrists and have her put away. He was bluffing; I'm sure he was. But he scared her, and after that she didn't say much."

"Did this happen more than once?"

"I can only remember one time."

I fingered the stacked pages of her record. In five months of investigating her childhood I had found no close healthy relationship with anyone.

I went on. "Were they ever affectionate?"

"They always slept together.'

"Did they often sit and talk pleasantly?"

"Not very much."

"Did he kiss her as he left for work or when he came from work? Did he kiss her when he returned from one of his two- or three-day business trips?"

"No, not very often."

"Did he give her presents, such as on her birthday and on their wedding anniversary?'

"I think he usually gave her something on her birthday. Other than that, I can't remember anything."

I silently wondered how she had turned out as well as she had. How had she developed the flexible interpersonal capacities and feelings that enabled her to function well as a wife and a mother?

"From an emotional point of view this was a somewhat painful home in which to be reared," I commented.

"I suppose so," she said, and looked aimlessly at her lap and hands in silence.

"How did you and your father get along?" I asked.

She went on sadly. "He was good to me, I guess. He almost never bawled me out, and he gave me things. He was much more generous with money, presents, and such things than my mother."

"Was he affectionate toward you?"

She became a little tense. "No, not really. But he was good to me."

"Did he talk to you much?"

"No.'

"Did he ever talk to you about your mother?"

"Once in a while he'd say she was nervous and not to let it bother me."

"In what ways did he say she was nervous?"

"I guess he meant all her cleaning and fussing and harping on things."

"Did he ever defend you against your mother?"

"Sometimes.'

"What, specifically, did he say or do?"

"Well, sometimes he'd say, 'Lay off the kid; she's not done anything.'"

"What else?"

"He told her she took her nervousness out on me and that she was in the wrong most of the time when she was after me and to leave me alone."

"And how did your mother react when he said those things?"

"She'd leave me alone for a while."

"Did he do anything else?"

"They had a few big arguments about me. In one of them he hit her and told her she was crazy and threatened divorce. Maybe there were others; I don't know."

"This must have aroused very uncomfortable, mixed feelings in you," I said.

She did not reply.

"We shall not attempt now to go into these feelings," I went on. "Feelings of fear, anger, and guilt. Many of them were probably woven into painful daydreams."

She looked silently at me.

"I am aware that these things are distressing to talk about," I added.

"They do upset me a little," she said.

"A little or a lot?"

"A lot, I guess."

"Some people say it's like a trip to the dentist," I said, "without an anesthetic."

She laughed tensely and replied, "I'd prefer the trip to the dentist."

"I suppose that you sometimes wonder if it's worth it to go on with this painful digging. I think it is," I said. "You're a more comfortable person than when you first started. Your fears are fewer and less intense."

She agreed, but the agreement of a passive patient is always difficult to evaluate.

The hour was over.

"Well," I said, "we must stop now and go on next time."

During the next couple of months we explored in detail the material that has been roughly sketched in the interview above. We examined the distorted feelings and conflicts these experiences bred in her and traced how they warped her views of herself and the ways in which people live intimately with each other.

However, there was one area of her early life that she rarely mentioned and never discussed, though I gave her repeated opportunities to do so. Toward the end of the sixth month of treatment I directed our attention to it.

"Mrs. Adams, we have never talked about your mother's psychiatric illness. I am not certain whether it had a significant role in the gradual accumulation of emotional stresses that eventually produced your problems, but we should—at least to a certain extent—examine her illness and its impact on you."

She said nothing in response; in recent months she had been talking more spontaneously, and such silences had become rare.

Since she did not speak, I went on, "Perhaps you might tell me how and when your mother's illness began, and what its major features were."

She leaned forward slightly and opened her lips to speak, but said nothing.

"Apparently this is a quite uncomfortable aspect of your life," I said.

"Yes," she answered, "I guess so."

For some time she had been employing phrases such as "I guess so" and "I suppose so" less than in the early stages of therapy, but as we now approached a difficult subject, she lapsed back into their use.

I again waited for her to begin, but she did not.

"How old were you when your mother's illness began?" I asked.

"Twelve."

"Are you sure it was when you were exactly twelve?"

She stared at me, wordless.

"Talking about this seems to make you quite uneasy," I said.

"Yes, I guess so."

"Is there any particular reason why you remember so precisely your age at the time your mother's illness began?" I inquired. "Did her illness begin abruptly or in relationship to some event you can easily identify?"

She twisted a handkerchief and did not reply.

After a minute or so I repeated my question.

"I just remember. That's all," she said.

"What time of the year did it begin?"

"Summer. July."

I was surprised at her answer. She was talking about something that had happened a quarter of a century before, and it is unusual that a patient can date an event of his early adolescence so accurately.

"Early or late July?" I asked, pushing the point further.

"Early July."

I silently speculated that her mother's illness did not, in fact, begin as precipitately as this, but that at some particular point her mother did something that abruptly brought it to the attention of her and her father. Nevertheless, what the patient *felt* happened was probably as important as what actually happened.

"Her illness must have begun in a very sudden manner, at least as you remember it," I said. "Do you relate the onset of her illness to any specific event or occasion?"

"It began on the sixth of July.'

"Can you tell me why you feel so certain about this date?"

"It began during the Fourth of July weekend. The Fourth of July was on a Friday that year. It made a long weekend."

"It is unusual," I said, "that her type of illness begins in such an abrupt, severe manner that it can be pinpointed to a particular day. It is much more common that it begins gradually over a period of weeks or months or even years."

She remained silent.

"Are you sure that you remember this date so exactly, or have you heard your father or others mention it since then, and perhaps you mistake what you have heard for what you remember?'

"No," she replied in a low voice, "I remember."

She was so visibly upset by this topic that I hesitated about going on with it at that time. However, clinical judgment, or curiosity, led me on.

"What were the initial features of your mother's illness? What were the first things that you or your father or anyone else noted?"

"She became very quiet, which was not like her. She hardly said anything at all," she replied.

"And when did you first notice this?"

"Sunday morning."

Again I was startled that she pinpointed this date so specifically.

"Sunday morning, July the sixth," I stated.

"Yes."

"And as you remember it, she was all right—or at least she seemed to be her usual self—on the preceding day, July the fifth?"

"Yes."

I did not believe that, but said nothing. I assumed that her memory had been distorted by subsequent speculations and fearful or guilty daydreams. However, the fact that she believed that her mother's illness had begun suddenly on this particular morning was probably of much emotional significance to her, especially since she seemed so upset about discussing it.

"As you recall it, did this alteration in her behavior begin at some specific time on Sunday morning?'

"She was like that all morning," she replied.

"Did she literally get up that way, in a changed emotional state?"

"Yes."

"To put the matter in what is probably an oversimplified way," I said, "as you remember it, she went to bed well, or at least in her usual personality state, on Saturday night and got up in a quite different state, a very sick one, on Sunday morning?"

She stared at the floor and mumbled, "Yes."

"Mrs. Adams, I understand that this is the way you remember it. However, from my knowledge as a psychiatrist I would assume that the onset of her illness was in fact more gradual. Nevertheless, that you remember it as beginning in such a precipitate manner is probably of some emotional importance to you."

She said nothing.

I went on. "Besides her unusual quietness, what else did you or others notice about your mother early in her illness?"

"She stopped doing the housework. She made the meals, but she let everything else go. She just sat in the kitchen or on the front porch and did nothing."

"Did she seem depressed? That is, did she seem sad, melancholy?"

"No."

"Did she seem frightened?"

"No. Not really."

"Did she seem disconnected from things—that is, lost in a world of her own inner thoughts and feelings?"

"I guess so."

"And you are quite sure that you first noticed all this on Sunday morning, July the sixth?"

"Yes."

"Did your father notice it on that day, and did he say anything then?"

"No, I don't think he paid much attention to her. He watched TV that morning and went to a baseball game in the afternoon. He didn't say anything special about her."

Again I was struck by the fact she seemed to remember the events of that day with such precision.

"Mrs. Adams, it is probable that you feel you can place the onset of your mother's illness on this particular day because you had more contact with her during this three-day weekend. Hence, you probably saw for the first time things that actually began from several days to several weeks or more previously."

As I watched her in uneasy silence, I abruptly realized that what I had just said was not valid.

I corrected myself. "No, this was in July, and so you had been at home virtually all the time for the preceding thirty

days or so, since you had been out of school since early
June.'

I paused. "Were you in any kind of activity program, such
as classes at the Sixty-fifth Street YWCA or anything of that
sort during that summer?"

"No."

She got up and walked quickly to the window behind her
chair. She pressed down one of the slats of venetian blinds
and looked out. She had not done this before. She was very
tense.

After watching her for a brief time I said, "This obviously
is a very upsetting thing for you to talk about. A severe psychiatric illness in a parent is often a quite painful experience
for an early adolescent. It apparently had a marked impact
on you."

She let the slat of the venetian blind slip back into place
and, making a strong effort to control her feelings, returned
to her chair and sat down.

"Perhaps you would prefer not to talk about this subject
anymore," I said.

"No," she responded, "go on, if you think you should."

I did not know if I should, but I went on. "Besides quietness and inactivity, what were the other symptoms of your
mother's illness?"

"For the first two or three days, nothing else. She didn't
pay any attention to me or Dad or anything. After a couple
of days Dad asked her what was wrong; she just stared at him
and went into the kitchen."

"And then?"

"Over the next few days she began to be afraid of things."

"Afraid?"

"Yes, you could see it in her face and in the way she acted."

"What did she seem afraid of?"

"Of anyone who came to the door—the mailman, salesmen, kids selling things, anyone."

"Did she also seem afraid of you and your father?"

"Yes."

"That was a marked change in her behavior toward you," I said.

"Yes, I guess so."

"Did she say anything that indicated what she was afraid of?"

"Not at first."

"And later?"

"Toward the end of the week, on Thursday or Friday, she began to say mixed-up things."

"What kinds of mixed-up things?" I inquired.

"She began to talk a little more, usually in a low voice. She said there were people outside the house watching us and that sometimes they drove up and down the street in cars, to keep track of us."

"What else did she say?"

"She began to imagine all sorts of things. She said that our telephone was tapped, and she wouldn't answer it anymore. She said there were wires and microphones in the walls of the house, and that people were using them to listen to everything we said. She said the water tasted strange and that people were putting dope or something else in it."

"Did she say that she heard voices outside the house or elsewhere saying malicious things about her, or did she say that she saw strange things?"

"Toward the end of the weekend, she did."

"When you say 'the end of the weekend,' do you mean about seven days after her illness began, or fourteen days?"

"Seven days," she responded.

"What specific kinds of hallucinations did she have?"

"She felt that people on TV were accusing her of ugly things, sexual things, and she said that people outside the house were saying the same sorts of things, especially at night. She sat for hours on end in the living room, very still, as if she were listening to something or someone outside the house. By Saturday she had stopped doing any housework at all. I made the meals and did whatever needed to be done. I didn't leave the house; my dad told me not to leave her alone."

"This must have been a very disturbing experience for a twelve-year-old girl," I said.

She did not reply.

I went on: "What did your father say and do about your mother's condition?"

"At first he didn't pay any attention to her. Then he said she was 'just putting it on, to be stubborn,' and he told her to 'snap out of it.' After a couple of days more he said that 'two can play this game,' and so he ate dinner out, came in late, and didn't talk to her. He said that he wasn't going to be pushed around by this sort of thing."

After a brief hesitation she went on. "But by the end of the week, when she was talking about people spying on the house and putting things in the water and so forth, he realized that she was having a nervous breakdown."

"And what did he do?"

"On Monday morning he took her to see Dr. Morgan; he was his doctor. Dr. Morgan sent her to Dr. Chambers. Late Monday afternoon she was hospitalized at Elmdale Hospital under Dr. Chambers." Dr. Chambers was a psychiatrist who had died in the early 1960's.

"Do you know what Dr. Chambers called her illness?"

"I didn't know then, but a couple of years later I learned that she had schizophrenia."

"How long was she in Elmdale Hospital?"

"A little more than a month, as I remember."

"Do you know what kind of treatment she had?"

"They gave her medications and electroshock treatment, and she also had occupational therapy and that sort of thing."

"Did you ever visit her while she was in the hospital?"

"No. Children under the age of fourteen were not allowed to visit."

"Where did you stay while she was in the hospital?"

"At home.'

"Just you and your father alone?"

"Yes. Dad arranged for the laundry to be picked up and done. I made my own meals, and Dad ate out a lot."

"It must have been a lonely, frightening time for you."

"I guess so. I watched TV a lot and read and played with my animal collection."

"Did your father suggest that you invite other children in to spend time with you or that a relative or a neighbor come over once in a while to help out while your mother was in the hospital?"

"No. He said he didn't want a lot of strangers prying around. He was a little worried about what the neighbors and the people he worked with would think about his wife being in a psychiatric hospital. He told people that she was just suffering from a little nervous exhaustion and that the doctor had put her there for a complete rest."

"And how was your mother when she came home?"

"She was better in some ways. She didn't talk about people spying on her and that sort of thing, but she was forgetful and not her usual self. In a couple of weeks the forgetfulness cleared up; the doctor said it was a temporary side effect of the shock treatment. But even then she was not, well, like she was before she got sick. She did the housework, and in a way she got along all right. But she didn't talk much, and sometimes she sat for a couple of hours or more, doing nothing. She never left the house, except to go to the backyard once in a while. Every two or three weeks my father took her to see Dr. Chambers, and he kept her on some medication. He said she'd made a 'social recovery,' but she was never really herself again."

"And how did she behave toward you?"

"She didn't seem to pay much attention to me."

"How did she seem to *feel* toward you?"

After a moment's vacillation she replied, "She didn't seem to feel anything about me or anyone or anything. Just blah, if you know what I mean."

"I think I do," I said. "Did she behave in any particular way toward your father?"

"No, she didn't pay much attention to him either."

"And was that all?" This general, nonspecific question gave her a chance to say anything further.

We sat wordless for a minute or so. Her face was almost haggard. She took a deep breath and said, "She seemed, well, just a little afraid of everything and everyone. She didn't say anything; but you could tell by the way she acted."

"Did she seem afraid of you and your father?"

She looked at me with sudden alarm in her face, and I was momentarily taken aback and puzzled. But she said nothing.

I quietly repeated my question, and she replied, "I don't know."

I watched her during another minute or so of silence, and then I went on. "As the weeks and months passed, did she continue to behave in the same manner?"

"Yes. That September I started my first year in Bingham Junior High. Everything went along the same way until about ten days before Christmas."

"And then what happened?"

"I came home from school one afternoon, and she wasn't there. I was worried and called my father. His office said he was out making calls on customers, and so he didn't call me back until a little after five. He said to look around the neighborhood and to check the two bus stops near our house and that he'd be home pretty soon. I did as he said, but I couldn't find her.

"When he arrived home about six, she still hadn't shown up, and he got worried. He said we'd wait until seven to see if she came back, but she didn't. At seven he checked with the neighbors on both sides and with the people who lived behind us, but they hadn't seen her. Then he called Dr. Chambers. Dr. Chambers suggested that he inform the police that she was missing and also check with the emergency rooms of the hospitals. Dad called the emergency rooms of all the hospitals, but there was no sign of her. So at about nine o'clock he notified the police.

"We didn't hear anything until the next day. When I came home from school, my dad was there. He was packing some of her clothes in a suitcase. He said that about eleven that morning he'd received a call at work from the downtown bus depot in the Pickwick Hotel. Apparently Mom had been sitting there all night. About the middle of the morning people at the bus depot had noticed her and had asked her if she were waiting for someone, or for a bus. She wouldn't answer, and after a while they called the Travelers Aid Society. She had nothing in her purse to identify her, and the Travelers Aid contacted the police. The police figured that she possibly was the person my father had reported as missing, and called him. He went to the bus depot and identified her. He called Dr. Chambers, and Dr. Chambers arranged for her to be admitted to the psychiatric ward at St. Catharine's. Dad took her there and admitted her and then came home to get her clothes and other things."

During the next twenty minutes or so, Mrs. Adams outlined the subsequent course of her mother's illness. She made another partial recovery and returned home, but remained there only a couple of months before her deteriorating condition made rehospitalization necessary. Since their hospitalization insurance policy would not cover more psychiatric care, she was admitted to the Municipal Psychiatric Receiving Center. She did not improve there over a four-month period and was transferred to the active-treatment division of the Missouri State Psychiatric Hospital at Fulton. She remained there for six months and then was moved for long-term care to another section of the same hospital. She had been there ever since.

Seven years after this illness began, when Mrs. Adams was nineteen, her father obtained a divorce from her mother, and he remarried shortly afterward. A few months later he was promoted by his company to the position of district sales manager in Milwaukee. At the time he moved to Milwaukee Mrs. Adams was in college in Kansas City, and she and three other girls rented an apartment near the college campus. Her father supported her during her two years in college and also during six subsequent months of business school. He stopped sending her money when she finished business school and went to work. Mrs. Adams had had little contact with her father after he moved to Milwaukee; he became absorbed in his new family. Their contacts became even less frequent after Mrs. Adams married.

Over the years Mrs. Adams visited her mother occasionally. After her first three or four years of hospitalization her mother was either mute or spoke in incoherent fragments of sentences when Mrs. Adams saw her. About six years ago Mr. Adams urged his wife not to visit her mother anymore, since it did her mother no good and left Mrs. Adams depressed and anxious for several days afterward. She accepted her husband's advice, and since then she each year sent her mother a box of Christmas gifts in response to a mimeographed letter to relatives from the hospital's social service department. Mrs. Adams periodically wrote the social worker assigned to her mother's ward inquiring about any clothing she needed, and sent whatever the social worker recommended. She also sent one hundred dollars four times each year to cover minor items such as cosmetics, beauty shop fees, and other things that hospital funds did not provide for.

After we finished tracing the course of her mother's illness we sketched the general outlines of other aspects of Mrs. Adams' life during her adolescence.

"Then," I said in summary, "from the time you were about thirteen, your mother was not in the home for any significant period of time?"

"No."

"Did you and your father live alone from then on?"

"Only until I was about fourteen and a half. When it became clear that Mother would probably never come home, he hired a housekeeper. He got her through the Family and Children Services Agency. Her name was Mrs. Caldwell. She was in her middle sixties, but she was very alert and active. Her husband had died, and her two married children lived on the West Coast. She was very good to me. She and I slept in the same room. She said she didn't like to sleep alone, and so she and I slept in twin beds in what had been Mom and Dad's room, and Dad took over my room. He was traveling more for the company then, and he also ate out at night with friends a lot."

"What kind of person was Mrs. Caldwell?"

"She was wonderful to me. She was like a real mother."

"What sorts of things did you and she do together?"

"Oh, she just talked to me. We spent a lot of time together."

"What did you and she talk about?"

"We talked about clothes and my school and the boys I dated and her kids and grandchildren and her husband and just about everything."

"She apparently was a healthy influence in your life at a time when you needed someone like her," I said.

"Yes."

"You must have been very fond of her," I added.

"I still am," she replied.

"She's still alive?"

"She's in a nursing home in Olathe. She's about eighty-eight. I go to see her once a month or so. Her memory is poor, but she still remembers me and talks about things that happened when she and I lived together. I contribute one hundred twenty dollars a month to her maintenance in the nursing home, and her children send something, too. With that and her husband's pension and Social Security she can stay in a good nursing home."

"Did you continue to see much of her after your father moved to Milwaukee and you lived with other girls in an apartment?"

"Yes. I'd go over to see her two or three times a week. She lived in a kitchenette apartment not far from where I lived. Sometimes I'd spend weekends with her, and I'd talk to her about school and what I was doing and the boys I was dating. She was the matron of honor at my wedding, and until she went to the nursing home four years ago she usually spent two or three days a week in our home. My husband is fond of her, too. She baby-sat a lot for us and often spent nights with us. I call her Aunt Margie. Her name is Margaret."

In this patient's entire childhood and adolescence this was

the only close healthy relationship she had. Even though she entered Mrs. Adams' development at a relatively late stage, Mrs. Caldwell probably was the most important single influence in giving her capacities for comfortable living with people and for developing that elusive thing we call love.

During the next three months we covered, from many points of view and in increasing detail, many aspects of Mrs. Adams' life that have been outlined above. We examined the connections between interpersonal traumas and her emotional turmoil, and traced the ways in which they had led to her current symptoms. She improved steadily. Her anxiousness, phobias, and obsessive fears of insanity and suicide diminished in intensity, and some of her minor phobias disappeared altogether.

I periodically dictate summaries on patients in treatment. These summaries are placed in their records and provide me with easily located synopses for later review during a course of therapy; they also can serve to refresh my memory if, after termination of treatment, a patient returns to see me in later years, or if in the future I receive a request for information about the patient from a psychiatrist in a distant city in which the patient is then living.

A summary that I dictated on Mrs. Adams at about this time went as follows:

"This patient was reared by a compulsive, emotionally cold mother who dominated her by guilt-laden, depreciatory tirades. In this relationship the patient grew during childhood and early adolescence into an anxious, passive, guilt ridden person with strong feelings of inferiority and inadequacy. She felt worthless, unloved, and unlovable, though she was not articulately aware of her feelings and of her views about herself and others.

"Moreover, because of her mother's fearfulness about the patient's involvement with people outside the home, the patient was shut off from any close relationships with persons in social groups and with relatives and friends who might, at least to some extent, have corrected the warped views she was developing of herself and the ways in which people live together intimately. The patient's father, except for putting occasional limits on her mother's domination and hostile harangues, played little part in her upbringing. He abandoned her to the mother during her formative years.

"Beneath a façade of frightened passivity the patient from early childhood onward had large amounts of inarticulate hostility toward both her parents, each of whom failed her and damaged her in his own way. This hostility was especially strong against her mother. Dimly, in ways of which she was largely unaware, she sensed that she was being reared in a loveless environment and was trapped in it. However, if at any time her hostility threatened to break into her awareness, even in a camouflaged way, she was flooded with panic and guilt, and her hostile feelings were pushed back out of consciousness.

"These traumas and personality warps, which might in themselves have produced later emotional difficulties, were increased by her mother's psychotic illness, which began as the patient was entering adolescence. At a time when her pent-up resentments and conflicts probably were pushing for at least minor expression in adolescent resistance, or even rebellion, and when moderate moves toward independence might have occurred, such healthy developments (at least in the context of her relationship with her parents) were made impossible by her mother's persistent, incapacitating schizophrenic disorder.

"Her mother's illness was traumatic to the patient in two major ways. First, it forever removed the possibility that the patient might work through some of her tumultuous conflicts with her mother in a direct relationship with her. The mother's removal from the home left the patient with, so to speak, a great deal of unfinished business. A second consequence of her mother's psychosis was even more damaging to the patient. In becoming psychotic the mother made a decade of guilt-laden tirades come true, for throughout the patient's childhood her mother had daily ranted that her daughter's misbehavior was causing her to become physically and mentally sick, and it seemed to the patient that her mother's psychosis proved that all her mother's accusations were confirmed. The patient thus came to view herself as a malicious, unlovable person who caused emotional pain, and even illness, in anyone with whom she lived intimately.

"Considering the marked emotional trauma to which the patient was subjected, and the fact that she had no close healthy interpersonal relationships until a housekeeper, Mrs. Caldwell, entered her life when she was fourteen, it is remarkable that her emotional symptoms have not been more severe. The constructive influence of this housekeeper, who lived in the home during the patient's middle and late adolescence and continued to be a confidante of the patient throughout her early adulthood, probably was very important.

"The connection between the patient's emotional turmoil and some of her symptoms is fairly clear. In her obsession with becoming suddenly insane she fears that what happened to her mother will happen to her, and that the debt she feels for having contributed to her mother's illness will thus be paid; in her obsessive fear of suicide while in a psychosis of abrupt onset, her guilt feelings find further expression. In her phobia of small rooms and elevators she feels symbolically that she, like her mother, will be confined in limited spaces from which she cannot escape. Her free-floating anxiety arises from the general turbulence within her, which threatens at times to break into consciousness. The patient's other symptoms may, with less precision, be traced to the kinds of damaging experiences she suffered during childhood and early adolescence."

These paragraphs are typical of the ways in which psychiatrists neatly summarize the agonies of patients and glibly explain their symptoms.

For another eight months we continued to discuss her feelings and interpersonal experiences, and to resolve the subtle anguish that had produced her disorder.

She improved, but in time reached a stage beyond which she did not progress. Her symptoms were, to use an artificial way of assessing them, about sixty-five percent better, and it began to appear that the remaining thirty-five percent would form an irreducible nucleus. I felt she probably would turn out to be one of the many patients who have been so traumatized during their formative years that psychotherapy can improve them only to a limited extent.

I do not believe in continuing indefinitely with such patients. When we reach a point where I feel reasonable goals have been achieved, and I feel that the odds are against further improvement, I tell the patient so, and we draw treatment to a close. In most cases I leave the way open for the patient to return for more treatment later if he wants it, and if I feel that it then offers reasonable chances of helping him further.

By the end of the fourteenth month of treatment I felt I had about reached that point with Mrs. Adams.

One Monday afternoon in late February, she was very restless and apprehensive when she arrived for her appointment.

She fidgeted with her cigarette, clawed the end of the arm of her chair, commented on the mildness of the weather for late February, and fell into silence.

"You seem somewhat tense today," I said.

"Yes, I guess I am," she replied.

"Is it only today, or have you been tense for the last two or three days?"

"Just yesterday and today."

"It began yesterday?"

"Yes."

"Did anything special happen yesterday to upset you?"

"No, at least nothing I can put my finger on."

"Do you remember what you were doing when you began to feel tense?'

"No."

"Did it begin in the morning or the afternoon?"

"In the morning."

"Did you do anything unusual in the morning, or did anything special happen that might have touched this off?"

"No, I don't think so."

"What did you and your family do yesterday morning, and during the day?"

"We stayed home all morning and had lunch at home. We spent the afternoon at the home of some friends and had dinner there; the man is a client of Tom's. We came home about eight thirty and watched TV for a while. That was all."

"What did you do at home during the morning?"

"A little housework, and I read for a while. Then I watched the Anne Christie program on TV."

"What did you read?"

"*The Eagle and the Hare.*" A current best-seller.

"Was there anything in the book that seemed to bother you?"

"No."

"Was there anything on the Anne Christie show that might have touched a sensitive chord?" The Anne Christie show is a talk program for Sunday morning.

"I don't think so."

"And what did your husband and Sharon do?"

"Sharon's birthday was last week, and we gave her a new set of golf clubs, expensive ones. She likes the game and is pretty good at it for a girl of her age. She plays once or twice a week when school is on, and much more during vacations. My husband was out in the backyard with her giving her a few pointers on teeing off and putting."

"Did you watch them?"

"Yes."

"For how long?"

"Only a few minutes."

She seemed suddenly tenser, which struck me as odd, in the context of what we were discussing.

"Where were you when you watched them?"

"In the dining room. I watched them from the dining room window."

She leaned forward in her chair and squeezed her hands together.

I stared at her in silence for a moment.

"Was it *then* that you began to get tense?"

"I don't know."

"About what time of the morning was this?"

"A little before ten."

"Is there any reason why you remember the time so exactly?"

"It was shortly before the Anne Christie show began."

"Do you watch the Anne Christie show often?"

"No."

"Until yesterday, how long had it been since you last watched it?"

"Several months or more."

"Why did you decide to watch it yesterday?"

"I guess it was because I was tense, to get my mind off myself."

"Did the TV program do that?"

"I suppose it helped a little.'

"Then, it's clear that by ten o'clock you were quite tense?"

"Yes."

"And what time did you eat breakfast?"

"Late. Nine o'clock. Tom slept late."

"Were you tense then?"

"No, I don't think so."

"What did you do after breakfast?"

"I cleaned up the kitchen and breakfast room and tidied our bedroom."

"Were you tense then?"

"I don't think so."

"This takes you up to at least nine thirty and probably to a quarter to ten."

"I guess so."

"And by this time you were not tense, but by ten o'clock you were tense enough to turn on a TV program you rarely watch, in order to try to relax?"

"I guess that's it," she replied. She watched me fixedly, motionless.

"And so it seems clear that it was during this fifteen-minute period, while watching your husband give Sharon a few pointers on golf strokes, that you became tense?"

"Yes, I suppose so," she replied.

"Was there anything particular about watching your husband give Sharon instructions on golf strokes that bothered you?"

"I don't think so."

"You said that the clubs were expensive?"

"Yes, for a girl of Sharon's age."

"Did you object to purchasing them?"

"No, Sharon plays a lot of golf, and I'd rather have her on a golf course than hanging around with kids at drive-ins."

"Had your husband done anything that morning or during the preceding day or two to upset you?"

"No."

Though this did not seem a particularly promising point to investigate, I went on. Psychotherapy depends, among many other things, on meticulous patience with seemingly unimportant details. In exploring such details an *interpersonally* oriented psychiatrist, such as myself, tends to use *interpersonal* events and relationships as starting points, whereas a *Freudian* psychoanalyst tends to use uninhibited free-flowing speech by the patient and examination of dream fragments.

"Exactly what did your husband do as he showed Sharon these pointers on golf strokes?'

"He showed her the correct way to grip the club and to swing, and then she'd imitate him. He'd tell her if she'd done anything wrong and how to improve it."

I tried to visualize the scene.

"How were they dressed?" I asked.

"Both of them had on slacks and sweaters."

"Did he place his hands over hers on the clubs, especially in showing her exactly how to use the driver?'

"Yes."

"Did he stand beside her?"

"Yes."

"And at other times did he stand in front of her?"

"A few times."

"And did he also at times stand behind her?"

"Yes."

"Then you must have watched for at least ten or fifteen minutes."

"I guess so."

I went on methodically, asking my questions with slow preciseness, as she sat rigidly. "When he stood behind her, did he put his arms and hands around and over hers, to show her the correct hold on the club, the proper body stance, and the right body movements in the swing of the club?"

"Yes."

"And were their bodies pressed against each other in this activity?"

"Yes."

"The front of his body against the back of her body?"

"Yes."

"In physical contact with each other?"

"I guess so."

"There must have been," I went on, watching her closely, "something about this that bothered you. It seems probable that it was at about this time that you abruptly became tense."

I waited for her to say something, but she did not.

"Did you watch them until they finished the lesson?"

"No."

"You left the window and turned on the television set to see a program you watch only once every several months?"

She did not respond.

"Did anything run through your mind as you watched your husband demonstrate these golf strokes to Sharon?"

She did and said nothing for a few moments, and then quickly shook her head from side to side.

After a short hesitation I said, "Did your father ever teach you to play golf?'

"No."

"Or any other game?"

"No."

"Did he ever teach you anything of this sort, in his workshop, or while repairing things about the house or in any other activity?"

"No."

"Nothing at all, ever?"

"Only to drive a car."

"When was that?"

"When I was twelve."

"That was young to learn to drive a car," I said.

"My father had a new car, and I guess he wanted to show it off a little. When I was ten, my father got his first car, to drive in his work, but it was a used one. When I was twelve, the company gave him a brand-new one. He was sort of proud of it and took me out one afternoon to show me how it ran."

"And he taught you how to drive?"

"Yes. I was tall for my age. I developed early, and I was almost thirteen. He asked me if I'd like to take over the wheel. There wasn't much traffic where we were, and so I sat beside him and steered, while he sat in the driver's seat and did the footwork."

"And then did he go on and teach you to drive?"

"Yes. He said I was young, but that I was big enough to learn."

"And did you have many driving lessons?"

"Yes."

"Where?"

"We drove out on county roads where there wasn't much traffic. Then he taught me parking and backing up and things like that in a supermarket parking lot on Sunday afternoons."

"How long did this continue?"

"A few months. We did it mainly on weekends."

"And then?"

"Well, then I knew how to drive. When we were going places, on errands or something, he'd let me drive, with him sitting beside me."

"This must have been one of the few things your father did with you in a close father-daughter way."

"Yes, I guess it was."

I paused and compared the two situations: Tom-Sharon-golf. Father-patient-car.

"Your father must have been in very close physical contact

with you a good deal of the time, as he put his hands over
yours to show you how to steer and how to use the foot ped-
als and so on."

"Yes." Her face was frozen and her eyes were glued on me.

"In our work, Mrs. Adams," I said slowly, "we ask all kinds
of questions. There are no questions we avoid, if we think
they might, however improbably, have any bearing on a patient's difficulties."

I hesitated a moment.

"Did your father," I asked quietly, "while teaching you to
drive, ever touch you in any way he ought not to have
touched you?"

She remained mute and motionless.

I repeated the question, and she still said nothing.

"From your silence and obvious discomfort, I take it he
did."

"Yes," she said softly.

"In what way?"

She said nothing.

"On the legs, the knees, the thighs?"

"Yes."

"The breasts?"

"Yes." She was breathing shallowly.

"Did he put one or both arms around you—that is, around
you in a way he ought not to have done?"

"Yes."

"Did he kiss you?"

"Yes." She began to cry. She took a handkerchief from her
purse and wiped her face with it.

I waited until she stopped crying before I went on.

"We have uncovered something that is very painful to
you," I said, "but I'm afraid we cannot leave it here. We must
look at it some more, even though it is distressing for you to
do so."

She stared at me, red eyed and haggard.

"Did he do anything more? Did he attempt anything
frankly sexual?"

In a sound halfway between a sob and a moan, she said, "Yes."

The words pushed out. "I tried to shove him away, but I couldn't. He always had his way about everything. He didn't say much. He just said that I was a big girl now, and there were things I ought to learn, and he was going to teach me. And he did it."

She shut her eyes and turned her face downward.

"In the car?"

"Yes."

"On a lonely road, as it was getting dark, or at night?" I asked.

She looked up. "In broad daylight, parked a little way off a dirt road, in the country."

I waited a minute before going on, while she once more gazed down at her lap and her flaccid hands.

"I know you were badly frightened by this," I said. "An experience of this kind often floods a young girl with panic, guilt, and shame."

I waited a minute or so for her to say something or to make some gesture, but she did not.

I came to the central point. "Did it excite you sexually?" I asked.

She was calmer. It was all out, the barriers were broken, and from then on she talked in a flat, mechanical tone.

" Not at first."

"Then it happened more than once?"

"Yes."

"Always in the car?"

"Only at first."

"And then?"

She did not reply.

"At home?"

"Yes."

"When your mother was out of the house, shopping, or doing something else?"

" Yes."

"And, after a while, you sometimes became sexually excit-
ed when he did it?"
"Yes."
"And did you sometimes reach orgasm?"
She chewed her lip briefly and said, "Yes."
"At home how did he approach you about it?"
"When Mom wasn't at home, he came to where I was, took
me by the hand, and led me to his and Mom's bedroom. He
sat me on the edge of the bed, patted me on the legs or the
stomach a few times, and then laid me out on the bed. He
slipped off my shoes and slid my panties down and off, and,"
she faltered, "did it."
"And afterward?"
"He took my chin in his hand and told me I was a good
girl. He didn't mean sexually. And that was it."
"And how often did this happen?"
"A couple of times a week."
"How long did it go on?"
"For about a year and a half. Until Mrs. Caldwell came to
live with us."
"Do you think Mrs. Caldwell guessed anything?"
"No, he stopped just before Mrs. Caldwell came. In fact,
that may be why he had her come. I think he began to be
afraid about what the neighbors and the people he worked
with might think about him and me living alone together."
An uneasy feeling crept over me.
I hesitated, but again clinical judgment, or morbid fascina-
tion, led me on.
"How long after this started did your mother get sick?"
"A little less than a year."
"Then it went on for somewhat less than a year while your
mother was in the home and for about another half year
while she was in and out of hospitals?"
"Yes."
"And she never suspected anything, never found out?"
Her gaze wandered aimlessly about the room.
Her hour was up, but we could not stop. I could not send

her home until we had in some way dealt with the terror and guilt that had been laid bare.

After a long pause I repeated my question. She parted her lips as if to say something, but remained silent.

I began to dissect.

"You lived in a bungalow on Oak Street between about Fifty-seventh Street and Fifty-eighth Street. Where are the bedrooms in those houses?"

"One is on the first floor," she replied, "and there's another one on the second floor, with a sleeping porch behind it."

"The kind of sleeping porch that is screened on three sides?" I asked.

"In the summer. In our house the screens were taken out in the winter, and glass windows in wooden frames were put in."

"Where did your parents sleep?"

"On the first floor."

"And you?"

"In the bedroom on the second floor."

"Did your father ever come up to your room at night, after you were twelve years old?"

"No."

"Did your mother ever return unexpectedly during the day when your father was with you?"

"No."

"Did she ever notice anything, such as stains on a bedspread or on your underwear, that caused her to comment?"

"No."

A blank.

I thought about the house on Oak Street and its three occupants. I was reared several blocks from there in a house that, though larger, was built on somewhat the same plan.

"In the summer," I asked, "especially when the daytime temperature was in the middle nineties, or over one hundred, where did the three of you sleep?"

The pupils of her eyes were widely dilated, black holes of fear, as she talked in a low, expressionless voice.

"Mother slept in the bedroom on the second floor, with a couple of electric fans going, and Dad and I slept in twin beds on the sleeping porch."

"You didn't have air-conditioning?" I asked.

"It wasn't much used in homes then, and Dad said it was too expensive."

"Were there any other rooms on the second floor, except the bedroom and the sleeping porch?"

"No."

"The only bathroom was on the first floor?"

"Yes."

"To get to the sleeping porch, you went up the stairs and passed through the bedroom?"

"Yes."

"And on a hot summer night the door between the bedroom and the sleeping porch would be open?" I said.

"Yes," she replied mechanically.

"And your mother slept in the bedroom, with the electric fans going, and you and your father slept in twin beds on the sleeping porch?"

"Yes."

"Did your mother sleep soundly?"

She did not answer.

I repeated the question, and again she did not answer.

Her face was now supported on her hands and was turned downward toward her lap. As I watched her, apprehensiveness stole through me.

Summer. July. Thirteen.

"In the middle of the night, did your father ever cross from his bed to yours, on the sleeping porch?"

"Yes."

"Often?"

"A lot of times."

"While your mother was sleeping in the adjoining bedroom?"

She said nothing.

"Did he have sex with you when he came to your bed?"

"Usually."

"He did this only in the middle of the night, long after you had all gone to bed?"

"Yes."

"Did he sometimes wake you up when he did this, so that you did not know what time it was?"

"Yes."

"And your mother never found out?"

She said nothing.

"This was a very risky thing for your father to do," I said slowly.

However, as I knew from other cases of incest, incestuous parents have, in regard to their incestuous acts, an almost psychotic loss of contact with reality; though they may seem reasonably prudent in all other areas, they often do rash, even dangerous, things in their incest.

She spoke in a monotone. "One night, after he had finished and was getting back into his bed, I saw something white out of the corner of my eye. I looked up, and my mother was standing in the doorway to the sleeping porch."

There was a long silence.

"Did you make any sound?" I asked.

"No."

"Did your father see her?"

"No."

"Are you sure?"

"Yes."

"And then?" I asked.

"I looked away," she replied. "When I looked up a little later, she was no longer there."

"Are you quite sure she was there? Could the white thing have been something else? Could it, for example, have been produced by the way moonlight or a light from a distant streetlamp fell on the wall or in the doorway?"

"It was my mother."

I hesitated for a few moments before I asked the next question.

"Was this before, or after, your mother became ill?"

"Before," she said.

"How long before?"

She did not reply.

I had gone too far, too fast, but there was no turning back now. I had not expected this.

"How long before?" I repeated.

"The night before she got sick."

I was stunned, and I fear my astonishment colored the way I put my next few questions.

"Do you mean that this occurred on the Fourth of July weekend on which she became ill?"

"Yes."

"On the Saturday night before the precise Sunday morning on which you first noticed her changed behavior?"

"Yes." ·

"Are you sure you're not linking two events that actually occurred at a wider interval? Are you sure that your sense of guilt and the burden of having carried this secret alone for twenty-five years have not caused you to put together in time two things that must have occurred at least a few weeks, if not much further, apart?"

"No," she said, staring at me with almost a touch of defiance in her haggard face. "It was that way." Then, while we sat in silence, she opened her purse, took out a cigarette, and lit it.

As I watched her, I realized for the first time that there was a certain hardness in this frightened, passive woman, and a dull, cold hostility that could come out in brutal ways at unexpected times. Perhaps there was something in the set of her jaw or in the untrembling movements of her hands as she smoked her cigarette, but I saw her clearly as a woman who could have sex with her father, while beyond an open door in an adjoining room lay sleeping a mother she hated.

There are times in psychotherapy when, with little time for reflection, the therapist must make a decision. He must decide to say something, or to remain silent; and if he decides to speak, he must determine what to say.

What do you tell a patient like this? Do you tell her that although her mother obviously was an upset woman for many years, the experience of seeing her daughter and husband in

incest was apparently the final emotional trauma that precipitated a psychotic illness from which she never recovered?

I made my decision.

I told her a lie.

I told her that for many years she had unjustifiably carried
a heavy burden of guilt and terror; I said that any fear she
had harbored that she had precipitated her mother's psychosis by sexual activity with her father, and discovery of it by
her mother, was not realistic. I stated emphatically that such
an event did not, and could not, precipitate an illness such as
her mother had. I said that her mother had obviously been a
very disturbed person all her adult life and that the early
symptoms of her psychotic illness undoubtedly had gone un-
perceived by those around her for weeks or months before
they became clearly evident. I stated that the opportunity of
observing her closely over a three-day weekend had revealed
an illness that had unquestionably begun earlier, perhaps
much earlier.

Approaching this theme from various vantage points, I
presented it with all the persuasiveness I could muster.

I then explained to her that in ways of which she was only
dimly aware she had long felt that inevitable retribution must
come to her because of the role she believed she had played
in causing her mother's psychosis. For twenty-five years she
had been haunted by a dread, always hovering on the mar-
gins of her awareness, that she one day must pay for her
transgression against her mother by following her into insanity, and perhaps beyond that into self-violence, eye for
eye and tooth for tooth. In her guilt and panic arising from
this, I went on, we could perceive the origins of her obsessive
fears of mental illness and suicide, and of her phobias and
other symptoms.

The basic trauma, I repeatedly emphasized, lay not in
what had happened to her mother, father, and her, but in
the unrealistic, fearful misinterpretations that she, as an early adolescent girl, had placed on these events.

I think I convinced her. It is easy for people to believe
what they desperately must believe.

Her fearful misinterpretations, I continued, were much

fostered by the traumatic relationship she had with her mother throughout her childhood, in which her disturbed mother continually stated that she was the cause of her mental distresses and physical discomforts. Some hostility and guilt about that hostility toward her mother had understandably smoldered in the patient throughout her formative years, and these feelings added to her inner tumult. Furthermore, I pointed out, she undoubtedly had very mixed feelings toward her father, who had so cruelly exploited her and had left in her confused sensations of guilt, shame, lust, and hatred.

I argued my thesis as skillfully as I could, and when she left my office, the terror was gone from her face.

We continued to "work through" these things during four more months of psychotherapy. By the end of that time we had come to the point where I felt that psychotherapy had little further to offer her. She was a much more comfortable woman, and the symptoms for which she had come to see me were nearly gone; from time to time her old fears nibbled briefly at her, but the discomfort was small.

Leaving the way open for her to return at any point in the future when she felt more treatment might be useful to her, we terminated. She never returned to see me.

The erudite Greek who more than a century after the death of Christ drew up the Gospel that bears St. John's name put into the Nazarene preacher's mouth the words, "You shall know the truth, and the truth shall make you free." Under some circumstances, however, this must be altered to, "You shall know the truth, and the truth shall drive you mad."

The French Disease

At a little past ten on a Thursday morning in early April I arrived on 4-South, one of the general medical wards of St. Catharine's, a five-hundred-bed general hospital in central Kansas City. I had just finished making rounds on the several patients I had on the psychiatric ward on the floor below.

After stepping off the elevator I pulled from the inner pocket of my suit coat the small black notebook in which I keep the lists, hour by hour, of my daily activities. Opposite the line for ten o'clock I had written, "Hayes, Nancy, St. Catharine's, 425, Crawford." This indicated that Dr. Andrew Crawford, a Kansas City internist, had asked me to see in consultation a patient named Nancy Hayes in room 425 at St. Catharine's Hospital. Dr. Crawford's s secretary had left this message with my secretary the preceding morning. Although my secretary always tries to get data on such referrals, she apparently could get no information about the nature of this patient's problems; she probably was told, " It's on the chart."

However, even before looking at the chart I could surmise a few things about Nancy Hayes, since I knew Dr. Crawford and his ways of handling patients. Dr. Andrew Crawford is a snob. He grew up in Topeka, went to medical school in Kansas City, and married a girl from an old, prestigious, but economically threadbare Kansas City family. With the combination of his good income and his wife's social connections they move in the best circles; they have two teen age daughters and live in a large house in a fashionable district.

Andrew derives about thirty percent of his practice from the well-to-do social circles in which he moves, and the other seventy percent comes from working-class patients who drift to his door. If he wants me to see a hospitalized patient from the socially favored section of his practice, he telephones me himself, gives me a three-minute rundown on the patient, and wants to know when I'll see the patient so he can inform him. However, if he wants me to see one of the socially unwashed, he merely leaves the patient's name and hospital room number with my secretary. Thus, I already knew that Nancy Hayes was from the less privileged sector of Andrew Crawford's practice.

I could also make some further speculations about this patient. Andrew Crawford handles his blue-collar patients in characteristic ways. Since they cannot comfortably pay fees for elaborate outpatient medical workups, and since through their employment they usually have hospitalization insurance that covers both hospital bills and doctors' fees for inpatient checkups, he hospitalizes them. He always has half a dozen or more of these patients on the medical floors of St. Catharine's. There they receive workups that include batteries of laboratory tests, X-rays studies, and other scientific procedures. Of course, about seventy percent of these patients have complaints, such as muscle-tension headaches, stress-induced backaches, anxiety states, psychogenic gastrointestinal problems, and obsessive worries over minor dysfunctions. As a rule, elaborate hospital workups only increase these patients' convictions that they have obscure physical diseases for which science will, sooner or later, provide curative medications or other appropriate treatments. These patients are admitted to the hospital with such diagnoses as "possible Addison's disease," "suspected thyroid dysfunction," "occult ileitis," and many others, and are discharged with such diagnoses as "migrainous headaches," "gastric irritability," "adaptive colitis," "subclinical thyroid malfunctioning," and many other conditions that medical nomenclature conveniently provides. These patients rarely have psychiatric consultations. After discharge from the hospital Dr. Crawford treats them with a wide variety of medications and shots. These patients also help Andrew Crawford in another way; they help him keep his medico-political fences mended, since they can be referred for special examinations to other specialists, who in turn refer patients to him. Andrew Crawford is a pleasant conversationalist and is, on the whole, well liked by the doctors of Kansas City.

When, as happens occasionally, Andrew refers one of these patients for psychiatric evaluation, it is because (a) the patient is openly delusional and hallucinating and clearly needs psychiatric hospitalization; (b) the patient is bothersome and Andrew wants to get rid of him; (c) the patient is out of money and, hence, "not the kind of person with whom I work well"; or (d) the patient is disquieting in some vague way and is referred, often on the spur of the moment.

Thus, I could make some shrewd guesses about Nancy Hayes before even knowing her age, her complaints, or any other things about her.

In psychiatry when you grow tired of studying the patients, you can always study your colleagues.

I walked down the corridor and entered the nurses' station by its swinging waist-high door. A chest-high counter separated the nurses' station from the ward corridor.

I found the patient's record in the large, circular, revolving rack in the center of the room. The record revealed that Nancy Hayes was a seventeen-year-old high school student from Shawnee Mission, Kansas, a large Kansas City suburb. A nine-day hospital workup for fatigue and vague upper gastrointestinal symptoms had resulted in nothing more than several pages of normal laboratory and X-ray reports. The nurses notes stated repeatedly that she was a quiet, cooperative girl who spent most of her time in her room looking at TV.

I took a sheet of record paper from my briefcase and wrote in its upper right-hand corner her parents' names, her home address, her home telephone number, her father's telephone number at work, her date of birth, and other routine information. I put her name on the left-hand side of the sheet, a couple of inches from the top, and put the date below it. This would be the first sheet of my record on her.

I turned to the ward secretary.

"How has Miss Hayes in 425B been getting along?"

"All right. She's a quiet kid; she sticks to herself."

"Have any of the nurses or aides made any particular comments about her?"

"No."

"Does she seem to get along all right with the staff and other patients?"

"Yes. She's very cooperative. Frankly, I don't think we've paid much attention to her. We've had a run of cardiac cases, and she's just in for a quick, routine workup. But she's gotten along okay."

"Is the other bed in her room occupied?"

"No, the patient in 425A went home yesterday. It's reserved for a patient who's coming in this afternoon."

This would enable me to use the patient's hospital room as an interview room. Otherwise I would have had to hunt for an unused treatment room, an unoccupied conference room, or some other handy space.

"Is she in her room now?" I asked.

"Probably," the ward secretary replied. "I'll see."

"Never mind," I said. "I'll look." I picked up my briefcase and walked down the hall.

In room 425 I found a thin, small-breasted, adolescent girl; she was sitting upright in bed, resting against the upper part of the mattress, which had been cranked to an almost vertical position. A sheet covered her body to the waist, outlining her long legs and up-pointed toes. She had a light bed jacket on over her pajama coat. She was in the bed nearest the door; the other bed was empty, and the drape that slid on a ceiling rod to separate the two beds was bunched against the wall at the head of the bed, so that I could sit on the other bed and talk with her.

She looked at me in an expressionless way.

"Good morning. I'm Dr. Chapman."

She stared at me silently.

"I presume Dr. Crawford told you that he had asked me to see you," I said, sitting down on the opposite bed.

"No."

"Well, perhaps he forgot to mention it," I went on. "Anyway, he called my office yesterday and left a message requesting that I drop by this morning to see you. I'm here at St. Catharine's each morning."

She continued to stare at me.

"Dr. Crawford also left a consultation request to me on your chart in the nurses' station." I mentioned this fact to assure her that I had not mistaken her for another patient.

"Are you a stomach specialist?" she asked.

"No, I'm a psychiatrist," I answered. "Dr. Crawford wants to find out if emotional factors are playing a role in causing your fatigue, stomach trouble, and other difficulties. That is, he wants to know if emotional stresses and tensions between you and other people are contributing to your symptoms. So he asked me to see you."

"Oh."

I put my briefcase on my lap for use as a writing board, and I took out the sheet of paper on which I had written her name and other factual data. My back was to the window and her face was well lighted as we talked.

"My job is to ask questions about the things that are going on in your life and have gone on in your life, to see if we can make any connections between stressful events or tense relationships with people and your symptoms."

She gazed blankly at me.

"Sometimes," I said, "difficulties in a person's life—with his family or with kids at school or with a boyfriend or with others—can cause him to get tense. And emotional tension can cause stomach muscles and other muscles to become tense, and thus produce the kinds of symptoms you have."

She made no response.

"Am I getting through? Are you with me?" I asked.

"Huh?"

"Nancy, when I explained just now how emotional tensions can cause symptoms like yours, were you with me?"

"I guess so."

Her motionless eyes did not leave my face, her lips were slightly parted, like those of a child who breathes through his

mouth. She did not appear frightened or depressed or perplexed or sullen or resistant. Her face was lineless, except for
the creases that run from the wings of the nose to the corners
of the mouth. I watched her for a few moments and wondered if she were stoned on marijuana, but the ashtray on
her bedside table was clean and a quick glance at the floor revealed no butts or debris.

"How do you feel about this consultation?" I went on.

"Huh?"

"How do you feel about my coming to see you?"

"Okay."

I wondered if she were mentally retarded; this type of flat,
expressionless face and behavior is sometimes seen in mentally retarded persons.

"Where do you go to school?" I asked.

"Shawnee Mission High."

"What year are you in ?"

"Third.'

"What kind of grades do you get?"

"Okay."

"Have you ever made the honor roll?"

"A couple of times."

"Did you ever have to repeat a subject or a year?"

"No.'

"Have you ever been put in a special class of any kind?"

"Huh?'

"Have you ever been put in a class for kids with special
kinds of problems?"

"No."

She apparently was of average or better intelligence.

"Do you like Shawnee Mission High?"

She did not reply.

"Do you have any particular hassles there?"

She remained silent, staring at me.

"Have you ever been in any kind of trouble with the teachers or with the principal or with the kids there?" I asked.

After a pause she said, "No."

"Do the kids at Shawnee Mission High use much pot or
coke or anything else like that?"

"No."

She responded in such a mechanical, detached manner that I asked, "Do you know what I'm talking about?"

"Huh?"

She was beginning to exasperate me, and so I sat back further on the bed and let my legs dangle over the edge. I slowed down and went methodically on.

"Nancy, I suppose you know what pot is?"

"Yes."

"And that there are other drugs like it?"

"Yes."

"Have you tried any of them a few times?"

"No."

I shifted to more easily covered subjects, and during the next few minutes she indicated, in answers of a few words each, that she lived with her mother and father, aged about forty and forty-two respectively, and her twelve-year-old brother Paul in a three-bedroom, one-floor home in Shawnee Mission. She had been born in the Kansas City area and had lived in it all her life; the family had lived in Shawnee Mission for about ten years. Her father was a computer programmer and analyst at the Department of Agriculture Data Processing Center at Eighty-ninth and Ward Parkway; her mother did not work outside the home; they were all in good health; and they all got along well with each other. Everything in her life was either "fine" or "okay."

"Nancy, do you have a boyfriend?"

"No."

"Have you ever had a serious, or steady, boyfriend?"

"Yes."

"Who was he?"

"A kid at school."

"What was his name?"

"Randy."

"Did you like him a lot?"

"I guess so."

"Are you still friends?"

"No."

"Why?"

"We broke up."

"Why did you break up?"

"We just broke up."

"Did Randy give any particular reason for breaking up?"

"No."

"Or did you?"

"No."

"Then you don't have any clear concept about why you broke up?"

"Huh?"

"Do you have any idea, Nancy, about why you and Randy broke up?"

"No."

She was neither evasive nor resistant. She simply seemed disconnected from our interview, and from everything else.

Her hands, legs, and body remained motionless as she looked steadily at my face.

"How do you feel this morning?" I asked.

"Okay."

"Could you tell me something about your various symptoms, for which Dr. Crawford has done all these tests?"

"Huh?"

"Your hospital chart says that you tire out easily and that you have various kinds of stomach complaints."

She did not reply.

"Well, Nancy, do you have these problems, and, if so, what do you think about them?"

After a pause so long that I was about to repeat the question, she said, "I don't know. I guess they don't bother me too much."

I looked at her carefully. I wondered for a moment if she were taunting me or mocking me. I decided she was not.

"Well, do *you* feel that you are tired and worn out much of the time?"

"No."

"Do you have stomachaches, or other kinds of intestinal difficulties?"

"No, not very much."

"Well, where did Dr. Crawford get the idea that you suffer from these complaints? They are the things for which he has been evaluating you here."

"Maybe Mom told him that."

"Were you with your mother when she said those things to him?"

"Yes, I think so."

We were talking, but no communication was going on.

"Nancy, do you feel physically ill or physically uncomfortable in any way at the present time?"

"No."

"Have you felt physically ill in any way at all in recent weeks or months?"

"No.'

"In your opinion is any part of your body not working as it should?'

"Huh?"

"Do you feel, Nancy, that your body is all right in all ways?"

"Yes, I guess so."

"And emotionally—in terms of tensions, fears and so forth—are you getting along all right?"

"Yes."

"Then why are you in the hospital? For what reason did Dr. Crawford put you in the hospital?"

"It's a checkup."

"Why do you need this checkup?"

She remained silent.

It was clear that further interviewing at this time would be fruitless.

"Well, Nancy, I'll come by tomorrow to see you again. Do you have any questions or comments at this point?"

She shook her head from side to side.

After sitting with her in silence for another minute or so, I rose and said good-bye. She mechanically said, "So long."

I went back to the nurses' station and sat down at the long desk behind the partition separating it from the corridor. In my own record I wrote, "This seventeen-year-old girl answers all questions in an expressionless way that suggests flatness of affect. Other than the few facts outlined above, it is difficult to elicit data from her. She seems uncertain about why she is in the hospital. She is cooperative, but her apparent detachment from the environment and indifference to what is going on around her make it hard to communicate with her."

On the Progress Notes sheet of her hospital record I wrote, "This patient was seen in an initial interview to evaluate possible emotional contributants to her symptoms. I will see her again tomorrow. A. H. Chapman, M.D."

I turned to two student nurses who were setting up medication trays and asked them what kind of impression Miss Hayes in 425 made on them.

One of them replied that she didn't know her; she was working with patients on the other side of the ward.

The other student nurse said, "She's not with it."

I asked her what she meant by "not with it."

"She's up on cloud nine all the time. She's just not plugged in to what's going on. She looks like a pothead who's half stoned most of the time."

"Most of the time?" I asked.

"Well, I don't see that much of her," the student nurse replied. "We have three coronaries and those emphysema cases, and they keep us busy. But every time I see her that's the way she is."

I thanked them and left the ward, as they returned to their work.

The next morning at about ten thirty I went by to see Nancy again, and this time I brought my Rorschach cards.

Relatively few psychiatrists do Rorschach tests; they are done mainly by clinical psychologists. However, when I was a first-year resident in psychiatry in 1948 we had a bright young instructor who was interested in the Rorschach test; he had devised a simplified technique for administering, scoring, and interpreting it, and had written a small book on his method. He taught his method, which was ingenious and clinically useful, to all the first-year residents, and he super-

vised our use of it for several months. I have used the Rorschach extensively ever since, have published a couple of ar-
ticles on it in psychiatric journals, and still administer it to
about half the patients I see. I use the same set of Rorschach
cards I bought for two dollars in 1948; once every few years I
clean finger marks and other smudges off them. Since 1955 I
have used the same black plastic case to carry them.

The Rorschach is the oldest, and by far the most reliable,
of the personality tests. It was devised by the Swiss psychiatrist Hermann Rorschach, who published his major work on
it in 1921 and died at the age of thirty-eight the following
year. The basic techniques for administering, scoring, and
interpreting the test have changed little from those Rorschach originally laid down. I have given Rorschachs to thousands of patients; while serving in a Coast Guard training
center during the Korean War, I spent six hours a day, five
days a week, administering and grading Rorschachs.

Ten seven-by-ten-inch cards are employed in the Ror
schach test; on each of them is lithographed a standard inkblot. These inkblots are still the original ten that Dr. Rorschach made by spilling ink on sheets of paper, which he
then doubled down the middle; the blots are therefore sym-
metrical, each half being more or less a mirror image of the
opposing side. The inkblots of five of these cards are composed of black ink only; two cards have inkblots with both
red and black parts; and the three remaining cards have
blots in which pink, orange, gray, green, yellow, and blue ink
merge into each other or form separate blotches. All ten inkblots have white backgrounds and are printed on stiff cardboard.

The Rorschach test is based on the principle that since the
cards contain only inkblots, anything the patient sees in them
must of necessity come from within him. As the results of
decades of research studies, Rorschach responses have been
correlated with the various kinds of psychiatric disorders and
personality characteristics, and the interpretation of the test
has become remarkably valid.

An elaborate code is usually employed in scoring a Rorschach test, but in the following account of Nancy's Ror-schach I shall simply list her responses and make short comments on them.

When I arrived in Nancy's room, I found that the other bed was occupied by a middle-aged woman. After exchanging a comment or two with Nancy, I explained to her that I was going to give her a brief psychological test which might help us discover if emotional tensions played a role in causing her symptoms. I indicated to the woman in the other bed that, with her permission, I would not draw the drapes between her bed and Nancy's, since in the test I would use some printed cards, and bright daylight made their designs clearer. The other patient, who did not appear to be in any distress, seemed pleased at the prospect of observing a psychiatric examination.

I turned to Nancy.

"Now, Nancy, although this psychological test may appear simple, it's quite useful. It has been employed in our field for a long time. In it I shall show you, one at a time, a series of cards on which inkblots are printed. They are simply inkblots and nothing more. You say whatever comes into your mind as you look at the cards. We like several responses to each card, if possible. All right, shall we begin?"

"Okay," she said.

I was sitting on a metal chair between the two beds, with my back to the other patient and the window; a sheet of notepaper lay on the briefcase in my lap. I handed the first card to her.

In taking it from me, she turned it upside down. I turned it around for her, explaining that the patient may do whatever he wishes with the card, but must begin with it in the proper position.

I wrote Nancy's name and the date in the upper right-hand corner of my sheet of paper and put the Roman numeral one in the left-hand margin on a slightly lower level. The ten Rorschach cards are conventionally designated by Roman numerals, and the patient's responses are numbered with Arabic numerals.

She looked at the inkblot, which was composed of black ink only, for about half a minute.

"A bird, flying," she said. I recorded all her responses verbatim. I put a one in front of this response. A flying bird is a common response to this card.

"A man or a woman, in the center, with his hands raised up," she went on. Two. A common response.

"A couple of witches dancing around in the center." Three. A fairly frequent response.

"A mask, with two white spaces, here, for eyes." Four. I put a circle around the number four, since the use of white space is suggestive of sensitive, self-conscious tendencies; however, it must be correlated with other things in the test.

The numbers of her responses were beginning to form a neat column in the left-hand margin of my sheet, with the responses written after them.

"A couple of little hills, far away, here at the top," she said. Five. I drew a circle around five, since three-dimensional landscape responses indicate emotional insecurity and anxiousness.

As I administer a Rorschach, I circle the numbers of those responses that are indicative of unhealthy personality features; I go back and score them later. The normal responses are left unscored. Most psychologists would not consider this an acceptable technique, but after many years of giving Rorschachs I feel I can make such shortcuts without impairing the usefulness of the tests for my purposes. I employ the Rorschach more as a screening tool than as an instrument for detailed personality evaluation.

She handed the card back to me and said, "That's all."

I took the card, put it face down on the formica-topped table beside her bed, and handed her the second card, which had both black and red ink spots. I put the Roman numeral two in the left margin of my sheet and wrote a six after it.

Six. "Two bears; they're dancing," she said. A normal response.

Seven. "Two bloody feet, down here." This is an unhealthy response, indicating anxiousness and in some cases preoccupation with violence and body deformities. Blunt use of color reveals strong, chaotic emotional forces hidden within the person.

Eight. "Two people playing patty cake." A normal response.

Nine. "Some blood smeared up here," she said, pointing to the top of the card. A response that is determined mainly by the crude use of color, especially when the object does not have a precise shape ("smeared blood" has no precise shape), is quite abnormal. The inclusion of blood in the response makes it even more pathological. I put a double circle around nine.

She handed the card to me and I gave her the third one, which had both black and red ink blotches.

Ten. "Two men carrying a bucket or a heavy box." A normal response.

Eleven. "A butterfly, here in the middle." A common response.

Twelve. "High-heeled shoes." A frequent response.

In a Rorschach test, even that of a very disturbed patient, half or more of the responses are normal. The abnormal responses are scattered through the test and usually constitute no more than a quarter or a third of the total.

I gave her the fourth card, which has only black coloring.

Thirteen. "Two big boots." A common response.

Fourteen. "The head of a snail, here at the bottom." A common response.

Fifteen. She frowned slightly. "Something all decayed and sort of rotted out, down here." A very sick response.

Sixteen. "There's smoke coming out of it," she added. Another very sick response.

She spent two more minutes looking at the card in silence.

"Anything more?" I asked.

"No."

I took the card and handed her Card V, which has a black inkblot on it.

Seventeen. "A black butterfly." A butterfly is a frequent response, but to specify it as black is somewhat abnormal.

Eighteen. "Two peninsulas sticking out here, like on a map." Geographical responses indicate insecurity and unsureness of oneself. I circled eighteen, as I had circled several preceding numbers.

Nineteen. "A bat." A common response.

Twenty. "Pincers, down here." A commonly given response.

"That's all," she said, and handed me the card. I gave her Card VI, which had only black ink on it. She studied it for a minute.

Twenty-one. "A furry thing." This was her first use of texture. It tends to indicate anxiety, and I circled twenty-one.

Twenty-two. "A totem pole." A frequent response.

Twenty-three. "A spinal column." A common response. Many anatomical responses indicate preoccupation with body functions, but a few scattered through the test are within normal limits.

Twenty-four. "A tree, with feathers growing out of it." The union of incongruous or even bizarre things in a response is called contamination in Rorschach scoring, and suggests schizoid personality features or, in some cases, a frank schizophrenic psychosis.

She handed the card to me and I gave her Card VII. She looked at it for a moment and then abruptly gave it back to me.

"Why are you giving it back?" I asked.

"It's too ugly." After her words I wrote, "Rejected the card." To reject a card with revulsion or other strong feeling is a sick response; I counted her rejection of the card as response twenty-five, and circled the twenty-five. I handed her Card VIII, which is multicolored.

Twenty-six. "Pink rats with bushy tails, climbing up these trees, which have a lot of gooey stuff at the top." Contaminated in two ways, this is a very disturbed response.

Twenty-seven. She pointed to parts of the card and said, "Orange. Green." In Rorschach interpretation this kind of color naming often indicates disorganized, poorly controlled feelings and ideas.

Twenty-eight. "A Christmas tree, a pine tree." This is a fairly common response.

She gave me the card and I handed her Card IX, which is multicolored.

Twenty-nine. "Two old men, or elves, with tall, pointed hats, tossing something back and forth." A fairly common response to Card IX.

After looking at it for another minute she returned the card to me, and I gave her Card X.

Thirty. "Down here, a rabbit's head, with two green worms coming out of his eyes." A bizarre, contaminated response. I put a double circle around thirty, as I had done to a few of the preceding numbers.

Thirty-one. "Crabs, here on each side." A common response.

Thirty-two. "A wishbone." A normal response.

Thirty-three. "Two faces, with frowns on them, looking at me." A personal reference of this kind is unhealthy.

Thirty-four. "Yellow leaves, like in the fall." A frequent response.

Thirty-five. "Two green bugs." A normal response.

She had finished. I stacked the ten cards and slipped them into their case while she watched me impassively.

"Well, Nancy," I said, "this test would seem to indicate that you have a certain amount of emotional tension, and it is probable that this tension is playing a role in causing the symptoms that brought you to the hospital. As a routine part of an evaluation of this kind, I always talk with the parents to get background data; sometime in the next two or three days I'll probably see your parents in my office. Is that okay with you?"

"Yeah," she said.

"Also," I added, "I think you'll be leaving the hospital soon. Dr. Crawford has probably done all the tests he wants. So we shall complete this evaluation in my office."

"Okay."

I said good-bye, nodded to the woman in the next bed, and left.

A psychiatric consultation on a hospital general medical ward usually is unsatisfactory. Often there is no comfortable place for holding the interview without observation by other patients or interruptions by nurses or intrusions by aides or lab technicians. The consultation in many cases is not requested until the physical workup is over, or nearly so, and by then both the patient and the referring physician want a speedy discharge; often it is requested late in the week for a patient who is to be discharged on Saturday morning.

In many cases, moreover, neither the referring physician nor the patient is really interested in the consultation. The referring physician has found no physical pathology during a ten-day workup, and he wants a psychiatric consultation to enable him to turn over to someone else a patient he cannot help. The patient usually did not contemplate a psychiatric examination when he entered the hospital for "tests," and is indifferent or frankly hostile to it.

Hence, unless the patient during the consultation states that he has hallucinations or persecutory delusions or other gross disturbances, the evaluation usually ends on an indecisive note.

That afternoon in my office I called Dr. Crawford to give him my usual three-minute telephone report on a consultation.

"Andy?"

"Yes."

"This is Harry Chapman."

"Hello, Harry."

"I'm calling about the Hayes girl in four twenty-five at St. Catharine's."

"Uh huh." From the tone of his voice I felt he was not sure which one of his patients I was talking about. I helped him out.

"She's the seventeen-year-old high school student from Shawnee Mission, an uncommunicative sort of girl."

"Oh, yes." He had placed her. "Her father is a computer operator at the government center out on Ward Parkway."

"That's right. Well, Andy, I think the girl has a lot of tension under her apparent calmness and detachment. She has some neurotic traits and some schizoid features. At any rate, there's a lot of evidence to suggest that there probably are large emotional factors in her physical complaints."

"Good. I thought she was more in your line than mine."

"I'll put a consultation note on her chart tomorrow morning, and my secretary will send a carbon of it to your office. My secretary will also telephone the girl's parents to set up an appointment for me to see them in my office, and I can complete the evaluation on an outpatient basis. You might emphasize to the parents the importance of completing this evaluation when you talk with them."

"All right, Harry. They're sound people; they're responsible for their obligations. They won't give you any trouble." By that he meant that they'd pay the bills I sent them.

I thanked him for the referral and we said good-bye.

Fewer than half of such patients accept recommendations that they complete their evaluations after they leave the hospital. A patient who has sufficient motivation to make and keep an appointment at a psychiatrist's office as a rule completes a several-interview evaluation, but a hospitalized patient who has psychiatric examination forced on him as "part of the workup" often has little interest in it.

In my office that afternoon I dictated a four-paragraph consultation report on Nancy; my secretary typed it, and the next morning I placed it in Nancy's chart. In the report I stated that I found Nancy an uncommunicative, emotionally detached adolescent girl with whom I could not establish effective contact. I said that a student nurse working on the ward also found her very withdrawn. A Rorschach test revealed marked schizoid, perhaps even schizophrenic, tendencies, with depressive and neurotic features; underneath her placid exterior there was a great deal of emotional turmoil. Full evaluation of the patient would require interviewing her parents to get more information, as well as further direct study of the patient herself. I indicated that this could be done on an office-visit basis after she left the hospital, and I concluded by saying that there was sufficient evidence to suggest that her physical complaints were to a large extent caused by emotional problems.

I talked briefly to Nancy the next day, Saturday morning, when I went to the ward to put my report on her chart. She was discharged from the hospital on Saturday afternoon. On the following Monday my secretary telephoned Nancy's mother and made an appointment for Mr. and Mrs. Hayes to see me in my office on Wednesday afternoon of that week.

Mr. Hayes was a thin man of medium height whose expressionless face resembled his daughter's. Nancy's mother was a tall, attractive woman who talked rapidly and dominated the interview.

I began by saying that, as they knew, I had spent a couple of sessions with Nancy in the hospital, but that I needed more information before I could definitely formulate my opinions about her. Mrs. Hayes broke in at my first pause.

"Doctor, she's always been a very good girl. Until this school problem began we'd never had a day's trouble with her. Now, Paul—he's the younger one—is a problem. If I've been called to the school once about him, I've been called fifty times. Nothing serious, of course, but the teachers and the principal complain constantly that he won't sit still in class, talks out of turn all the time, and pushes other children down on the playground. But it's just that he's what I call a natural-born leader. He simply takes over a group of other boys and becomes the leader of whatever is going on. And in class he's simply one to express himself about things, which is all right, but some of those teachers want the children just to sit there like bumps on a log. But he gets good grades, and they've never had a serious complaint about him. He's just one to say what's on his mind. I guess you might say that .Paul's like me and Nancy's like Norman. Paul and I are extroverts. But Nancy and Norman are introverts, the bookish type—Norman with his stereo set and all those electronic gadgets at home, and his computers at work. He knows more about those computers than the engineers out there at the center. Sometimes they call him at two o'clock in the morning when something goes wrong out there during the rush sea-

son, when they're making out the checks to send the farmers
for the wheat subsidies or the soybean subsidies or other
things, and sometimes they call him on Saturdays and Sundays. They keep track of all the wheat acreages and subsidies
and so forth for a seven-state region and mail out all the
checks to the farmers and give the orders when it's to be
shipped and where to and all that sort of thing. Like I said,
Nancy is bookish. Which is all right. I'm a great reader myself. I belong to the Friends of Literature Book Club and buy
more books than I have to, and I read them all. But Nancy is
too much that way. I've talked to her about it. And she
doesn't date enough. She's shy. She gets that from her father." She went on for five minutes more in this way.

I interrupted, saying, "How do you view Nancy's problems, Mr. Hayes?"

He had been looking alternately at the floor and at me. He
started slightly when I addressed him, glanced anxiously at
his wife, and said, "Well, it's this school thing."

"Yes," said Mrs. Hayes, "that's the whole problem. She
hasn't been to school since Christmas."

"Christmas!" I said, with perhaps more surprise in my
voice than should have been there. "Why, that's more than
three months ago."

"Didn't Dr. Crawford tell you about that?" Mrs. Hayes
asked.

"He was mainly concerned with making sure she had no
physical causes for her problems," I said, evading her question.

"'She wouldn't go back to school after the Christmas vacation," Mrs. Hayes went on. "No matter what I did, she
wouldn't go, or at least she wouldn't stay there. I took her to
school myself half a dozen times, but she just stayed for one
or two classes and then came home, without telling anyone
there. And when I asked her why she came home, she'd just
say that she was too tired or that her stomach hurt or something else. And I said, all right, then she'd go see a doctor.
She didn't want to, but it dragged on and on, and so I took
her to Dr. Crawford, who put her in the hospital for tests. I

personally don't think it's psychological; she's never done this before. But then, of course, I'm no doctor."

"Did she refuse to go other places?" I asked.

"Oh, she'd go to the supermarket and the dry cleaners and a few other places, but always under protest. But I insisted. It isn't normal for a girl to sit home all the time and do nothing. I tried to get Norman to take her out of the house more, but he's as bad as she is, except for his work."

"What has Nancy done at home for the last three months?" I inquired.

"Well, she's read and listened to records and cassettes and watched TV," Mrs. Hayes replied.

"Has she had any friends over?"

"No."

"None at all?"

"Like I said," Mrs. Hayes answered, somewhat impatiently, "she's an introvert. I've told her to invite girls over, and she says she will, but she never does."

"Do any boys or girls ever call her on the phone?" I asked.

I think Mrs. Hayes was a little embarrassed as the full extent of her daughter's social isolation became apparent. So instead of answering she lit into her husband.

"It's her father's influence. He's never encouraged her to develop friends. I've told him to talk to her about it, and to set a good example for her. But between his work and all that stereo stuff of his he never has. And," she continued, turning on me, "like I said, she's an introvert. I'm no psychiatrist, but I can see that. Didn't she tell you she hadn't been to school since Christmas?"

She leaned forward and stared at me, waiting for my answer. The obvious implication was that my examination in the hospital had been so slipshod that I had not even discovered the central problem.

"No," I admitted.

"Well, I'm no psychiatrist, like I said, but it would seem to me that that is the main problem. She's probably lost the whole school year and will have to repeat it. Then, what *did* you find out? What *is* her problem?"

"Well, as you yourself have pointed out," I replied quietly, "Nancy is a very uncommunicative girl. In a two-bed hospital room she perhaps was even less communicative than usual." I was making awkward excuses for myself.

"Well, now that you know what her problem is," Mrs. Hayes said, "what are you going to do about it?"

I replied that the question was rather what *we* were going to do about it.

It was hard to avoid fencing with this woman, who had aroused more emotion in me than a psychiatrist is supposed to feel while dealing with patients and their relatives.

"*We!*" she said. "Well, I'm sure I've done everything possible to get her back to school." She glanced irritably at her husband and then stared at me.

"Mrs. Hayes, I'd like to ask a few questions to get some things clear in my mind," I said.

"Of course," she replied, "we want to cooperate in every possible way." With that, she sat back in her chair, folded her hands tightly together in her lap, and looked fixedly at me. She was now ready to "cooperate."

"We must consider all possibilities," I said, "no matter how unlikely some of them may seem. First of all, do you have any reason to feel that Nancy is taking drugs or has been doing so in recent months? For instance, when she is staring at a book or watching TV or listening to a stereo set for hours on end, is it possible that she's under the influence of marijuana or some other drug?"

"No," said Mrs. Hayes. "I'd have noticed something. Besides that, she doesn't have the money to buy that stuff. When she wouldn't go to school, I cut off her allowance, because if she can't carry out her responsibilities—and that includes going to school—she doesn't deserve her allowance. So she's had no money since the middle of January. Moreover, nobody's been to the house, and she's not been out, except with me. So how could she get it?"

"We must merely try to rule out all possibilities, no matter how unlikely," I replied. I began to understand how being reared by this abrasive, domineering woman had warped her daughter into a withdrawn, disturbed person, and how living with her probably had accentuated whatever shy, passive tendencies her husband had.

"Other than the physical complaints that she has mentioned occasionally," I proceeded, "has Nancy offered any reasons for not attending school?"

"No," she replied.

"Nothing?" I inquired.

"Nothing," she said, obviously annoyed, "except for silly things once in a while.'

"What kinds of silly things?"

"Oh, just nothing at all," Mrs. Hayes said impatiently. "For example, she said she imagined that the kids at school didn't like her and didn't want her around. But that's just her shyness coming out. Anyone who keeps himself shut up all the time will begin to think like that."

"Did she say anything else like that?" I went on. "For example, did she say that she felt that other kids at school were whispering unpleasant or malicious things about her?"

"No, of course not. Why would she say a thing like that?"

"In our work," I said, "we sometimes see adolescents who do not attend school because they're afraid, or even panicky, at school, and in their panic they may feel that other people are saying malicious things about them."

"Well," she said emphatically, "there may be cases like that, but Nancy is not one of them."

"Has Nancy seemed at all depressed?" I asked. "That is, has she seemed melancholy, sad, and blue?"

"No," Mrs. Hayes answered, "she's been her usual self."

"In terms of her general behavior, has she always been as she is now?"

"She's *always* been an introvert," Mrs. Hayes replied, clearly implying that we'd been over this three or four times before.

"Then, other than her refusal to attend school since the Christmas vacation, you haven't noticed any changes in her behavior in recent months?" I inquired.

"No," she answered firmly.

I turned to Mr. Hayes.

"Do you have anything to add to this, Mr. Hayes?"

"I think my wife has covered it all pretty well," he said, glancing at her uneasily.

I waited for him to say more, but he was silent.

"Well," I said, "perhaps I might summarize my impressions of Nancy at this point. I feel she is a very frightened, isolated girl who, for unclear reasons, finds attending school a painful experience. I would imagine she verges on panic when she attempts to leave home to go to school or is in school for a brief time. To some extent she has a similar apprehensiveness about going other places, but the problem centers on school, since school attendance is her major obligation outside the home at this time. I do not know why she feels this way, nor what her specific fears about school attendance are.

"The physical complaints Nancy has mentioned, such as fatigue and vague intestinal discomforts, are merely excuses she has found to justify to herself and to others her inability to go to school. It's easier to say 'I feel bad' than 'I feel scared,' both to herself and to others. The basic task with Nancy is to understand better the kinds of fears that are preventing her from attending school, and then to decrease the emotional turmoil within her that is producing her fearfulness.

"Since in the hospital I could not talk to Nancy as freely and extensively as was necessary, I would like to see her for another interview or two here in the office before outlining specific treatment plans. After a week or so I shall want to see both of you again to discuss those plans."

"And in the meantime," said Mrs. Hayes, "what are we going to do about school?"

"When is school over this year?" I replied.

"The last week in May," she said.

"That's only about seven weeks off," I said. "It's very unlikely that Nancy will return to school soon enough to salvage this year. I can give you a letter to the school asking that she be excused for the whole year, by reason of illness, so that any failing or incomplete grades she has received so far will not be recorded on her permanent record."

"She can make it up at summer school," Mrs. Hayes declared.

"She can do that only if she's well enough to attend summer school," I said.

"Well enough?" Mrs. Hayes retorted angrily. "Dr. Crawford found nothing wrong with her, and in two sessions you say you've found nothing particularly wrong with her."

"I think," I said firmly, "that she's a very frightened girl, and that the panic she experiences when she enters school is beyond her control. This is the basic problem she has. It is an illness, an emotional illness, and she will need some help to get over it."

Mrs. Hayes glared at me while her husband sat motionless, staring at the rug.

"When I've seen Nancy for another session, or maybe two, I'll see you and Mr. Hayes to outline Nancy's treatment."

After a few moments' pause, Mrs. Hayes said, "Well, I suppose we have no choice."

The hour was up. We agreed that one of them would bring Nancy to see me later that week at a time they could set with my secretary in the waiting room, and they left.

Nancy came three days later. I went to the waiting room and found her sitting alone. When I asked if her mother or father had brought her, she replied that her mother had accompanied her but had left to do some shopping; she would be back to pick her up at the end of her hour.

We went into my office. My clipboard with its notepaper was lying flat on the back corner of my desk, away from the patient's chair. I rarely take notes during an office interview with an adolescent; the only time I take notes while talking with an adolescent is during a consultation on a general hospital ward, when one must cover much ground rapidly on both the physical and emotional state of the patient. Note-taking frequently stifles the spontaneity of an adolescent, and it also detracts from the special alertness and flexibility a psychiatrist must have in talking with a teen-ager.

On the desk there were two bottles of a cola drink that my secretary had got from the drugstore on the first floor of the office building, and after Nancy and I sat down I offered her one of them. She accepted it, and I opened both of them. During the first ten minutes of the interview we drank from them occasionally. Adolescents talk better in an informal setting.

She was dressed in blue jeans, a white blouse and a thigh-length, brown corduroy jacket. She looked at me, motionless, expressionless, and silent, as she had in the hospital. Knowing that it would be useless to wait for her to begin, I started.

"What have you been doing since you left the hospital, Nancy?"

"Nothing much."

"Have you been staying mainly at home, or have you managed to get out a few times?"

"I've been sticking around the house."

"Doing what?"

"Just messing around."

"What do you do when you mess around at home?" I asked.

"Watch TV, read, listen to tapes, and that sort of stuff," she replied.

"Well, Nancy, we psychiatrists are always fussing around with details," I said. This apology was to take the sharp edge off my prying. "How many times have you been out of the house since you left the hospital?"

"This is the first time."

"And how many telephone calls have you received?"

"Nobody called."

"Have any of the kids from school or the neighborhood dropped by to see you?"

"No."

She had the same flat, detached manner she had had in the hospital.

"You're sort of a loner, I guess."

"Huh?"

"I mean, you do things by yourself. You don't have a lot of friends."

"Yeah."

"Have you always been like this?"

"I guess so."

"When you were younger—say, in grade school—did kids from the neighborhood or from school come to your house once in a while to play or to listen to records or to do other things?"

"Yes."

"How often?"

"A lot," she replied.

"Up to three or four times a week?"

"Yes."

"And how did you like that?"

"It was okay."

"Then you've changed in this respect?" I asked.

"Huh?"

"I mean, you used to have more friends than you do now."

"I guess so."

"But now you stay home most of the time," I said.

"Yes."

"And very few kids come over to see you."

"I guess so."

"When did you change, so far as you can tell?"

"Change what?" she asked.

"Change into a loner," I said. "When did the kids stop coming to the house, and when did you stop going out?"

"When they started it," she replied.

"Whom do you mean by 'they'?"

"The kids," she answered.

"The kids at school or the ones in the neighborhood or some other kids?" I asked.

"All of them."

"But mainly at school?"

"Yes."

"And in the neighborhood, too?"

"More at school."

"And what is it the kids at school started to do?"

She shifted her body a couple of times from one buttock to the other and began to play restlessly with the arms of the chair. After a minute I repeated my question.

"It was all that talk," she answered.

"By talk do you mean the kids were saying things?"

"Yes."

"About what?"

She did not reply.

"About whom?"

Silence.

"Nancy, was it about you?"

"Yes."

"What did they say about you?"

"A lot of things."

"Malicious things?"

"Huh?"

"Did they say unkind, false things about you?" Her tension had gone; she sat motionless and responded in a flat, unemotional way as I proceeded with my methodical questioning.

"Yes."

"Such as?" I asked.

She did not reply.

"Did they accuse you of things?"

"Yes."

"What kinds of things?"

She did not answer.

Long experience in talking with patients guided me in the ensuing questions.

"Did they accuse you of doing things you ought not to do?"

"Sort of."

"Did they accuse you of ugly sexual things?"

"Yes."

"Can you tell me what kinds of ugly sexual things?"

She did not respond.

"Sexual things with boys?"

"Sort of," she said.

"And sexual things with girls, too?"

"Yes."

"They said you were doing improper, ugly sexual things with both boys and girls?" I said.

"But I wasn't."

"I'm sure you weren't," I replied, "but I can understand how you were very upset by the things you felt they were saying."

After a pause I went on. "What did they say you were doing with the girls?"

She stared at me and said nothing.

"Did they say you were having sexual relations with girls?"

"Yes."

"With girls at school?"

"Yes."

"And also with girls or women outside of school?"

"I don't think so."

"Can you tell me exactly what kind of homosexual activity they were accusing you of?"

Silence.

I repeated the question.

"Diking it," she answered.

"By that, you mean rubbing your body, and your genitals, over another girl's genitals, face to face?" I asked.

"Huh?"

"By rubbing your cunt on other girls' cunts?"

"Yes."

"It must have upset you a lot to feel they were talking about you in this way."

"I guess so."

"Especially since it wasn't true."

"Yes."

"Since you never did anything like that." I was taking nothing for granted.

"No," she said.

"Did you actually *hear* them talking about you in this way, Nancy?"

"Huh?"

"Could you actually hear their voices when they said these things, just as you can hear my voice now?"

"No, but I could tell by the way they were talking."

"Where?"

"At school."

"But where at school—in the corridors or in classrooms or in the gym or elsewhere?"

"Yes."

"In all those places?" I asked.

"Yes."

"Did you see little groups of them talking and whispering about you?"

"Yes."

"Did they do anything else?"

"They made signs."

"What kinds of signs?"

"With their hands."

"Can you show me what kinds of signs they made?"

She remained silent and motionless.

"By the nature of these signs," I went on, "did you feel they were saying that you were a homosexual?"

"Yes."

"Did this occur every day?"

"Yes, I think so."

"Did it occur many times each day?"

"Yes."

"And what was the reaction of the teachers to all this?"

"They just laughed."

"At you?" I inquired.

"Yes."

"Did the teachers laugh only when talking to other teachers, or when talking to students, too?"

"Both."

"Was the principal also involved in this?"

"Yes."

"Did the principal do anything particular that indicated he was involved?"

"He talked about it in an assembly."

"In the main auditorium?" I asked.

"Yes."

"How often do they have such assemblies at Shawnee Mission High?"

"Every Friday morning."

"What did the principal say about you?"

"He said that some of the kids were doing things that couldn't be tolerated, and that if there was any more trouble, some of them would be expelled.'

"And you felt he was talking about you?"

"Yes."

"And about others, too?"

"I don't know."

"But mainly about you?"

"Yes."

"Do you have any specific reason for feeling that he was talking about you?"

"He mentioned my name, in code."

"In code?'

"He said that ever since the beginning of the year some of the older students had been hazing the freshmen, and that it had gone too far and had to stop."

After a moment's puzzlement I saw what she meant. "And by *hazing* you felt he was talking in code about you, since your names is *Hayes?*"

"Yes."

"When did this assembly occur?"

"In October, just before Columbus Day."

"That was some time ago," I said. I counted the months silently. "Six months ago."

She said nothing.

"Nancy, when did people start talking about you in this way?"

"Right after school began."

"Last September?"

"Yes."

"Until that time you had noticed nothing unusual?"

"No."

"Your birthday is in early December," I said, again counting months, "and so you were sixteen when this began."

"Yes."

"And once these things began, did they grow steadily worse?"

"I guess so."

"Until last September, had people ever said such things about you? Have you ever gone through a similar experience in past years?"

"Not so far as I know," she answered.

"Nancy, do you have any ideas about why they said these ugly things about you?"

"Because I wouldn't do it," she replied.

"Do what?"

Silence.

"Because you wouldn't do something they wanted you to do?" I asked.

"Yes."

"Was this something the kids wanted?"

"Yes."

"Did the teachers and the principal also want you to do it?"

"No, I don't think so. It was just the kids."

"All the kids?'

"I guess so. Most of them, anyway."

"Exactly what was it the kids wanted you to do?"

"To do it with them," she said.

"To do homosexual things with them?"

"Yes."

"What did the boys want you to do?"

"To do it with the girls, mainly, but with the boys, too."

"In other words, the kids at school, including the boys, wanted you to have homosexual relations with girls, and also heterosexual activities with boys?"

"Yes," she answered, "it was about like that."

"Did any girl, or any group of girls, come right out and invite you to engage in homosexual acts with them?"

"Not right out. But I could tell."

"How could you tell?"

"I could tell by the way they looked at me, and by the signs they made to me."

"Signs?"

"They did things with their hands," she said, "and sort of winked and smiled at me."

"But you wouldn't do it?"

"No."

"So what did they do then?"

"They spread it all over."

"Spread it all over?" I asked.

She did not reply.

"Do you mean they spread it all over school that you were a homosexual?"

"Yes."

"That must have been very upsetting to you."

"Yes."

I paused, deciding on my next line of inquiry.

"You said, Nancy, that they also accused you of doing improper sexual things with boys."

"Yes."

"Can you tell me what these things were?"

She did not respond.

"Was it to have sexual intercourse with boys?"

"Sort of," she replied.

"Did it involve some kind of unusual or abnormal sexual activity?"

"I guess so."

"Can you tell me what kind of abnormal sexual activity?"

She stared at me and said nothing.

"Was it sexual activity in which you use your mouth or anus?"

She remained silent, expressionless.

"Your mouth?" I asked.

"Yes."

"Did they accuse you of sucking boys' penises?"

"Yes."

"That must have upset you a lot."

She made no response.

"Did they accuse you of anything else?" I asked.

"Yes."

"What was that?"

"Of being pregnant."

"Did they say you got pregnant by using your mouth in sex with boys?"

She did not respond.

"Or did they accuse you of having regular sex with boys and getting pregnant that way?"

"Yes."

"And all the time you were a virgin?"

"Yes."

"You've never had sex with a boy?"

"No."

"Just some heavy petting?"

"Well, sort of."

"But nothing more than that?"

"No," she replied.

"And when did they begin to accuse you of being pregnant?"

"Just before Christmas."

"And was that the main reason you did not return to school after the Christmas vacation?"

"I guess so."

"And have not gone to school since then?"

"I suppose so."

"And your physical complaints—the tiredness, the stomach distress, and others—did they really bother you much, or were they in the main excuses you offered your parents for not attending school?"

"I didn't feel so good."

"But if it had not been for the things the kids and other people were accusing you of at school, would the tiredness and stomach trouble have prevented you from going to school?"

"I guess not."

"Did these physical symptoms bother you every day?"

"No."

"How many times a week did they bother you?"

"I don't know. Maybe a couple of times."

"Did you have them mainly when your mother tried to get you to go to school?"

"I guess so."

"Perhaps it was easier to tell your mother and father that you felt bad physically than to talk about the things they were accusing you of at school."

"Yeah," she said.

"Now, Nancy, until you told me now about these problems at school, had you told anyone else?"

"Only Dad," she replied.

"You hadn't told your mother anything?"

"No."

"Why not?" I asked.

"She'd only get mad."

"And you didn't tell your brother or any girlfriend or Dr. Crawford or anyone else?"

"No."

"When did you first tell your father about these problems at school?"

"A little while after they started."

"And your father never told your mother about them?"

"No."

"Did he tell anyone?"

"I don't think so."

"Do you have any idea why he never told anyone?"

"It would only have caused more trouble," she replied.

"Where and when did you tell your father?"

"A couple of weeks or so after it started he was driving me to school because it was raining. I didn't want to go, and he asked me why, and I told him."

"And what did he say?" I asked.

"He said I'd just have to face it. If I did that, they'd stop in time; but if I ran away from it, they'd talk about me all the more."

That stalled me for a few moments. I watched her face carefully as I slowly put the following questions to her.

"Did your father attempt to persuade you that perhaps

you had misinterpreted the school situation, and that maybe these things were not really going on?"

"No. He just said that the only thing to do was to tough it out."

"And as the weeks and months passed, did you talk further with your father about what was going on at school?"

"Once in a while," she said.

"Did he bring up the subject, or did you?"

"He did. He asked how things were at school."

"And what did you say?"

"I told him things were the same."

"And did he make any comments about the situation?"

"He said I'd just have to tough it out, and when they saw it wasn't getting me down, they'd lay off.'

"Did he at any time say anything else?"

"Once he said that maybe he and I ought to talk to the principal about it."

"And what did you say?"

"I told him about what happened at the assembly."

"You mean," I said, "when the principal referred to you, in talking about the hazing, and threatened expulsion?"

"Yes."

"And what did your father say about that incident?"

"He didn't say anything."

After a moment's pause I started to explore another area.

"I take it, Nancy, that you and your father are pretty close to each other."

"I guess so," she said.

"And that sometimes you can talk to him about things that bother you."

"Yes."

"Can you talk occasionally to your mother in that way?"

"No. I guess not."

"Can you talk about things like this to your brother Paul?"

"Not very much," she replied.

"Can Paul talk to your father, or your mother, when something bothers him?"

"He's closer to Mom."

"They're both fairly aggressive and outspoken, I take it."

"Huh?"

"Both your mother and Paul speak up for themselves pretty well and don't let people run all over them."

"I guess so."

"How do your mother and Paul get along with each other?"

"They fight once in a while, but they get along okay."

"Would it be accurate to say that Paul is closer to your mother and you're closer to your father?"

"I suppose so."

"Do Paul and your father often go places together and do things with each other?"

"Not very much," she responded.

"Putting it in other words, would it be fair to say that your mother and Paul are on one side and your father and you are on the other side?"

"We get along okay," she said.

I left this topic. It is unwise to push a girl like Nancy too far on any particular subject. If an area is explored beyond the limits of comfortable tolerance, such a patient may balk or panic. I turned to another aspect of her interpersonal life.

"Did your inability to return to school after the Christmas vacation seem to bother your father much?"

"No. Mom was the one who got upset."

"Did your father more or less accept the situation?"

"I guess so."

I went on, phrasing my questions carefully.

"Is your father what you would call a nervous person, Nancy?"

"No. Mom's the nervous one."

"Has your mother ever seen a psychiatrist, so far as you know?"

"I don't think so."

"Has your father ever seen a psychiatrist, so far as you know?" This was the main question I wanted to ask; I had asked about her mother merely to cushion this inquiry.

"Not so far as I know," she replied.

"Are both your mother and father usually in good health?"
"Yes."
"Does your mother get along reasonably well with people in the neighborhood and elsewhere?" This was merely preparatory to the next question.
"Yes. I guess so."
"And does your father get along reasonably well with people at work, in the neighborhood, and elsewhere?"
"Yes."
"In recent weeks or months has he lost time from work for any reason?"
"He had the flu in February," she said.
"How many days' work did he miss with the flu?"
"About three or four."
"Other than that, has he missed any time from work since last fall?"
"I don't think so."
"Has he recently seemed upset about anything?"
"No."
"Has he seemed angry or worried or upset about your trouble at school?"
"He didn't like it, but he didn't get upset."
"Have either you or your father taken any steps to correct this situation at school?"
"Like what?" she asked.
"Such as writing a letter to the school board or speaking to anyone in authority," I answered.
"No."
"Have you ever considered such action?"
"Dad once said that the school board ought to know what was going on, but he didn't do anything."
"Now, Nancy," I said, shifting my line of inquiry once more, "in the course of your life has anyone or any group previously mistreated you in this way?"
"How do you mean?" she asked.
"Has anyone or any group ever before said ugly things about you or tried to hurt you in any manner?"
"No."

"Did your father say whether anyone or any group has ever said ugly things about him, or has tried to hurt him in any way?"

"Not until all this started."

"By 'all this' you mean your trouble at school?"

"Yes."

"Has your father become involved in your school problems in some way?"

"In a way, I guess. He didn't like what they started to say at work."

"*At his work?*"

"Yes."

"At his place of work, the Department of Agriculture Record Center out on Ward Parkway?'

"Yes."

"What did they say out there?"

"A little after Thanksgiving they learned about it. Some of the men who work there have kids who go to Shawnee Mission High; I guess they heard about it from them."

"Do you mean that the people who work with your father found out from their children who attend Shawnee Mission High what the kids there had been saying about you?"

"Yes."

"And what did these people who work with your father do then?"

"They talked and laughed about it," she replied.

"All the people with whom your father works?"

"It was mainly the men."

I continued cautiously.

"Did your father feel that the people he worked with were whispering ugly sexual things about you, just like the kids at Shawnee Mission High?'

"Yes."

"Did your father say he could actually hear them talking about you at work?"

"No, but he could tell."

"How could he tell?"

"By the way they became quiet or laughed when he entered a room, and the way they avoided him in the cafeteria and whispered and made signs to each other."

"Was he sure, or did he just suspect they were talking about you?"

"He could tell," she said.

"Did your father feel they were saying unkind things about him, too?"

"No, just about me."

"Did the things they said at his work differ in any way from the things the kids said at school?"

"No."

"Did all this malicious talk at work upset him much?"

"No, not much."

"Not much?" I echoed.

"He got sort of upset when they started to say I was pregnant, but he got over it. He said that once they get started there's no limit to what they'll say."

"Has he spoken to anyone at work about these things? Has he complained to anyone there or elsewhere?"

"I don't think so. It wouldn't do any good; they'd just deny it."

"Does he feel that just about everybody at the Record Center knows about this?"

"Yes."

"And all these months neither you nor your father have discussed these things with anyone except each other?"

"Yes."

"I take it your father is a loner. That is, he tends to do things by himself, like you."

"I guess so," she responded.

"Does he have any hobbies?"

"His stereo set and other electronic things."

"Does he collect anything?"

"Huh?"

"Does he collect stamps or guns or anything else?"

"No."

"Does he have any firearms at home—rifles, pistols, and so forth."

"Not so far as I know," she replied.

This inquiry about hobbies, with its follow-up questions, is a devious way of finding out if he has firearms at hand for impulsive acts, and how well he can use them. It is better than asking, "Does your father keep any guns around the house, and how good a shot is he?"

I went on. "And what does your father think about your coming to see me?"

"He didn't say anything," she answered.

"He didn't object or say that it's a waste of money or that it's not necessary or anything else?"

"No."

"Do you think your father would come to see me if I requested an appointment with him—that is, an appointment with him alone?"

"I don't know," she replied.

The electric clock on the table in the corner behind Nancy indicated that the session was nearly over.

"Let me see if your mother has arrived," I said. "If she has, the three of us will talk together for a few minutes."

Her mother was in the waiting room and joined us, sitting on a cushion-seated wooden chair I had drawn from the rear of the office to a position beside Nancy.

"Well," Mrs. Hayes said, "when will Nancy be going back to school?"

"I don't think it will be this school year," I replied. "However, it's quite possible she will be able to go back next fall."

"Next fall!" her mother exclaimed. "She at least has to attend summer school and make up some of the time she's lost."

"That may be possible," I said, "if treatment goes better than expected, but I think next fall will be a surer time to count on."

Mrs. Hayes was plainly exasperated. "Well, what *is* her trouble, and what are you going to do about it?" she asked.

I was tempted to emphasize, as I had in my previous session with her, that it was not what *I* was going to do about Nancy's problems, but rather what *we*—Nancy, Mrs. Hayes,

Mr. Hayes, and I—were going to do about them; however, I felt this would only annoy further an already irritated woman.

"Nancy and I have spent the session today," I said, "discussing her problem and getting a better understanding of it. I want to set up another interview for all four of us to discuss the situation. I have time on Monday afternoon; my secretary can give you the exact hour."

"My husband can't take any more time off from work," Mrs. Hayes said. "What about Saturday?"

"Saturday morning is full," I replied. "Mr. Hayes has been at the Record Center for a number of years, and it usually is easy for long-term government employees to get time off for medical visits."

"All right," said Mrs. Hayes. She stamped out, with Nancy behind her.

On the following Monday at four I found Nancy, her mother, and her father in the waiting room, and I sat down with them there briefly. I explained that in evaluating a patient in my kind of work I often needed information from the people who lived with him; family members frequently could provide data that the patient could not give. I said I wanted to spend a few minutes speaking with Mr. Hayes, since I had not yet had a chance to talk separately with him. After assuring Mrs. Hayes that this was routine practice, I escorted him down the corridor that leads from the waiting room to my office.

He sat on the edge of his chair with his elbows on his knees and his hands clasped together. He eyed me with a stare that resembled his daughter's, but there was more tenseness in his face.

"Mr. Hayes," I began, "I would like to verify with you a few things your daughter told me. As I explained in the waiting room, in my kind of work it's often useful to check various aspects of a patient's problems with members of his family."

I paused to allow him to talk, but he said nothing.

"Nancy told me," I went on, "that her fatigue and stomach

complaints do not really bother her much. It seems that her main problem is worry about what people at school and elsewhere think about her and may be saying about her. It is this worry that has prevented her from attending school since Christmas."

I again halted to give him a chance to speak, but he merely gazed at me in a frightened way.

"Nancy told me," I continued, "that she has spoken to you a number of times regarding her worries and fearful speculations about what people at school were saying about her. I would like to know what your feelings are about her worries and fears."

He opened his mouth as if to talk, but did not, and then looked aimlessly around the room for a few moments.

"Do you," I said slowly, "feel that her fears are justified, or do you feel that she has misinterpreted the situation?"

"It's like she says," he mumbled.

"Could you elaborate on that a little?" I asked.

He rubbed one hand over the other and frowned at them.

After a brief silence I said, "What exactly has she told you about the school situation?"

"She told me all those things the kids are saying about her," he replied.

"What sorts of things?"

"Sexual things," he said in an awkward way.

"What was the worst thing they said about her?"

"That she was pregnant."

"Then you feel that the school situation is really as bad as she fears it is?" I asked.

"Yes."

"Have you yourself had any opportunity to observe these things directly?"

"At school?" he asked.

"Yes, at school."

"No," he answered.

"Anywhere else?" I inquired.

After a brief hesitation he said, "They spread it all over the place where I work."

"That must have been very disturbing to you."

"I can take it," he said, "but it's too much for her."

"You mean," I went on, carefully making sure that I understood each thing he said, "that you can go on at work despite such malicious accusations, but that Nancy can't face going to school when they are talking in this way against her."

"Yes."

I started on a different line of inquiry.

"Mr. Hayes, has anyone else in your family or any person close to you ever been subjected to accusations and slanders of this kind?"

Looking steadily at the carpet, he slowly nodded his head up and down.

"Was it against some member of your family?"

"Yes."

"Was it, by any chance, against yourself?"

He nodded his head up and down in silent affirmation.

"When did this occur?" I asked.

"It was fourteen years ago," he replied.

"Where?"

"At work."

"At the Record Center on Ward Parkway?" I asked.

"No. It was when I worked at the Blake-Mathiessen Company."

"About how many years ago was that?"

"I left there twelve years ago."

"What happened at the Blake-Mathiessen Company?"

"The same thing, more or less. They started the story going around that I was a queer."

"How did you find out they were spreading this story?"

"I could see them laughing and whispering about me, and I overheard a few of the things they said." His voice was firmer now, and slightly tinged with anger.

I thought it would be unwise to probe the precise details of this further; he was becoming upset.

"How long did this go on at the Blake-Mathiessen Company?"

"About six months."

"Then what happened?"

"It just died down."

"They stopped talking about you?"

"Yes."

"How long was this before you left the Blake-Mathiessen Company?"

"About a year or so."

"Then this was not the main reason you left Blake-Mathiessen?"

"No. I took the exams for a computer-programmer position at the Record Center and got it. It was a better job."

"At any other time in your life, with the exception of this trouble of Nancy's and the difficulty at the Blake-Mathiessen Company, have you or anyone close to you had problems of this kind?"

"No."

We sat in silence for a minute or so. I made no notes during this session; I would write or dictate them after the hour was over.

I was trying to decide what to do with this family.

I felt it would be useless to try to convince Mrs. Hayes that both her daughter and her husband were psychotic. However, since she completely dominated her husband and Nancy, no treatment plan would have a chance of success without her support. If she rejected my treatment suggestions, declaring them "outlandish" or "ridiculous," nothing would be done, and the situation would probably deteriorate until Nancy or her father, or both, were precipitated into psychiatric hospitalization by socially intolerable or tragic acts. Moreover, if treatment were delayed for weeks or months, the chances of recovery by Nancy and her father would be less.

I decided on a course of action, but at best I gave it a fifty percent chance of success.

I told Mr. Hayes I was ready to talk to all three of them together, adding that I would never reveal to his wife or Nancy anything we had discussed.

I brought forward from the rear of my office a couple of

high-backed, cushion-seated wooden chairs and placed them, with the upholstered chair, in a small semicircle before my chair. I asked Mr. Hayes to move to one of the wooden chairs, leaving the upholstered chair for Nancy or Mrs. Hayes. I then fetched Nancy and Mrs. Hayes from the waiting room, and soon we were seated for a conference.

The main person I had to deal with was Mrs. Hayes. If I could persuade her to accept my treatment regimen, it was probable that Nancy and her father would accept it. If I could not get Mrs. Hayes' cooperation, the ball game was over.

"As you know," I began, "I've spent four interviews evaluating Nancy's problems. As is customary in studying a teenager, a good deal of that time has been devoted to talking with you, the parents. I'm now ready to tell you what I think about Nancy's difficulties, and what we can do about them."

Nancy gazed at me in her wooden-faced manner, Mr. Hayes stared at his clenched hands in his lap, and Mrs. Hayes, clutching her purse, was making an effort to let me say what I had to say.

"First of all," I said, "let us cover Nancy's physical complaints—her fatigue, stomach symptoms, and others. Dr. Crawford found no physical basis for them, and both he and I feel they are caused by tension. Tense abdominal muscles can cause many kinds of abdominal and gastrointestinal symptoms. Muscle tension also is exhausting; it can produce the kind of fatigue Nancy has. Nancy has a lot of muscle tension because basically she has much emotional tension. One of the main things we must treat is her emotional tension."

"And exactly why is she so tense, if I may ask?" interrupted Mrs. Hayes.

"Because she is very shy," I shot back firmly. "I am sure that you have observed that. Her shyness makes her tense and fearful in situations in which she must face a lot of people."

The apparent logic of this left Mrs. Hayes temporarily without a comeback. There are several times in psychiatry when I feel somewhat like the proverbial salesman whose task was to sell refrigerators to Eskimos.

I barged ahead before Mrs. Hayes had a chance to get her bearings. "Our job is to help Nancy get over her shyness and her fears of public places, and to get her back to school. Willpower alone is not going to get the job done. She's going to need some help."

"Precisely what kind of help?" asked Mrs. Hayes, eyeing me closely.

I stared squarely back at her and said, "It's a kind of help in which you are going to play a central role, Mrs. Hayes."

She clamped her jaws together in attentive silence, and I went on.

"Nancy needs a schedule," I said, "and she needs medication. She needs a schedule so that she will not go too fast or too slow in getting back to her usual pattern of activities, including school. She needs the medication because she is very tense. She is so tense that unless she takes the medication exactly as I prescribe it she could even proceed to the verge of a nervous breakdown. I need somebody to run the schedule and to take over the administration of the medication each day at home, and that's where you come in, Mrs. Hayes. I feel you're the one to handle these things."

Her face relaxed slightly. I had the feeling that she considered my last sentence the first sensible thing I'd said.

"I'll prescribe the medication and Mrs. Hayes will administer it. When Nancy begins to unwind, we'll set up a schedule for her social rehabilitation, and Mrs. Hayes will see that it's carried out."

I paused.

The three of them were silent.

"Now, are we all agreed on this plan?" I asked.

"Well, I guess there's nothing else to do," Mrs. Hayes replied.

I proceeded to explain that I was putting Nancy on 300 milligrams of chlorpromazine each day, given in long-release capsules of 150 milligrams at twelve-hour intervals. As we evaluated its effect on Nancy, I said, we could adjust the dosage either downward or upward, so that she would be relaxed but not drowsy. I then covered a few precautions and other details in the use of this medication.

When chlorpromazine, an antipsychotic medication, is prescribed in this way on an outpatient basis without the use of other treatment measures, it has about a fifty percent chance of clearing a schizophrenic disorder of recent origin, which Nancy had. If a patient who recovers on this regimen continues to take small maintenance doses for two or three years, his chance of relapse is small. The phenothiazine antipsychotic group of drugs, of which chlorpromazine is a member, was introduced during the 1950's and has dramatically improved the prognosis of schizophrenia.

Of course, Nancy's chances for recovery would have been higher if, in addition to taking chlorpromazine, she had been psychiatrically hospitalized and had group or individual psychotherapy and a hospital environment adapted to her emotional needs. However, I felt I had little chance of selling such a plan to Mrs. Hayes. Moreover, I had to manage Mr. Hayes, whose condition would probably worsen if Nancy were hospitalized and he were left to flounder alone on an outpatient basis. To convince Mrs. Hayes that both her daughter and her husband were psychotic and that both should be hospitalized in separate psychiatric wards under different psychiatrists was out of the question. If such a plan were presented to her, she would merely stomp out of the office, dragging her psychotic husband and daughter with her.

If Nancy did not fall in the fortunate fifty percent who can recover on outpatient chlorpromazine, I would in time have to try to convince Mrs. Hayes that hospitalization was imperative for both her daughter and her husband. I told myself that I would cross that bridge when I came to it, but I was doubtful that I could ever get the Hayes family across so rickety a span.

I wrote the prescription and handed it to Mrs. Hayes, explaining exactly how the medication was to be given and putting her in charge of keeping and administering it.

"And now," said Mrs. Hayes, "what about the schedule? When is she going back to school?"

"The schedule," I declared firmly, "will be put into operation once Nancy is completely relaxed. However, once the

schedule goes into operation, school will be given top priority."

"When you say 'top priority,'" Mrs. Hayes demanded,
"does that mean she will go to summer school or are we supposed to wait until next fall and let her lose a whole year?"

"Every patient is a different case," I said, "and we can't give
specific dates of delivery. I would if I could, but I can't. No
doctor can, and we must be satisfied with that. As I said, the
schedule will go into operation as soon as Nancy is completely relaxed."

Mrs. Hayes made a guttural noise of disgust. I repeated
what I had just said and, fortunately, carried the day.

My talk about the "schedule" was, of course, merely a device to get Mrs. Hayes off Nancy's back until she could comfortably leave the house and attend school.

"All right," said Mrs. Hayes, "when do you want us to come
back?"

"Well, there's one other point we must cover," I said.

"And what's that?" said Mrs. Hayes, leaning forward in her
chair.

I went ahead steadfastly, eyeing her squarely, "Nancy will
unwind and get over her emotional tension and fearfulness
more quickly if everybody in the family is relaxed."

Mrs. Hayes tried to butt in, but I barged ahead, drowning
her out.

"You, Mrs. Hayes, do not need anything to relax. However, I feel that Mr. Hayes is much more upset by all this
than you would imagine by looking at him. He's the kind of
man who tends to keep things to himself too much."

"I've told him that for years," Mrs. Hayes declared. "He
lets those people at work run all over him."

Avoiding any discussion of where else in his life he possibly
was "run all over," I hurried on. "We must get Mr. Hayes to
relax, too. Mr. Hayes, you're a tense, worried man," I said,
turning briefly to him, "and I'm going to prescribe a relaxing
medication for you. I'll give it to Mrs. Hayes and she'll administer it to you twice a day. I know you want to help Nancy
in every possible way, and this is the way you can help her."

I wrote a prescription for thioridazine for him and careful-

ly explained its use. The antipsychotic medication thioridazine is closely related chemically to chlorpromazine, and the
two drugs can be used interchangeably. I felt it best not to
give him the same medication his daughter was receiving,
since I was presenting their problems as somewhat different
from each other. In reality their disorders were identical.

I reemphasized a few points to Mrs. Hayes, set an appointment for all of them to come back in a few days, and saw
them out.

Did Nancy and her father recover? They did; each of them
fell in the fortunate fifty percent. Within ninety days Nancy's
delusions and hallucinations had receded, and she began to
leave the house comfortably. By manipulation of the "schedule" I maneuvered her mother out of forcing her to go to
summer school. By the time September came Nancy was taking only a moderate maintenance dose of chlorpromazine at
bedtime. She reentered school and did well there in her usual shy way. I saw her in once monthly follow-up visits for
three more years, regulating the nighttime dose of chlorpromazine and making occasional recommendations about
her activities. As Nancy got well her father also recovered; I
discontinued his medication the following November.

Did the Hayes family live happily ever after?

No.

Four and a half years after I first saw her, and about eighteen months after I discontinued my contacts with her, Nancy
had a return of her schizophrenic psychosis. This time she
was so obviously psychotic that I had no trouble convincing
her mother to hospitalize her. Mrs. Hayes dismissed this illness as a "nervous collapse" brought on by studying too hard
in college. As a preventive measure, I put her father on thioridazine again and, though he became apprehensive and
taciturn, he did not become delusional. Nancy had three
months of hospital care, with an antipsychotic medication,
group psychotherapy, and a therapeutic hospital activity
program. She recovered, and I followed her for two further
years, during which I kept her on maintenance doses of an

antipsychotic medication and carried out supportive psychotherapy to the extent that she could engage in it.

Years passed.

Like many physicians, I usually scan the obituary columns of the newspaper each day to see if any former patients, or their relatives, have died, and of what causes. Eight years after I last saw Nancy I read the obituary of her father in the Kansas City *Star;* it consisted of two short paragraphs. He died of a heart attack after a short hospitalization. Besides his wife and an unmarried son, Paul, he was survived by a married daughter and two grandchildren in Indianapolis. She was Nancy.

We have a name for it, of course. It is called *folie à deux,* which may be literally translated as "madness for two." It was first described in 1877 by two Parisian psychiatrists, Drs. Charles Lasègue and Jean Falret, in an article in a French psychiatric journal; the article was titled "*Folie à Deux, ou Folie Communiquée.*" The French name has stuck, despite occasional efforts to substitute other names for it.

Folie à deux consists of the simultaneous development of identical psychotic illnesses in two members of the same family. Paranoid schizophrenic disorders with delusions of persecution constitute the most common type of *folie à deux.* One member of the family becomes psychotic, and then "communicates" the disorder to a second person. The two individuals are usually emotionally close to each other.

Folie à deux is more common than is generally recognized. If disorders owing to organic brain disease (such as cerebral arteriosclerosis and head trauma) are excluded, about two percent of all psychotic patients admitted to psychiatric hospitals are involved in a *folie à deux* process.

The French-disease is fairly common.

A Golfing Psychosis

Aт a little after eight o'clock on a warm June night I was called from my home to the emergency room of Mt. Sinai, a large general hospital in midtown Kansas City, to see a patient whom Dr. McArdle of Manchester, Missouri, had sent to me.

Although Dr. McArdle had been sending me patients for ten years or more, I had never met him; he originally got my name from one of my former patients. He sent me four or five patients a year, and almost all of them were good referrals. He did not treat a neurotic with shots and pills for years until he was tired of the patient or the patient ran out of money, and then refer him. He did not refer patients for whom the cost of hospitalization would be a difficult burden, because of poverty or their lack of hospitalization insurance, and whom I could only send back on the one-hundred-fifty-mile trip to Manchester with recommendations that the family hospitalize the patient at the nearest state psychiatric hospital. He did not send deteriorated senile patients for whom there was no treatment or sullen adolescents who steadfastly refused to be treated. I could almost always do something for the patients Dr. McArdle sent.

I have about thirty small-town referring physicians like Dr. McArdle. They are scattered over the western half of the state of Missouri and the eastern third of the state of Kansas, and they give a much broader social, as well as geographic, dimension to my practice. Some of these physicians send me a patient once every couple of years, and others refer four or five patients a year. I do not send these doctors small presents, such as baskets of fruit and desk-top gadgets, at Christmas, to keep in touch, and I do not invite them to lunch or dinner when they come to Kansas City. However, I always give them a three-minute telephone report on each of their patients after the initial interview, and I send them a fifteen- or twenty-line letter when the patient is about to be discharged from the hospital, or when I have clear ideas about what an outpatient's treatment and his probable reaction to it will be.

At most times the emergency room of Mt. Sinai is a mess. It is crowded with adolescents and children with wet casts, young suburbanites with hands and feet cut on power mowers, old women wheezing with cardiac disease, and confused, elderly men whose adult children shout reassurances into their ears. Over this melee a harassed nurse presides, assisted by several scurrying aides. An intern, recently arrived from Indonesia or the Philippines, attends the crowd at a leisurely pace.

It was not hard to locate my patient as I entered the emergency room. A tall, heavy-set, red-faced man of about forty, with abdominal fat ballooning his sport shirt over the tight belt of his slacks, was standing in the middle of the waiting room; everybody else, temporarily silent, was staring at him. He looked beyond me, as if into the distance, with his arms stretched stiffly before him at a forty-five-degree angle. He abruptly pulled his arms back over his right shoulder, shouted "Fore!" and let fly with a drive that could have sent a golf ball two hundred yards down the fairway.

As he shaded his eyes and looked past me, a short, stocky man attempted to get him to sit down on a nearby bench where a woman was sobbing. Another man stood at his side, not certain what to do, while a nurse was trying to convince them all to go into a treatment room where the golfer's behavior would cause less disturbance. A slender, olive-skinned intern in starchy white sat at a metal table filling out a form, as if nothing unusual were going on; he looked up and smiled politely to me.

The nurse turned to me. "Dr. Chapman," she said, "thank

God you're here. This man is disturbing the whole place and scaring the other patients half to death."

"I take it this is Dr. McArdle's patient from Manchester," I said.

"Yes, and he's been here for twenty minutes," the nurse replied.

"I came as soon as you called," I said apologetically. Pointing to a corner, I asked, "Is that treatment room empty?'

"Yes," she responded eagerly, and called to an aide to hold the swinging double doors open.

I approached the patient, who shouted at me, "Glad to see you, George. We're teeing off and need a fourth." With that he raised his beefy hand and gave me a hearty slap on the shoulder.

I took him by the arm and said, "Come on, Mac, let's go in here for a quick snort before we tee off."

He pulled back and didn't move.

"Just one quick bourbon on the rocks, and then we're off," I said.

He hesitated and then said, "All right, George." Turning to the other two men, he shouted, "Come on, this guy's paying," and we all marched into the treatment room, with the crying woman behind us. A psychiatrist is not supposed to encourage the delusions of his patients, but I have to live with the people at Mt. Sinai and it was necessary to clear the emergency room.

As soon as he entered the treatment room, the patient eyed a spot on the floor about fifteen feet from him and announced it was the fourth hole. He then got down on his hands and knees to study the line the ball would take to reach the hole. Standing up, he winked at one of the men, carefully assumed a putting position, and putted. He tensely watched the ball in its brief course, and then suddenly raised his arms and shouted, "Hot damn, I made it!" He grinned at us, went over and fished the imaginary ball out of its hole, and put it in his trouser pocket.

"Pitiful," murmured the stocky man and shook his head sadly.

The other man watched silently, and the woman gulped sobs while the putter looked at us in happy satisfaction.

"Come on, fellows," he hollered, "let's get going on the next one."

"Wait a second, Mac," I said, "these guys are tired. Let's rest here for a few minutes." I persuaded him to sit down, and I took a place beside him.

Turning to the stocky man, I said, "I need a little information to get oriented here. First of all, does this man have any kind of physical disease?"

He waved his hand toward the woman, to whom I repeated the question.

"Not so far as I know," she replied.

"You're his wife, I take it?"

"Yes," she replied.

"And these two men?" I asked.

"Friends," she answered.

"I haven't had a chance to talk to Dr. McArdle in detail yet; what did Dr. McArdle say about his condition?" I said, addressing the three of them.

"He said the problem was mental and that physically he was all right," the stocky man replied.

"All right," I said. "All of you wait here for a couple of minutes, and don't let him leave this room." Turning to the patient, I said, "Take it easy for a couple of minutes, Mac. I'll be right back."

"You're the pro," he shouted. He looked around the room and broke into a loud guffaw.

I went through the swinging doors and called for the nurse. "Get me a five-milligram ampule of perphenazine and a five-centimeter syringe. I'll put the medication into the syringe myself. And make it fast."

She sent an aide flying to the pharmacy down the hall.

I returned to the treatment room, where the patient was trying to get out of a sand trap.

With a little cajoling I got him out of the sand trap and back into a chair. Sitting beside him, I kept up a stream of calming patter until the nurse came in a couple of minutes later with the ampule and the syringe. I thanked her and she left.

After checking the lettering on the ampule to make sure it contained exactly five milligrams of perphenazine, I scratched a line on the neck of the ampule with the forked, rough-toothed cardboard cutter that accompanied it and broke off its tip. After sucking the fluid into the syringe I quickly searched a surgical dressing table in a corner and found alcohol and cotton. I then approached the patient, syringe in one hand and an alcohol-soaked cotton ball in the other.

"Mac," I said, "you're too tense right now to get anything done. I'm going to give you this shot to help you unwind; it won't hurt any more than a mosquito bite."

"What the hell is it for?" he yelled, and drew away from me.

"It's good for what ails you," I said firmly and gently pushed him back down onto his chair. Sitting down beside him, I rapidly rubbed alcohol over a wide area on his upper arm and tossed the cotton ball into the corner.

"Hold still," I said sternly, and caught a wad of his upper arm between the thumb and forefinger of my right hand. I quickly jabbed the needle into his muscle, pulled back on the bore of the syringe to make sure I was not in a vein, and injected the medication. After pulling the needle out, I got a Band-Aid from the surgical dressing table and put it over the injection site.

It takes experience and a certain amount of luck to carry off a thing like this with a disturbed patient.

With my arm laced through his, I sat beside him and kept up a flow of gentle chatter during the next ten minutes as he became increasingly drowsy.

"You should lie down for a few minutes, Mac," I said, and, summoning the other two men, I soon had him up on the treatment table in the center of the room, where he at once went to sleep.

I called an aide and we passed a waist belt around him to secure him firmly to the table and prevent him from falling off. However, I told one of the two men to remain constantly at his side to diminish further the chance that he might fall.

I got my briefcase, which I had left on top of a locked instrument cabinet near the entrance to the room, and sat down again on a metal chair. I pulled a sheet of notepaper from the briefcase and motioned to the stocky man to sit beside me. The woman, who was no longer crying, sat a few feet off.

"I'm Dr. Chapman, as you know. Dr. McArdle's secretary called me late this afternoon to let me know that this patient was coming in. She couldn't give me much information; everything was hurried because of the patient's very disturbed state. So I shall begin at the beginning. First of all, what is the patient's name?"

"Hammond, John Hammond," the stocky man said. During the next few minutes I learned that John Hammond was forty-three and his wife Shirley, the woman with us, was forty-one. They had been married eighteen years and were childless. Mr. Hammond was vice-president and cashier of the Marshall County State Bank of Manchester, Missouri. He was active in the Rotary Club, the Lions Club, the Marshall County Country Club, and other local organizations. His father was dead, and his mother was living, age seventy-one, in Manchester; his only sibling was a thirty-eight-year-old married sister in Cleveland. His marriage was good, he had no financial problems, and he had no obvious difficulties or marked stresses in his life situation. Until he had abruptly become ill earlier that day he had been considered a well adjusted, successful member of his community. The two men described John Hammond as a cheerful, outgoing man who was well thought of in the community and competent in his work.

He had graduated from the University of Missouri at Columbia and had worked at the Marshall County State Bank since his discharge from military service at the age of twenty-four. In the bank he had gradually risen from teller to its second highest executive. He was a minor stockholder in the bank, which was owned by a group of local businessmen, lawyers, and dairy farmers. The two men with him in the treatment room were long-term, close friends; the stout man was named Collins, and the other was named Novack. After getting this data I proceeded to inquire about his psychiatric illness.

I asked his wife when it had begun.

"At three o'clock this morning," she replied.

"At exactly three o'clock?" I asked.

"Yes," she said. "Perhaps a little later, but more or less then."

"And until that time he had seemed perfectly all right?" I asked.

"Well," she answered, "he'd been a little tense and hadn't been sleeping well; he'd get up and wander around the house at night or read until he got sleepy, and then he'd come back to bed. But until today he seemed all right."

"And what happened at three o'clock this morning?"

"I woke up and heard him shouting in the living room. I put on my robe and slippers and went there right away. He was . . . " She broke down crying. I waited in silence for her to recover and go on, while the stocky man went and sat down beside her. He put his arm around her shoulder in a brotherly way and said, "There, there, Shirley, he'll be all right; pull yourself together."

She stopped crying and continued. "He was in the living room, just like you saw him. He was waving a golf club around and shouting that he was five over par, and had just made a birdie, and so on. Then he teed off again and went on and on like that."

"And until three o'clock this morning," I repeated, "you are sure there had been no signs of emotional disorder, other than some slight tenseness and difficulty sleeping?'

"There was nothing else. He was all right," she replied.

"Does Mr. Hammond drink heavily?" I asked.

·"No. Social drinking, but nothing more."

"Does he ever drink to excess?"

"Hardly ever; once a year at a party, at the most."

"In our kind of work we must ask all kinds of questions in

evaluating a patient," I said. " Does he use any kind of drugs, so far as you know?"

"Do you mean marijuana and that sort of thing?" she asked.

"Yes."

"No, he'd never do that."

Mr. Collins, the man standing beside him at the table, said, "He's not the kind to do a thing like that."

After stating again that I had to rule out all possible causes of his condition, I went on.

"Has he been exposed to any kind of toxic substances lately? For example, has he been using insecticide sprays in the yard during the last day or two, or has he been crop spraying in an orchard or on a small farm, or has he been painting inside a garage or some other small space, or has he been exposed to kerosene or turpentine fumes or any other kind of aromatic chemicals?"

"No," she answered, shaking her head from side to side.

"Have they been painting or putting down a new floor or installing new equipment at the bank in any way that produces irritating or noxious fumes?" I continued.

She shook her head. I went on looking for other possible toxic substances to which he might have been exposed, and also asked if he were taking any medication, but my search was fruitless.

"And he has never been like this before?" I inquired.

"No."

"Has he ever had any kind of psychiatric disturbance?"

"No, none at all."

"He seemed the most stable person you could imagine," Mr. Novack said from his chair beside Mrs. Hammond, and Mr. Collins agreed.

"What happened after you found him in this state at three o'clock this morning?" I went on.

"I didn't know what to do," Mrs. Hammond said. "I tried to calm him down, but the more I talked, the louder and more excited he got. And he went on driving and chipping and putting. I thought he might be drunk, even though that wouldn't be like him. But he didn't have any smell of liquor on him, and he didn't seem drunk; he wasn't unsteady on his feet and his speech wasn't slurred. Still, I checked the liquor shelf, but nothing had been touched and there weren't any empty glasses around. So, I just kept on trying to reason with him, but it wasn't any good. He went on and on, just like you saw him. I didn't want to call Dr. McArdle at that time of the morning. Also, I thought it would be embarrassing to John if it turned out he really was drunk, or was high on something else, and I had called people in. So I made coffee and got him to take some, and I talked with him and tried to get him to go to bed, until it began to get light at about five o'clock. Then I called Mr. Collins, who lives down the block. My family all live in Jefferson City, and I didn't know who else to call."

I turned to Mr. Collins, who was now sitting on a white metal stool, which he had drawn to the table beside the sleeping patient. "What did you observe when you went to the home, Mr. Collins?"

"I found him just like Shirley says he was," he responded. "He was rampaging around and shouting and acting like he was on a golf course. But he knew who I was and slapped me on the back and told me I was just in time to tee off. He asked where Bill Novack was; he said Bill was late and that if he didn't come soon, we'd have to tee off without him."

"What happened then?" I asked.

"I tried to calm him down," Mr. Collins replied, "but it didn't do any good. So I told Shirley that the only thing was to call Dr. McArdle. I figured John was on some sort of a jag. I also told her that I thought we should get somebody else in . . . in case John, well, became violent. So we called Ted Novack, and after he came we called Dr. McArdle. It was about six thirty by that time."

"What did Dr. McArdle do when he arrived?"

"He watched him shout and run around the living room for a couple of minutes. Then he said he'd give him a shot to calm him down and got the things out of his bag. John held still and let him do; he didn't object. But then he's known Frank McArdle for twenty years or more, and I guess that even in the state he's in he sort of felt that Dr. McArdle knew what he was doing. Doc McArdle said that John would calm down in a while, and he said he'd drop back later in the morning."

"Did Dr. McArdle say what he thought was wrong with him?"

Mr. Novack broke in. "No, he didn't. As he left, I went out to his car with him, because I figured he might not feel free to talk frankly in front of Shirley, for fear it might upset her too much. I asked him what he thought, and he said it was a very strange case. He said he'd sent a lot of mentally upset people to the state hospital and to you, but he'd never seen anything like this before."

"What happened next?" I asked.

"Well, pretty soon, at a little before eight o'clock, John went to sleep," Mr. Novack said.

"Have you and Mr. Collins been with him most of the day?" I inquired.

"We haven't left him all day. My wife brought over something for lunch and made a snack for us to eat on the way up here. We came in my car."

"After Mr. Hammond went to sleep at about eight, how long did he sleep?" I asked.

"About an hour," Mr. Novack answered.

"And how was he when he woke up?"

"He was groggy for a while, but then he got up and started golfing again. It was awful. George Carson, he's president of the bank, dropped by, and he was shocked. He said for us to do whatever was necessary, and that the bank would manage to get along until John was all right again. John has enough vacation time piled up; he hasn't had a vacation in three years. He's the mainstay of the bank. George Carson is out looking after his herd of Herefords all the time, and John more or less runs the bank. I've told him he ought to take more time off, but he always said he was too busy to get away."

"What did Dr. McArdle say and do when he came back?"

"About eleven thirty he came by and saw what was going on. He checked John's blood pressure and listened to his heart and all that. We told John it was a checkup for the sum mer golf tournament at the club; that was the only way we could get him to sit still for a while. Then Dr. McArdle gave him another shot. He left Ted to watch John while he took Shirley and me into the next room. He said it was a very puzzling case, but that John obviously had to go to a psychiatric hospital; he said he'd arrange it with you. John went to sleep for about three hours after the shot. About two o'clock Doc McArdle called and said he couldn't get hold of you, but to take John to the emergency room at Mt. Sinai here in Kansas City anyway and put in a call for you. He gave us your office telephone number and your home number."

"I spend Wednesday afternoon at the med school supervising med students or residents," I said. "That's why he had trouble reaching me. It wasn't until five thirty that I got the message that Dr. McArdle was sending in a patient." After a pause I added, "Is there anything else you feel I should know?"

"I think that's all," Mrs. Hammond said.

"And Mr. Hammond has no physical illnesses, and has had none in the last several years?" I repeated.

"No," Mrs. Hammond replied.

"Well, it's clear he must be psychiatrically hospitalized," I said. "The exact nature of his problem is not immediately clear, but after a few days' study we ought to understand what's wrong with him and how to help him get well."

I turned Mrs. Hammond. "I take it you agree to his entering the hospital?"

"Yes, of course, whatever is necessary," she replied.

"It's the only thing to do," I assured her.

"Will it be here?" she asked.

"I don't know," I answered. "After I got Dr. McArdle's message I called Mt. Sinai, St. Catharine's, and Bethesda to reserve a bed; they were all full. We can put him in Elmdale, of course, but I think you'll be happier with one of the other hospitals. I'll make a few phone calls to see what I can arrange.'

I went to the emergency-room nurses' station, sat down at a desk, and dialed the Mt. Sinai admission office. It was on the floor above in another wing, and since I felt I would have several calls to make, I telephoned instead of going there personally.

"Hello, this is Dr. Chapman; I'm calling from the emergency room here at Mt. Sinai. I have a very sick man down here who just came in from Manchester, Missouri. I called you about three hours ago when I learned he was coming in, but the psychiatric ward was full and had one on the waiting list. What's the situation now?"

The admission office clerk replied that the ward was full, but there was now no one on the waiting list; there had been a late-afternoon discharge, and the patient on the waiting list had come in.

"All right," I said, "thanks just the same." I hung up and dialed the psychiatric ward at Mt. Sinai. "Hello, this is Dr. Chapman. May I please speak with the ward secretary? . . . Miss Nelson? Hello, this is Dr. Chapman. Look, honey, how many patients did you discharge since you came on this afternoon at three? . . . Two? And how many came in? . . . One? You must have an empty bed, then. . . . Okay, what's the room number? Is it a single? . . . Good. Apparently they don't know about this in the admission office. Don't worry, honey, I'll cover for you. You're a doll. Good-bye."

I dialed the admission office again. "Look, sweetheart, this is Dr. Chapman down in the emergency room again. I just went up to the psychiatric ward to get an ampule of perphenazine to calm this patient down, and I noticed the chart in slot one fifteen was empty. I checked around and found out that they had two discharges late this afternoon, and somehow or other you got informed about only one of them. The memo telling you about the other one is probably in their mail tray or on the way right now. So I guess I can have one fifteen for my man here in the emergency room. . . .

Sure, you check it out with the ward. I'm at extension four three six. I'll wait."

Two minutes later the phone rang and I answered. "Good. I understand. The man's name is Hammond, John, and his wife's name is Shirley." I went on to give the other information the admission office needed and assured them that I would send the patient's wife and two close friends up to them in about sixteen minutes; they could give the patient's hospitalization insurance data and sign the admission papers.

I then called the psychiatric ward, gave them a brief sketch of the patient, and left orders on him. The night head nurse asked for his diagnosis. "It's a confused picture," I said, "but admit him as a schizophrenic disorder, schizoaffective type, with manic features. That'll do, and it may be what he has."

I returned to where Mrs. Hammond and the two men were, and informed them of the arrangements I had made.

"Do you think I should stay in Kansas City or go back to Manchester?" Mrs. Hammond inquired.

"Do you have any relatives or close friends in Kansas City?" I asked.

She said she did not.

"Then go back to Manchester," I advised her. "You can check with my office or the psychiatric ward every day and can drive up a couple of times a week to see him when he's ready to receive visitors. I shall restrict visitors to you, but I would prefer that you not visit him until he's a little better; it would not help him and would only upset you."

She requested that Mr. Collins or Mr. Novack be allowed to accompany her during her visits to him, and I said I'd put both of them on the visiting list.

"How do you think he'll do?" she asked hesitantly.

"When a psychiatric illness begins abruptly and dramatically like this in a person who previously has made a good adjustment throughout his life," I replied, "the chances of recovery and return to his usual level of functioning are good. It's the patients who have been sick a long time and whose disorders began so gradually that it's hard to know exactly when they started, with whom we do less well. Mr. Hammond's chances for full recovery are ninety percent or better."

I was telling what she wanted to hear, and it was also the truth.

I shook hands with the men and parted from the three of them.

During the following days Mr. Hammond continued his golfing activities on the psychiatric ward of Mt. Sinai, which he insisted on calling the Five Oaks Country Club of Manchester, Missouri. Dozens of times each day he teed off or blasted out of sand traps or chipped or putted in the day room, the corridors, and his bedroom. The nurses and aides discouraged his golfing since it bewildered other patients and confirmed in the minds of their visitors their worst suspicions about the nature of a psychiatric ward. One of the aides hit upon the ingenious idea of telling him that it was raining or about to rain whenever he started to play golf; the aide then hustled him into the day room, which he said was "the bar" or "the locker room" of the country club. There Mr. Hammond would watch television for long periods of time, while occasionally looking out the window "to see if the weather had cleared up." In time Miss Spitzer, the head nurse, caught the aides using the rain ploy to control Mr. Hammond and gave them a severe reprimand for "treating the patient's delusions and hallucinations as reality." Thereafter, the aides, and some of the nurses used the rain ruse and others ("they're cutting the grass on the fairway") only when Miss Spitzer was off the ward.

At times Mr. Hammond played Chinese checkers and card games with other patients; they were at first startled by his references to golf games he had just played or was going to play as soon as the game was over. However, they soon became accustomed to such comments and overlooked them.

The occupational therapy department's annual budget was based on the number of patients who used that facility and the amount of time they spent there. Thus, the occupational therapists were not above humoring patients to keep them coming to their department.

Owing to my uncertainty about what was wrong with Mr. Hammond, and my innate tendency to compromise on doubtful issues, I let the aides, nurses, and occupational therapists manipulate his delusions to manage him. Moreover, getting along comfortably with the personnel of a psychiatric ward has practical usefulness for a psychiatrist; if the ward personnel like a psychiatrist, they'll often slip his patients ahead of those of other psychiatrists on treatment schedules, and they'll find him beds when the ward is technically full. I have long been a believer in the law of the sloppy compromise, live and let live. Nobody wins a fight.

In order to rule out the possibility that Mr. Hammond had some type of acute physical brain disease, I ordered a comprehensive battery of laboratory procedures on him during the first few days; the results were all normal. I had a neurologist evaluate him, and he found nothing wrong. Mr. Hammond did not fit the picture of a patient with organic brain disease well, but when a patient is puzzling, all possibilities must be considered.

I wondered at first if he had a dissociative hysterical disorder, somewhat similar to hysterical amnesias and hysterical trances, but he didn't fit that category well. Hysterical dissociative disorders are rare in men over the age of forty who have never before had any kind of psychiatric difficulty, and such disturbances usually last no more than a few days at the most. After five or six days of continued golfing on the psychiatric ward I decided that this was an unlikely explanation for his condition.

Though we had him listed as a schizophrenic, he did not act and think as a schizophrenic should, and he also did not fit the pattern of a manic disorder. In addition I had no data that could make clear the underlying psychological processes in him that were causing his disturbance.

On about the fourth day of Mr. Hammond's hospitaliza

tion Miss Spitzer, the psychiatric ward's head nurse, caught me as I was reading my charts in the nurses' station. Miss Spitzer does not think highly of me. Though presumably she admits that I am intelligent enough to have gotten through medical school and psychiatric training and to have published a few things, she ranks me far down on the list of Mt. Sinai psychiatrists in terms of clinical skills and capacity to understand patients.

Miss Spitzer has been psychoanalyzed, and I have not. Miss Spitzer believes that everything Freud wrote is revealed truth, whereas I have marked reservations about many things the Viennese bard proposed. Depending on Miss Spitzer's mood, she views me as an erring sheep to be gathered to the flock or a pagan to be converted or a pernicious influence to be combated. My discussions of patients with Miss Spitzer are unpleasant, and I avoid them when I can; they occur only when she corners me in situations from which I cannot escape without being rude.

When I say that Miss Spitzer has been psychoanalyzed, I am exaggerating the case a bit. She has been in and out of psychoanalysis for the last half-dozen years or more. She gets analyzed until her money runs out, and then she takes a "vacation" from analysis "to consolidate her gains." When she has paid off the arrears to her analyst and has accumulated another wad, she starts again.

I don't know what Miss Spitzer is looking for in analysis, but I suspect that among other things she is seeking salvation in this world. Like many other young Jews, she has lost her faith; she can no longer accept the Mishnah and the Talmud and has found nothing to put in their place. She doesn't know exactly what to do in this world and hasn't figured out why one should bother to stay alive and plod on in so silly and meaningless a place. So she has taken up the cause of psychoanalysis, with its intricate intellectuality and cabalistic rituals of treatment, with the same zeal and tenacity with which her forebears clung to their dogmas in the villages of Poland and Russia. For Miss Spitzer, the Messiah has already come; he practiced medicine in Vienna for fifty years. Miss Spitzer is, unlike her forebears, evangelical; she feels it is her duty to convert everybody to the Gospel According to Saint Sigmund.

When I was an adolescent in the 1930's, people talked about the "black Irishmen." They had been reared devout Catholics, but during adolescence they lost their religion. They had a sore emptiness where their faith had been and often spent the rest of their lives looking for something to put in its place. Their quests often led no further than alcoholism, but in some cases they ventured into intellectual creativity. The black Irishmen included James Joyce, Eugene O'Neill, the distinguished American psychiatrist Harry Stack Sullivan, and many others. One of my early teachers in psychiatry was a black Irishman. Miss Spitzer is a lost Jew.

Miss Spitzer is not a happy person. I had a patient, a nurse, who knew her well. Miss Spitzer often leaves her analyst's office crying. At times she is depressed for a week or two, and she is unpredictably irritable with her staff. She formerly dated black men, and felt quite liberal about it, but the ones she picked treated her badly and she now dates very little. I suspect, from sly comments that some of the aides have made, that she has begun to drink too much. However, my compassion for Miss Spitzer is tested when she goads me about how badly she feels I am mismanaging my patients.

Having trapped me as I was seated reading my first chart, she dug into me on the subject of Mr. Hammond.

"Dr. Chapman, have you come to any conclusions about Mr. Hammond?" she inquired in a tone that conveyed her doubt that I had.

"Well, no, Miss Spitzer. He's a puzzler, all right. He's probably one of those cases who will go down the drain and we probably never will know what was wrong with him." I fear I sometimes adopt an attitude of bumbling ignorance to nettle Miss Spitzer.

"Don't you think it's about time we get an effective treatment program going for him?" she retorted.

"Well, there's really no hurry," I answered. "He's pretty well off financially, and there are no kids; there are just he and his wife."

"I wasn't thinking of *that,* Dr. Chapman," she said. "I was thinking of his psychiatric state."

"Oh," I replied, as if that aspect of the case had not yet occurred to me.

"What diagnosis have you put on him?" she asked, struggling to control her impatience with me.

"Well," I said, "let's see what I put on the chart." I made a great to-do of finding his chart in the stack of four metal-cased patient records before me and thumbing through its pages.

"Here we are. I have him listed as a schizophrenic reaction, schizoaffective type, with manic features." I smiled blandly at her, as if I had solved all his problems by putting that label on him.

"A diagnosis," proclaimed Miss Spitzer, "is merely an administrative convenience. It tells us little about the inner turmoil that is producing the patient's emotional distress and clinical picture."

"Yeahnnnn," I said, staring at her in an expressionless way as if I had never heard this point of view before.

"However," I added, after thinking it over I've been wondering if it might be something organic."

"Clearly, it is *not* organic," Miss Spitzer said.

"You may be right," I replied. "None of the tests checked out."

"Well, if Mr. Hammond's problems are not organic, and if the term schizophrenia tells us virtually nothing about his inner emotional difficulties, what *is* wrong with him?"

"Well," I answered, "like I said, it's just one of those cases, and we'll just have to coast along and see how things work out."

"By 'things,' " she said, "I presume you are referring to the patient."

"Yeahnnnn," I replied. After a brief pause I added, "What do you think is wrong with him, Miss Spitzer?"

This is what she had been waiting for; however, if I had not asked this question, she soon would have given me her opinion anyway.

"It appears to me," she said, "that Mr. Hammond has marked conflicts about his masculinity. He basically is a fearful little boy who covers his insecurity with a veneer of masculine bravado. Hence, we have all this talk about golf and his prowess in it and his physical agility in it. The sexual symbolism is self-evident. Driving golf balls with the use of a long rigid stick has obvious references to the male role in sexuality, and sinking balls into holes is a clear symbol of vaginal penetration. His anxiety about his capacity in the masculine role verges on panic much of the time. Thus, the reassurance he gets about his sexual capacity and his integrity as a man by symbolic golfing achievements is short-lived. He constantly must reassure himself that his maleness is intact; and he must proclaim it in a loud, ostentatious manner to everyone around him, both men and women."

The reader who has had little association with persons in the mental health professions may feel that I am exaggerating, or perhaps parodying, Miss Spitzer's speech. However, this is the way some Freudians talk. During my psychiatric training I one day was present at a seminar in which one of the young psychiatrists presented a case to a pipe smoking, fortyish psychoanalyst with whom we had weekly two-hour teaching conferences. During the first few minutes of the first presentation of data on his patient the young psychiatrist mentioned that, as one of his various symptoms, the patient had occasional headaches in the back of his neck. The analyst interrupted to comment that these headaches obviously indicated repressed homosexual feelings in the patient, a man. The young psychiatrist looked up from his notes and asked the analyst how he came to that conclusion. "The pain in the back of the neck represents anxiety about penetration of his rectum from behind by the penis of a paramour," the analyst replied; with a wave of his pipe he indicated that the young resident psychiatrist could go on.

Thus, Miss Spitzer continued, "His golfing is an exhibitionistic caricature of masculinity. I presume you've noticed the underlying homosexual factors."

I confessed I had not.

"They are obvious," she said. "In his golfing delusions and hallucinations he speaks only of male partners; he invites only male aides and male patients to participate with him in his golfing activities, and he discusses his golfing prowess only with men. He has never included any of the female staff or patients in any of his golfing delusions. Can you cite a single instance in which he has included a female in his golfing activities?"

I admitted I could not.

Triumphantly she went on. "He feels comfortable only with men. He has marked anxiety about closeness with women and hence drifts into associations involving only men. In the male camaraderie of golfing activities and golfing talk, and in the crude jokes and banter of the locker room, his homosexual urges find releases in socially acceptable ways. However, these avenues of expression do not give adequate expression to the homosexual forces within him; these forces press toward the surface, and as they approach consciousness, they arouse overwhelming anxiety. Rather than come to grips with these homosexual forces he has fled, unconsciously, into the psychiatric illness that we see."

I listened attentively. I must get along with Miss Spitzer, and as long as she views me as a possible convert she will take a strong interest in my patients and will ease many problems for me on the ward. Also, she is a good psychiatric nurse. She often works twelve hours a day on the ward, though her position demands only eight, and she makes Sunday-morning rounds and occasional night spot-checks to make sure everything is in order.

She went on for another couple of minutes about his castration anxieties and unresolved Oedipal complex.

"Well," I said, in my best country-boy-trying-to-get-along-in-the-big-city drawl, "I hadn't analyzed it quite that deeply yet."

"The choice of golfing," she continued, "is not happenstance. I suppose you have reflected that it is a sport in which men are traditionally superior to women?"

I said I had not thought of that, but agreed that it appeared to be so.

"Yes," she said, "golf is particularly associated with men, and the major stars are, almost without exception, men. In identifying himself with these outstanding golfers he is, in a forced way, adopting a role that is characteristic of men and thus drawing an even sharper cleavage between the masculine and feminine roles. This is one more way in which he is protecting himself against coming to grips with the homosexual forces within him."

She had finished her analysis of Mr. Hammond.

"What do you think we should do with him, Miss Spitzer?"

"These things must be worked out," she said.

"How do you propose we work them out?" I asked.

"Psychotherapy is the usual method," she retorted, somewhat archly.

"You mean that I should talk to him about all this?" I inquired.

"One does not assault the patient with such insights," she said with a tinge of exasperation in her voice. "Such an assault would only mobilize more panic and make him worse, unless, of course, one agrees with Rosen's methods of direct analysis."

Her tone indicated clearly that one should not agree with Rosen's methods of direct analysis, and I hastened to assure her that I did not favor that approach.

"Or Melanie Klein's methods, using what she calls 'deep interpretations,'" Miss Spitzer added. She was showing off more than usual today.

"Melanie *who?*" I asked.

"Melanie Klein," Miss Spitzer replied wearily. "She is a prominent British child psychiatrist."

"Well," I said, "I don't use those techniques."

"I am *aware* of that, Dr. Chapman," she replied with the patient tone of a missionary explaining the Trinity to a Hottentot.

"How *do* you tell a man like Mr. Hammond about his castration anxiety?" I asked. Miss Spitzer has no sense of humor, or at least I have never discovered it, and though the nurses and aides hold back giggles as they overhear my sessions with her, she seems never to catch on to the fact that I am egging her on.

"One begins with the most superficial layer and works gradually downward," she said, "always being careful not to mobilize more anxiety than the patient can handle."

"Well, I've tried to talk to him," I said, "but I can never get him to talk about anything except golf. Apparently he plays a pretty good game."

Miss Spitzer stared at me and gave it up as a hopeless job. She probably felt that if the patient got well, it would indeed be a lucky accident for him.

I think, in fact, that it annoys Miss Spitzer when my patients get well; however, she probably comforts herself with the reflection that most of my patients will soon relapse because "their basic problems have not been worked out," and that, rather than face her none-too-silent reproaches if I should rehospitalize them at Mt. Sinai, I send them all to St. Catharine's or ship them off to one of the state hospitals.

"At least," she said, "we can work out a ward activity program and organize the therapeutic milieu to encourage his return to a comfortable contact with reality."

I agreed that that would be a good idea.

"Perhaps you would sign the activity program sheet and the therapeutic milieu order sheet," she said.

I signed them.

"I'll assign Mr. Fox to work with him," she said. "He's very good with this type of patient." Mr. Fox was a senior aide in his forties.

"Thank you, Dr. Chapman," she said with a compassionate smile. She rose and went onto the ward.

Only a minority of Freudians talk like Miss Spitzer, but they are a conspicuous minority.

I went back to reading my charts.

While Mr. Fox and Miss Spitzer worked on Mr. Hammond, I sat for twenty minutes each day and listened to him talk about golf; he occasionally strayed into other subjects, but soon returned to the golfing theme. I kept him on a phenothiazine antipsychotic medication since it would do him no harm and, if he were in a schizophrenic illness, it would help him get over it.

I asked Harold Waxman, the clinical psychologist at Mt. Sinai, to do psychological testing on Mr. Hammond.

When Harold arrived at Mt. Sinai fifteen years previously, fresh from his training in New York, he was somewhat like Miss Spitzer, but he has been burned enough times to become more flexible than she is. Harold's position is different; as a clinical psychologist he must, at the end of a report, give a diagnostic opinion, estimate the patient's likely course in treatment, and make a statement about his probable outcome. In the last fifteen years Harold has learned a lot from the people who in the end are the best teachers of psychiatry— the patients.

I shall quote some sections of Harold's report on Mr. Hammond. Throughout these excerpts I have expanded the usual abbreviations; for example, the TAT is enlarged to the Thematic Apperception Test.

"Mr. Hammond was a difficult patient to engage in testing. He boisterously talked about his golfing delusions and hallucinations, and I could get his full cooperation only for limited periods. I saw him in three sessions, and his performance in the last two sessions was better than in the first. The results of his testing are uneven and inconsistent. Whether this reflects the nature of his disturbance or my inability to get his attention persistently is not clear.

"I performed the Wechsler Adult Intelligence Scale on him twice, in the first and third sessions. On the first Wechsler his combined verbal and performance IQ was 61 [in the range of moderate to marked mental retardation], obviously far below the level that would be expected in a man of his vocational and social position. There was marked scatter, not only from one section to the next but also within individual sections. For example, a response compatible with severe mental retardation often was followed by one that would indicate superior intelligence, and vice versa. Many responses were irrelevant to test items, or only obliquely related to them. The second Wechsler, in which his degree of cooperation was better, gave an IQ of 96 [within the range of normal intelligence, but still below what one would expect of a college educated bank executive]. However, this test also had much of the scatter of the first one. One would be tempted to say that 96 represents a recent fall of at least 20 points from his former IQ level, indicating organic brain dysfunction. However, comparison of the performance and verbal scores, which differ by only 4 points, does not substantiate such an impression. It is therefore probable that his low IQ is due to poor cooperation because of his grossly disturbed state. . . .

"He rejected so many items on the Minnesota Multiphasic Personality Inventory, and many of the responses he gave were so erratic, that the test could not be scored. He rejected many items with comments such as 'It's all Greek to me,' 'You know more about this than I do, Mac,' and 'Well, that beats the hell out of me.' To many items he gave golf responses of a completely irrelevant nature. . . .

"His Thematic Apperception Test was difficult to interpret. Despite repeated urgings to give other types of stories, he persisted in telling golf stories in response to all cards. Example: 'This guy doesn't want to stay inside. He wants to go out and play golf. They won't let him. That's why he's so down in the dumps.' All the persons in his stories were male; he avoided references to female figures or interpreted obviously female figures as males. The poverty of ideas and the briefness and simplicity of his stories are what one would expect in a mentally retarded or brain-damaged person, but this is not consistent with the results of his neurological work-up, as recorded on his chart.

"On the Sentence Completion Test his answers to most items were so irrelevant that if his psychotic state were not obvious, one would suspect him of deliberately mocking the examiner; such answers are sometimes given by resistant patients as part of their general refusal to cooperate in testing. His few appropriate responses were well organized and suggested, if anything, a depressive trend. However, the results of this test are at this time uninterpretable. . . .

"About one-third of his responses to the Bender-Gestalt Test were typical of those of a person with organic brain damage; some of his errors in the reproduction of geometrical designs were gross. The other two-thirds of his responses were only tangentially relevant to the test material or were not related to it at all. Examples: 'Some guy scribbled all over his golf card.' 'This guy had one hell of a time getting out of the rough.' The test could not be graded.

"On the Draw-a-Person Test and the House-Tree-Person Test he drew stick figures for both the male and female figures, and the female figure did not differ in any way from the male figure. His drawings of a house and a tree were on a general level that one would expect of a four-year-old child, but they contained some items that were consistent with average or superior adult intelligence. . . .

"He gave eight responses to the Rorschach; he rejected Cards II, III, and VI. Two of his responses were 'an inkblot,' and one was 'ink smeared all over.' The other five responses were animals. He saw three dogs, one cat, and one bird. He used no color, and his five animal responses were determined by form. . . . The test could not be scored, but Rorschach configurations of this kind are occasionally seen in persons with marked organic brain dysfunction. . . .

"*Impression:* No clear diagnostic or psychodynamic picture emerges here. The entire examination, with the exception of the second IQ, suggests either mental retardation or gross organic brain damage, but there is no evidence for either of these in his socioeconomic status, his current clinical picture, and his extensive neurological workup. There is little in his testing to suggest schizophrenia or a manic disorder or any of the other functional psychoses. No concept about his psychodynamics or underlying personality structure can be drawn from these test results.

"I shall visit Mr. Hammond on the ward in ten or fourteen days, and if he appears able to engage more effectively in testing, I shall examine him again."

This was an unusual report for Harold. He is not afraid to stick his neck out. He telephoned me at my office to give me a brief verbal report on the testing, and this too is unusual; as a rule he puts his report on the patient's chart and discusses the patient with the psychiatrist if he happens to meet him on the ward or elsewhere within the following week or two. He told me on the phone that he had seen such test results only once before. That was when, during military service, he did testing on soldiers awaiting courts-martial; several of them had test results somewhat like this. We agreed that this information was not of much help with Mr. Hammond.

When a psychiatrist or a physician in any other specialty is in doubt about a patient and is not sure what to do, he may get a consultation. At his request another physician goes over the patient's records, examines him, and puts on his chart a written, often detailed, opinion about the probable diagnosis and advisable treatment.

A consultation may serve various purposes. Sometimes the consultant notes things that had gone unobserved or considers possibilities that had not been explored or sees treatment from a new, better viewpoint. In other cases the consultant merely confirms what is being done. At times a consultation is sought for the legal protection of the requesting physician. For example, a psychiatrist may be uncertain about whether or not a patient is suicidal; if the consultant and the requesting physician agree that the patient does not present significant suicidal risk, and if the patient then kills himself a few days after discharge from a psychiatric ward, the attending psychiatrist is in a much better position to refute charges of negligence and any resulting malpractice suit. Lastly, a consultation reassures the attending physician; if the patient does poorly or if unexpected things later occur, he can, with justification, feel that he did all he could to help the patient.

At the end of a week I was still uncertain about what was wrong with Mr. Hammond and how to treat him. I therefore asked Dr. Mark Bromberg to see him. Except for some conservative political opinions that verge on the eccentric at times, Mark is a sensible, well-adjusted man who does a broad general practice of psychiatry. He is systematic and careful and is not padlocked into any particular school of psychiatric thought; he grinds no axes. His report was as follows:

"At the request of Dr. Harry Chapman I today examined this forty-three-year-old, married, male bank executive from Manchester, Missouri, who for the past eight days has been hospitalized on the psychiatric ward of Mt. Sinai Hospital. I reviewed the patient's chart, which reveals a negative physical and neurological workup, and talked with the patient in his room. I shall not repeat the history of this man's nine-day psychiatric illness of abrupt onset, without prior history of psychiatric disturbances; it is recorded in detail on his chart.

"The patient is a florid, husky man of more than average height and weight who, within the limits of his disturbed behavior, cooperated fairly well on the examination. I felt that he understood what I was doing and what was required of him, despite frequent references to his delusions and hallucinations.

"His affect was often inappropriate and was subject to abrupt changes. He greeted me with effusive geniality, stating that I was an old friend of his, and he frequently talked loudly and gesticulated excitedly. However, for brief periods he became sober and perhaps even a little depressed for no obvious reason; these periods occupied, at most, about one-fifth of our interview time.

"He was at times physically overactive. He paced about the room or went through golf-playing actions, saying that he was putting or driving or hunting for lost balls. However, by firm persuasion I could always distract him from these activities. More than half of these golfing episodes occurred in the first fifteen minutes of the interview.

"When not otherwise distracted, his thought content drifted to golfing topics. He spoke at length of particularly good shots and scores he had made. However, when the golfing theme and its related facets could be excluded, he demonstrated no delusional thinking. He had no persecutory or delusional or nihilistic thoughts. Although he skipped rapidly from topic to topic he had no true flight of ideas or fragmentation of thought processes.

"Many of his responses, however, were strikingly oblique to the questions asked. For example, when asked where he worked, he gave a telephone number; subsequent questioning revealed that this was his business telephone number. When asked his age, he said thirty four, which is the number formed when the digits of his true age are reversed; with leading questions he corrected this response to forty-three. When asked to give his wife's name, he said Dolly Madison; with cajoling he corrected this to Shirley, the name listed on his chart, which I had with me during the interview.

"His memory, though in general intact, had odd defects. He said he remembered nothing of his admission to the hospital, but later spoke of the injection of medication he received in the emergency room. After first stating that he did not know the name of his psychiatrist or the aide assigned to him, he later gave their names accurately. Of particular interest is the fact that, while searching for the correct name of the aide, he called him Mr. Rabbit, Mr. Hare, and Mr. Raccoon before getting his true name, Mr. Fox.

"He showed similar anomalies in orientation. He stated that we were in the clubhouse of the Five Oaks Country Club of Manchester, Missouri, but later statements indicated that he understood clearly that he was on the psychiatric ward of a Kansas City hospital. Thus, he referred to other persons on the ward as 'psycho patients' and comprehended the functions of the nurses and aides. . . .

"He had no hallucinations other than those associated with golf. (He saw golf clubs, balls, greens, and so forth.) These hallucinations were all visual, except for the accompanying tactile sensations (as when picking a ball out of a hole and when handling a club). He had no auditory, olfactory, or gustatory hallucinations, and he had no other disturbances of perception. . . .

"His fund of information and judgment showed the same incongruities found in other areas of his mental and emotional functioning. When asked the name of the current president of the United States, he replied Abraham Lincoln, but he could be persuaded afterward to give the correct reply. He gave the population of Manchester, Missouri, as fifteen million, but then corrected it to fifteen thousand. When asked what he would do if he were the first person to notice a fire in a crowded theater, he responded that he would summon the State Highway Patrol, and when asked what he would do if he found an addressed, stamped, sealed envelope on the sidewalk, he said he would deliver it to the nearest drugstore. . . .

"He had no apparent insight. He stated that he was not ill and had no problems other than a slight hook in his golf drives. . . . He accompanied me to the door of the ward as I left, slapped me on the back, and told me to return at any time as his guest to play a round of golf with him. . . .

"*Impression:* This man presents a confusing clinical picture. There are four possible processes going on here:

"1. The general picture suggests an atypical organic brain syndrome, with spotty defects of orientation and memory, fluctuating disturbances of contact with reality, and visual hallucinations. However, an extensive neurological workup and one week of inpatient observation have not substantiated this impression.

"2. The clinical picture also suggests a hysterical dissociative reaction. However, such disorders are extremely uncommon in men in their forties with no history of previous emotional problems; the few cases I can recall offhand were men who were involved in workmen's compensation disputes or other litigation after industrial accidents. In the absence of clear financial or other gain, a hysterical disorder of this type would be expected to terminate, or at least to improve or to show marked fluctuations in intensity, during a one-week period. In addition psychological testing does not support such a diagnosis.

"3. If there were any conceivable gain or motive, one might suspect this patient of malingering, but not once in eight days has any interruption, however brief, of his psychotic thinking and behavior occurred. I carefully questioned his special aide and a couple of nurses on this point, and went over the nurses' notes on his chart with this point in mind. Although this possibility seems very unlikely, I feel it should not be dismissed altogether.

"4. A schizophrenic psychosis, paranoid type, with manic features is statistically the most probable diagnosis, but he does not present fragmentation of thought processes, withdrawal from people, and many other things that would support this diagnosis. . . . Moreover, except in paranoid schizophrenics with fixed persecutory delusions, I cannot recall a schizophrenic whose delusions and hallucinations were so narrowly constricted to one kind of activity.

"I can make no suggestions about the past or current stresses in his life that might have contributed to his condition, if in fact it is a functional disorder, and it is impossible to get clear information about any premorbid personality difficulties. Any comments on psychodynamics in this man would be very speculative. . . .

"*Recommendations*: 1. On the assumption that this is some kind of functional psychosis, I would continue the phenothiazine medication, but on a somewhat higher dose level. I would continue the therapeutic milieu and ward activities program, and as he improves I would consider his inclusion in group psychotherapy. Lack of insight that he is ill will make individual psychotherapy or counseling unworkable until he is convalescent.

"2. There is still a possibility that this is an organic brain process that will become clear in time. A silent tumor in the parietal or occipital regions or a subtle demyelinating disease or an obscure toxic process may later become evident. I would order a brain scan and urine examination for heavy metals.

"3. I would have the social-service department interview his wife, and any other close persons, to try to discover any emotional or situational factors that may be playing roles in this process."

Mark Bromberg, MD

I ordered the examinations Mark suggested, but they revealed no abnormalities. I raised his phenothiazine medication slightly and requested the social-service department to interview his wife.

For nine more days Mr. Hammond golfed on the psychiatric ward of Mt. Sinai, but he golfed with less enthusiasm and spent less time at it. He was less talkative and was more cooperative in ward activities and in occupational therapy. He sat for periods of an hour or more looking glumly out the window or staring impassively at television.

Miss Spitzer cornered me for more tête-à-têtes; she stated that as the result of the work of Mr. Fox and others in implementing the therapeutic milieu, Mr. Hammond's delusions and hallucinations were ebbing away, revealing underlying depressive features. I agreed that in some ways he looked better. She predicted that within two months he would recover entirely.

After his first ten days in the hospital his wife, often accompanied by Mr. Collins or Mr. Novack, visited him a couple of times a week, and they found him somewhat better.

On the morning of the eighteenth day he seemed somber and tired as I sat with him in his room. From a chair by the window he gazed at the grassy slope that rose to a distant parking lot.

"You seem a little sad today, Mr. Hammond," I began.

"I'm okay," he replied, without looking at me.

"How long have you been here now?" I asked.

"It's going on three weeks," he answered. The correctness and matter-of-fact tone of his reply surprised me.

"I think you're a little better," I said.

"I'm okay," he responded, continuing to look out the window.

"I suppose you find life here a little boring and confined."

"It's all right," he replied. "I played thirty six holes of golf yesterday. I guess that's why I'm so pooped today."

"I've never mentioned it before," I went on, ignoring his

golfing comment, "but we've found you a bit of a puzzler. You don't fit into any of the usual categories into which we can put most patients."

He sat motionless, looking out the window, and did not respond. I wondered if he were listening.

"Are you with me?" I asked.

"I'm with you, Doc," he answered.

"Sometimes," I continued, "patients come here, and we give them a little medication and talk with them and work with them in our various activity programs, and they get well; and in some cases we're never sure what was wrong with them and why they got well. I'm beginning to think that perhaps you will be one of these patients."

"I'll be all right," he said.

"I agree with you," I replied. "In the long run I think you'll be all right."

We sat in silence for another minute or so. Then he abruptly rose and said, "Doc, you'll have to excuse me. The boys are about to tee off; they want to play a round before it gets too hot." He walked out of the room, and later I saw him slumped in the dayroom before the television set.

On the afternoon of Mr. Hammond's twentieth hospital day my secretary received from the social-service department of Mt. Sinai a request that I call them between patients.

At my next break I called the Mt. Sinai social-service department, indicating that I was Dr. Chapman returning a call from Mrs. Smart.

"She's with a client, Doctor," the social service department secretary replied, "but she said to interrupt her when you called. I'll buzz her."

I heard the buzz and then Mrs. Smart's voice.

"This is Dr. Chapman returning your call, Mrs. Smart."

"Thank you, Doctor. Will you hold on for a moment? I have a client in my office and I'll take this on another phone." Muffled voices were followed by clicking and a silence, and then Mrs. Smart was back on the line.

"I'm calling about your patient Mr. Hammond," she said. "As you know, you requested that we interview his wife to get additional information on him. There was a delay in working out the time of her first appointment, and I didn't see her until last Wednesday. I got a detailed history of his early life, his college years, and his adult adjustment. She's known him since childhood; they were both raised in Manchester. So far, there's nothing remarkable in any of this material. However, today Mrs. Hammond came in very upset with some news I thought you ought to know about right away."

"What's happened?" I asked.

"Shortly after Mr. Hammond entered the hospital the state bank examiners arrived in Manchester for their twice-yearly examination, and it appears that there are some marked discrepancies in the books of the bank where Mr. Hammond works."

"What kind of discrepancies?"

"It appears that more than four hundred thousand dollars can't be accounted for."

I did not reply.

"I thought you'd want to know this," she said.

"Yes, yes, of course," I said. "Look, Mrs. Smart, do they suspect anyone in particular in regard to these discrepancies?"

"Well," she replied, "as Mrs. Hammond sees it, they're not sure. However, they're very anxious to talk to Mr. Hammond. I get the impression he's high on the list of suspects. Mrs. Hammond is very upset; I think she knows, or fears, more than she told me."

"How long have the bank examiners been down there?" I asked.

"A little over two weeks, which is much longer than they usually stay, and they've called in the federal bank examiners and the FBI, since the bank's deposits are insured by the federal government."

After a pause I inquired, "Is any of this public knowledge?"

"Apparently most of the town of Manchester knows about it, and the news is spreading fast," Mrs. Smart replied.

Then she asked the sixty-four-dollar question: "Do you think I should inform the hospital administration?"

People in the various mental-health professions—psychiatrists, clinical psychologists, psychiatric social workers, psychiatric nurses, and others—are *ethically* bound to keep confidential almost all information about patients and not to divulge it to individuals not directly involved in the patient's care. However, the situation *legally* is confused on this issue; the law varies much from one state to another and is the focus of much current debate. This problem is further complicated when, as in Mr. Hammond's case, some of the patient's difficulties are in the process of becoming public knowledge.

If Mr. Hammond were to slip out of the occupational therapy department or the outdoor recreational area or some other hospital section and disappear, it would be very embarrassing for Mt. Sinai Hospital, especially since his flight in time would be reported prominently in the newspapers and on television; an embezzlement of this size usually attracts much attention. Moreover, when a man like John Hammond faces a life crisis of this kind, there is always the possibility of suicide; if he were to flee and commit suicide, it would place everyone concerned with his care in a painful, vulnerable position.

Rightly or wrongly, I make most decisions quickly, and alone.

"Well, Mrs. Smart," I said, "I have suddenly become very concerned about Mr. Hammond as a suicidal risk. I shall immediately call the psychiatric ward and put him on strict, around-the-clock suicidal precautions and elopement observation. I shall restrict him to the ward and cut off all visitors except his wife, his clergyman, and any attorney whose admittance he and his wife request in writing." After a pause I added, "These steps are not quite so brutal as they sound. He *has* looked somewhat depressed lately, and it appears that he has something to be depressed about. It looks as though his world is collapsing around him."

"And will you inform the administration, Doctor?"

"Yes, I'll call the administrator's office right now and talk to Bill Elkins or Harvey Rosen. I'll fill them in and I'll emphasize that although much of this is rapidly becoming public information in Manchester, Missouri, it's still in the rumor stage. I'll leave you out of it and I'll stress that until formal charges are made any talk could be considered slanderous. That will enable the administration to handle any inquiries from the Board of Directors or any of the medical-staff committees or anyone else who contacts them."

After a moment's silence I went on. "I'll have Mark Bromberg, who's seen him in consultation, drop by to see him again and put an appended note on his consultation report backing me up on the patient's depressiveness, the suicidal precautions, and the other things. I'll also advise Harold Waxman, and he can redo some of the psychological testing if he wants. After that we'll just sit tight.'

"What shall I do about my records on this?" Mrs. Smart asked.

"Well, whatever Mrs. Hammond told you is clinical information, regardless of whether it's rumor or fact. So put it down. However, stamp each sheet of your record 'confidential,' and put a note on the front of the chart that it is not to be made available to anyone without the written permission of the hospital administration and me. Also, Helen, please do me a favor. Take your ink pad and stamp to the psychiatric ward and stamp every page of his chart 'confidential,' and tell the ward secretary and the others that only people directly concerned in caring for the patient are to be allowed to read it. Okay?"

"Okay," she said.

"Be a good girl, Helen, and do this right after you finish with your present client, or at least before you go home today."

"I'll take care of it," she said.

I then telephoned Bill Elkins and Mark Bromberg and left a message for Harold Waxman to call me when he could.

Miss Spitzer was waiting for me the next morning as I came into the nurses' station. With one hand on the chart desk and the other one crooked on her hip, she let fly.

"Dr. Chapman, will you kindly explain why yesterday afternoon you suddenly put Mr. Hammond on suicidal and elopement precautions and restricted him to the ward, thus completely destroying the therapeutic milieu we have created for him and ruining all we have accomplished?"

Without waiting for me to respond, she charged on. "It seems to me that we are supposed to have what is known as the 'team approach' here. In the team approach important therapeutic decisions are made only after at least limited discussion with the various professional persons working with the patient. I was under the impression that highhanded, autocratic acts by godlike psychiatrists were a thing of the past, at least here at Mt. Sinai."

"Ruth," I replied, "I'm sorry about it. I really am. I knew it might upset you and the staff, but some new information has come to light. In fact, I just learned of it late yesterday afternoon, and it makes these things necessary."

"Exactly what kind of information?" Miss Spitzer demanded.

"Well," I said lamely, "until the situation is a little clearer it's not the kind of thing I can discuss. It is possible that Mr. Hammond has some very severe troubles down in Manchester."

"I am sure that Mr. Hammond has 'some very severe troubles down in Manchester.' It usually requires 'some very severe troubles' to precipitate a schizoaffective psychosis. Unfortunately, since you destroyed his entire therapeutic program yesterday he has some even severer troubles right here on the psychiatric ward at Mt. Sinai."

"Ruth, I know it seems a little brutal, but—"

"Brutal!" she exploded. "It's barbaric."

"Look, Ruth, you've just got to trust me on this one. I know we see things a little differently, but until the situation becomes clearer we must make sure that this man does not elope from the hospital. It probably will all be clear in a few days."

She glared at me furiously, and then she began to cry. The ward is all she has. It's mother, father, brothers, sisters, and children to her.

"Let's go into your office, Ruth, and I'll tell you what the score is." I put my arm around her shoulder and led her onto the ward, while the nurses and the aides stared. They probably had never seen her cry before, and the running battles between her and me had for years been a source of amusement and satisfaction to them since, though they respected her, they did not like her.

In her office I explained everything to her, indicating that none of us could say anything until the suspicions against Mr. Hammond were put into formal charges.

"Besides," I said, "we both know that you and Irv Weiner are always trying to get more money from the administration for psychiatry, and the boys in medicine and surgery think that entirely too much money is already put into this ward. If this man should elope and throw himself under a truck on Brookside Drive, they'd be down on you and Irv like a bunch of hyenas; they'd want to know why, where, how, and when—especially after it hit TV and the newspapers. Sometimes we have to be a little nontherapeutic with one patient in the interests of all the others."

After a pause, I went on. "Moreover, he's been depressed lately, as you yourself have mentioned. On top of his intrapsychic problems he will have to face a very painful situational crisis as this thing comes to a head. Suicidal precautions and restriction to the ward may be more justified than they seem at first glance."

She wiped the tears from her face and agreed that perhaps I had done the only possible thing.

"Let's go back out to the nurses' station and agree on these steps in front of the staff. It'll be better for both of us. I couldn't explain all this on the phone yesterday. I'm sorry."

Three days later, as I entered the psychiatric ward of Mt. Sinai, the ward secretary asked me if I'd seen the morning paper. When I said I had not, she handed it to me. The upper right-hand corner of the front page was doubled inward to the second page where a column-length article under a one-column headline stated that $434,000 had been embezzled from the Marshall County State Bank of Manchester, Missouri. It said that formal charges had been made in the western Missouri district federal court in Kansas City against John Taylor Hammond, vice-president and cashier of the bank, who was hospitalized in Mt. Sinai Hospital. The administration of Mt. Sinai had no comment on the matter.

I took the paper onto the ward and, alone with Mr. Hammond in his room, showed the article to him. I said that even in his present state he should see it, since other patients on the ward would be receiving copies of this newspaper and there might also be brief reports of this on television newscasts. After looking at the article briefly he laid the paper on the bed, got up, and left the room.

That day his wife, haggard and not so neatly groomed as usual, came to see me in my office. She was accompanied by her sister, a middle aged woman from Jefferson City. She defended her husband weakly. She said she was sure it was a mistake and would be cleared up. "What would John do with four hundred and thirty-four thousand dollars?" she asked. "We live as we've always lived. He hasn't spent large amounts of money on anything. If he had taken the money, I'd have noticed something. If it's not a mistake, John will return the money, and it'll be all right. When he gets out of the hospital, he'll straighten everything out." And she cried.

John Hammond spent almost two months more on the psychiatric ward of Mt. Sinai. He continued to receive moderate doses of an antipsychotic medication and a sleeping capsule each night. He did not go off the ward. To the extent that she could Miss Spitzer continued his activity program, and the occupational therapists brought material to the ward for him to work with.

Mr. Hammond grew quite friendly with Mr. Fox, the aide assigned to him. Mr. Fox is black, and he was the first black man Mr. Hammond had ever known well enough to call a friend; so he probably learned something during his stay at Mt. Sinai.

He gradually stopped talking about golf, and did not mention it at all during his last three weeks on the ward. The depressiveness he had at the time his embezzlement was revealed lasted about a month; at the end of his hospital stay he was pleasant with the staff and with a few of the patients. With his consent and his wife's, two weeks before his discharge I put an order on his chart permitting two United States marshals to enter the psychiatric ward and serve papers on him. Shortly before he left the hospital a Kansas City lawyer whom he and his wife knew came to see him. He did not want a lawyer from Manchester.

When he was discharged from the psychiatric ward on a hot August morning, two federal marshals were waiting to take him into custody. His wife had spent an hour with him earlier that morning and on my recommendation did not wait to watch his arrest. He thanked the nurses and aides for all they'd done for him. One of the marshals slipped handcuffs on him and led him by the arm, while the other carried his two suitcases. They left the hospital through the emergency room and entered a waiting car.

I never saw him again. In October I read in the newspaper that he had pleaded guilty as charged and had been sentenced to five to seven years' imprisonment. With time off for good behavior and an early parole he was probably out of prison within three years. In a presentence statement his lawyer explained that Mr. Hammond had taken money from customers' accounts to make stock-market purchases; he had planned to sell the stock after it rose, replace the money and pocket the profit. A steady lower drift of the stock market over a two-year period, combined with some sharp falls, had caused him to take increasingly large sums of money to try to recoup his losses and cover his thefts, until his position had become hopeless.

The psychiatric term for John Hammond's disorder is the Ganser syndrome. It is named after Sigbert Joseph Maria Ganser, who practiced and taught psychiatry in Dresden, Germany, and first described this condition in 1898. Ever since I was a medical student, one of my dreams has been to discover a disease and have it named after me, thus securing for myself a comfortable coast into medical immortality. I have not achieved that dream, just as I have not achieved a lot of other dreams, and time is beginning to run out on me.

The Ganser syndrome most commonly occurs in prisoners awaiting trial, but it may occur in other persons for whom severe mental disease offers a temporary shield from their difficulties. It is characterized by extravagantly irrational behavior, in the midst of which the patient retains much of his contact with reality. Psychiatrists disagree about whether a Ganser syndrome is a hysterical dissociative disorder or a true psychosis that merits a diagnostic category of its own. Few psychiatrists consider it a malingered condition; the patient is not pretending, and he cannot control his behavior and mental state. In retrospect, Mr. Hammond presented a classical picture of this disorder.

The prognosis of a Ganser syndrome is good; in almost one hundred percent of cases the patient recovers in two to three months, and those whose trials or other legal problems are delayed because of the condition go on to face the painful crises from which their illnesses for a time protected them. Ganser syndromes are rare; I have seen only two patients with this disorder since I entered psychiatry in 1948.

A patient with a Ganser syndrome usually has a dramatic clinical picture and attracts much attention. For several months after he left them, the personnel of the psychiatric ward of Mt. Sinai continued to discuss Mr. Hammond and his golfing psychosis.